WALL STREET, REFORMING THE UNREFORMABLE: AN ETHICAL PERSPECTIVE

WALL STREET, REFORMING THE UNREFORMABLE: AN ETHICAL PERSPECTIVE

BY

David E. McClean

Routledge
Taylor & Francis Group

LONDON AND NEW YORK

First published 2015 by Pickering & Chatto (Publishers) Limited

2 Park Square, Milton Park, Abingdon, Oxfordshire OX14 4RN
52 Vanderbilt Avenue, New York, NY 10017

Routledge is an imprint of the Taylor & Francis Group, an informa business

First issued in paperback 2020

BRITISH LIBRARY CATALOGUING IN PUBLICATION DATA

McClean, David E., author.
Wall Street, reforming the unreformable: an ethical perspective.
1. Securities industry – Moral and ethical aspects – United States.
I. Title
174.4-dc23

ISBN-13: 978-1-84893-505-1 (hbk)
ISBN-13: 978-0-367-66893-8 (pbk)

Typeset by Pickering & Chatto (Publishers) Limited

CONTENTS

For
Egbert ('Eddie') McClean
(1925–2005)
He rose early often, and to the occasion always.

LIST OF FIGURES AND TABLES

GLOSSARY OF SELECTED TERMS

Alignment of Identities   Recollection on the part a commercial actor that persons to whom one is selling products or services, or involved in the production or delivery of such products or services, are not anonymous 'others' but rather have the same basic needs and desires as does the commercial actor. The alignment of identities requires moral imagination and the activation of sympathy, so that there is an emotional response to betrayal.

Animal Spirits   The emotional energies that impel action toward preservation, flourishing and the acquisition of 'goods' broadly construed. Herein, it is divided into **primal** and **positive** (also referred to as the 'The Spirits of the Sacred'), which more or less refer to egoistic emotional impulses, on the one hand (preservation, flourishing and acquisition for oneself and one's limited circle of family and friends), and, on the other hand, emotional impulses rooted in commitments to larger *communal* needs and aspirations, and which revolve around trust, loyalty and care for others.

Culture   In the aggregate, knowledge, belief, art, law, morals, customs, and other capabilities and habits acquired by human beings as members of societies or groups.

Dodd-Frank   The 'Dodd-Frank Wall Street Reform and Consumer Protection Act', signed into law by President Barack Obama in 2010, contains many reforms aimed at reducing systemic risks in the financial system, and at increasing transparency regarding financial institutions and the use of certain financial instruments. Dodd-Frank was a legislative response to the weaknesses in the financial system revealed during the financial crisis of 2007/8. Among other things, it imposed registration requirements on hedge fund managers, the regulation of certain swaps, and 'living wills' for large financial institutions.

Ethics   Consideration of (study of) behaviors and habits of mind that are conducive to the benefit and welfare of others and not merely to oneself. Consideration of (study of) what is due to others in virtue of their being human beings.

Existential Needs   Those good (or perceived goods) that are necessary for one's bodily existence and that provide a secure position within one's society and/or community, and that contribute to a healthy sense of self. Food, clothing, and the respect of peers and authorities are Existential Needs. What I am including in Existential Needs, for the sake of simplicity, are a collection of physiological and psychological needs that are divided and categorized differently in both Abraham Maslow's famous 'hierarchy of needs' and in Clayton Alderfer's 'ERG theory', in which needs are divided into existence needs, relatedness needs, and growth needs.[1]

Existential Threats   Things, conditions, or perceptions that may undermine procurement of **Existential Needs.**

First-Wave Economic Imagination   In the typology employed herein, the classical view of the role and place of business firms over and against the rest of civil society. It is perhaps best exemplified during the years of and by the actions of the robber barons, whose large trusts and extensive business interests were at their zenith during the years just preceding the twentieth century up to the Progressive Era (1890-1920), and whose successes often were the result of government/regulatory capture, ruthless business practices and disregard for the interests of workers and communities.

Frame   A conceptual scheme that allows one to order one's ideas, beliefs, perspectives and values.

Fully-Cognizant Corporate Conduct   Corporate conduct that proceeds from an executive's or other manager's (or other corporate actor's) **Third-Wave Economic Imagination.** That is, it is conduct that emerges out of an awareness of the ways social institutions depend upon one another, and that construes all human institutions as parts of a dynamic process within a commercial and economicecosystem of relations.

Libertarianism   A moral and political philosophy that holds that government intervention in markets and firms, as well as other spheres of civil society, must be kept to an absolute minimum. Libertarians believe that the individual, as a bearer of rights, is sacred, and so his or her activities may not be regulated, constrained or determined by others, especially government, other than for specific, limited and exigent purposes. Thus, libertarians oppose many government regulations and hold that such regulations are a form of unjust interference with the entitlement of people to run their lives (including their commercial affairs) as they see fit, whether their efforts succeed or fail (many libertarians view a robust welfare state, which serves to protect the members of society from suffering the shocks that come with failure or misfortune, as a form of government interference and 'unjust takings' or 'theft' from others through the mechanisms of the tax system). Libertarians believe that society is self-regulating and reorders itself spontaneously when there are shocks that disrupt the equilibrium (e.g., financial crises or recessions). Thus libertarians tend to be anti-Keynesian in that they believe that robust government actions (such as economic stimulus) designed to restore the equilibrium are forms of 'unnatural' interference with an economy that is best left to 'reset' itself. The notion of *laissez-faire* ('let the individual do as he will') is rooted in these libertarian ideas.

Metanoia A radical change in how one thinks and perceives. The word *metanoia* is the transliteration of the ancient Greek μετάνο. The word has critical importance in the Christian religion, with cognates in Buddhism and other faith traditions.

(The) Ministerial Model A management and organizational model that places acute emphasis on the needs or goals of those persons or institutions whom/that the firm or organization was established to serve. The expedients of the model are satisfaction and retention (whether or not the organization is engaged in commerce).

Positive Animal Spirits See **Animal Spirits**

Risk The possibility that an undesirable event or condition will hamper or thwart the achievement of valued goals (and the calculation of the probability of such event or condition). Otherwise framed, it is the meeting of the utility and uncertainty of desirable outcomes. Where there are no valued outcomes there are no risks. Risk is, then, a function of human desire and human need.

Second-Wave Economic Imagination In the typology employed herein, the commercial and public imagination that emerged during and immediately subsequent to what is commonly called the Progressive Era (1890-1920). It is constituted by a growing sensitivity to the needs and rights of workers for fair treatment and fair pay, workplace safety, and the hidden and overt problems of class.

(The) Self-Centered Model A management and organizational model that places acute emphasis on the needs or goal of the firm or organization, rather than on the needs or goals of those persons or institutions whom/that the firm or organization was established to serve. The expedients of this model are revenue and profit (if a commercial enterprise).

Social Imaginary	Refers to the way that one conceptualizes society as a whole, which conceptualization is structured by or around certain ideals, ideologies, and myths of origin and purpose.
Soulcraft/Soul-making	The process of internalizing the values and goals of a community or of society. Civics education, for example, is a process of soulcraft or soul-making.
(The) Spirits of the Sacred	See **Animal Spirits**
The Other Wall Street	The internal drive to gain control of and enhance one's social position, i.e. to meet one's **Existential Needs** and to vanquish or mitigate **Existential Threats**.
Third-Wave Economic Imagination	In the typology of economic imagination employed herein, a view of markets, firms and government as comprising, conjointly, an ecosystem, with various stakeholders and contributors, each interpenetrating the other and in partnership with the other. It rejects as chimerical the notion (popular with Libertarians and statists alike) that there are isolated 'realms' of policies, practices, and institutions, and abjures dualistic thinking in approaching social, commercial and economic problems and goals. It emerges out of the growing awareness of the ways social institutions depend upon one another, and from a shift in perspective that views all human institutions as parts of a *dynamic process* within an ecosystem in which one affects and depends upon the other, to varying degrees. It views the institutions that comprise government and commerce and that emerge to serve other social needs as *tools* for furthering diverse human interests and for the creation of social welfare. While holding personal choice and property in very high regard, it balances this against the needs of the political community, and accepts the fact that there will always be tensions.
Wall Street	The international financial services industry. It includes commercial and other banks, brokers, dealers, securities and commodities traders, investment managers/advisers, hedge funds, private equity funds, venture capital funds, mutual funds, and the various institutions (clearing houses and transfer agents, for example) that service them.

INTRODUCTION: A CITIZEN'S MEDITATION ON A PROBLEM

The proper role of the government, like the proper role of the advice-book parent, is to set the stage. The stage should give full rein to the creativity of capitalism. But it should also countervail the excesses that occur because of our animal spirits.

George A. Akerlof and Robert J. Shiller[1]

As for the life of money-making, it is one of constraint, and wealth manifestly is not the good we are seeking, because it is for use, that is, for the sake of something further.

Aristotle[2]

This book is a meditation on a social problem from the perspective of someone who is a citizen as well as a philosopher and an 'operative' in the industry that presents the problem – that is, the international financial services industry (what is often referred to as 'Wall Street'). I have, as well, written it from the perspective of a member of a rich and vibrant political community, a political community that, in recent years, seems to have lost its way, having become saddled with ideological disputes and the effects of its materialism and consumerism. These have, in different ways, eroded the sororal and fraternal bonds that should be the touchstones of public policy, with markets and market mechanisms (as important as they are) serving in a ministerial role only – serving as mere tools for the life and the flourishing of the community.

As part of this meditation I have drawn on the theoretical framework and foundation texts of our political community, on the work of philosophers and theologians, on aspirational literature that expresses our core ideas and beliefs, from academic and Wall Street colleagues, and on the practical experience I have derived from over thirty years in the securities and investment management businesses. The result is that in this book the reader will find a mix of the theoretical and the practical, rubber-meets-the-road prescriptions not usually found together in a book dealing with the reform of the culture of the financial services industry – or any other industry for that matter (and, indeed, some of the proposals for reform contained herein are applicable to any industry).

The reason for conjoining the theoretical and concrete policy prescriptions has, to some degree, to do with biography and temperament rather than a schema formulated *a priori* or to fit with more typical treatments of the subject matter. As for the theoretical, I have made efforts to keep it connected to practical realities. At the same time, the practical cannot be divorced completely from principles or theory, so the proposals that I introduce in Chapter 5 (and there are many of them) are rooted in certain philosophical commitments that speak to the larger purposes of firms, markets, and the political communities they are supposed to serve. Those proposals, most of which were sketched during the 'Occupy Wall Street' movement in 2011, are rooted in the values of civic virtue and certain dominant schools of American philosophy (which I will not elaborate upon in these pages but which have conditioned my philosophical temperament, including my distaste for needlessly abstract and often useless philosophical and theoretical rumination). In these pages the theoretical and the practical are in constant dialogue, largely because they are supposed to be, although that dialogue is often in the background and not apparent.

With those prefatory remarks out of the way, let me get to the heart of the matter.

Wall Street is broken. It has been broken for a long time. *Partly*, this is because *we* are broken. We seem to have lost our way as citizens. Yet I am optimistic that serious reform of the culture of Wall Street is possible, just as I am optimistic that we can regain a robust sense of civics, of common purpose, a common purpose that extends beyond the next fashion and the next technological trend. That is, I am optimistic that the current culture (and this book is primarily about culture rather than regulation or operations) can, in time, be replaced by a new one. But such will require, at least in part, the proper leadership – as well as time.

Cynics and fatalists continue to tell me that I am seriously mistaken, and often I am told this in even more colorful language than that. They say this, it has become clear to me, because they believe they have an insight into 'human nature' that they presume I lack. But those who believe that there are aspects of human culture or human enterprise that are beyond improvement or reform are the ones who are mistaken, and *demonstrably* mistaken. Their views, in fact, run *counter* to the historical evidence, however counterintuitive that may sound. That point needs to be made at the outset. The tables on that sort of cynicism and fatalism must be turned, for it invites us all to labor under a false assumption and to accept a *status quo* that is unacceptable, something that we must never do as we strive to improve the quality of our lives and of the lives of our neighbours. To paraphrase a point made by John F. Kennedy, the problems we face (the problem of scandal and corruption) are of human origin, and so they can be solved by human thought and action.[3]

Yet, cynicism and fatalism are as pervasive as the problem itself, or so it at times seems. There are many people who hold that 'business ethics' *simpliciter* is an oxymoron, as they like to say, and so the notion of the reform of Wall Street culture (*of all things!*) is naïve at best. To the contrary, the history of Wall Street cannot be told without reference to the history of its reforms, which are constant if not always timely and effective. One need only survey the laws, industry rules, barriers to entry, and regulatory organs that have been enacted or have been set in place since the early years of the twentieth century – the passage of various federal, state, and international securities laws, the creation of the Securities and Exchange Commission and of the Commodities Futures Trading Commission, the establishment of various self-regulatory organizations such as the National Association of Securities Dealers (now the Financial Industry Regulatory Authority) and of the National Futures Association, pervasive state regulation of financial institutions of all types, from insurance companies to banks, and a blizzard of regulations that make the financial services industry (in the United States and in many of the rich, North Atlantic countries often referred to as 'the West') one of the most regulated industries in the world – a fact seemingly unknown to many, especially on the far left who continue to assert that the financial services industry is 'unregulated'. More generally, those who mock 'business ethics' *per se* are mistaken insofar as business (legal activity based upon economic exchanges and *sustained* by profits), like horticulture and sport, is a dimension of human culture and enterprise (indeed, the word 'enterprise' is not the property of commercial interests alone). Mocking the very notion of reform would seem to imply that business operates, at least to some degree, outside of civil society and according to rules that have no truck with the basic moral and communal considerations that make horticulture and sport possible (bearing in mind, of course, that the arch often sprung over both horticulture and sport is a commercial one).

The false but pervasive assumption that business operates in a world of its own, outside of the bounds of moral constraint or the ethical considerations that are applied outside of business, is itself based, in part, upon certain false assumptions about what is commonly referred to as 'human nature'. Otherwise, it rests upon dogmas.[4] Unfortunately, certain assumptions and dogmas are hard to kill once they get going (take the assumption that women are not fit for commercial and political engagement, or that blacks should not live in the same neighborhoods as whites, or that families headed by gay couples are not 'real' families). This book will attempt, nevertheless, to kill these assumptions and dogmas. The killing of these assumptions and dogmas will require taking aim at Wall Street culture (and we will see, in due course, *where* culture actually 'resides'), as well as at the psychology and spiritual malaise that enables and perpetuates it. This psychology and malaise – call them, together, 'The Other Wall Street' – supervenes upon commercial intercourse. *Ultimately*, the reform of Wall Street culture will require the reform of The Other Wall Street. The Other Wall Street will be the subject of the final chapter of the book.

In particular, this book will take aim at the following hackneyed assumptions that are endemic to thinking about business in general, and that are especially robust on Wall Street:

1.   Businesses exist to make profits;

2.   The word 'public' and the word 'private' refer to two hermetically sealed *realms* of human activity and interest that should only be perforated on rare occasions (we see this most clearly in the hackneyed, libertarian prescription, 'Government should get out of the market!');

3.   In order to incentivize managers, executives, brokers, analysts, bankers, and traders, firms must pay outsized levels of compensation ('outsized' relative to the average employee's compensation);

4.   The 'special' nature of Wall Street requires that it have different rules of the road than other industries; and

5.   Wall Street firms, as agents, are *entitled* to a portion of the wealth that they create for their customers and clients.

All of the above can sound correct, at least facially, but are in fact sheer dogma and are elements of a feedback loop that (in this is, perhaps, the most important point) increases systemic risk and continues to lead to scandals and crises (i.e., human harm and human suffering, sometimes on a grand scale). Each element will be refuted. Refuting each element should not be construed as an attempt to suggest that the free market (a misconstrued term in the hands of market fundamentalists who labor under the curious assumption that a market can be detached from guiding principles and cultural constraints) or Wall Street does not have a vital role to play in improving the quality of life in society. *To the contrary, it is the importance of that role that calls for the refutation.* But that does not mean that one must agree with market fundamentalists (i.e., radical economic libertarians), who view free markets (literally or practically) as ends in themselves rather than as *tools*, as natural kinds rather than as *social constructs*. In operating under both a long-discredited notion of social Darwinism and a classic fallacy, they mistake outcomes for intents, thus forgetting that the social compact requires that the well-being of the political community's members be *intended* rather than be the emergent result of blind forces or tendencies that sometime will serve to undermine the well-being of many, while serving the well-being of the few. It may be that the currents and winds will, serendipitously and consistently, take a ship, with its passengers and crew, a great distance toward its destination, but the price of the passage is not paid so that the voyage may be determined by serendipity (or emergent conditions). To the contrary, the price of passage is for the use of a worthy and well-appointed vessel, and to ensure that the contingencies and dangers of the voyage are confronted by a well-seasoned, intelligent, and alert crew. The ship alone is but a tool, and its proper employment requires the lights of reason. However useful the sun and currents, they are no substitute for the employment of the intelligence of the captain and crew. Likewise, the 'invisible hand' must work in concert with the visible hands that steer the ship of state and are charged with, and *intend*, the welfare of all, not just some. The 'invisible hand' is the label for an emergent phenomenon, but it is human reason that must take over where emergence leaves gaps or leads to excesses. Markets, like ships (and governments), are but tools. That's *all* they are. That's all they ever will be.

One of the fathers of market fundamentalism was the libertarian economist Milton Friedman (1912–2006). Friedman essayed to warn us, using rather alarmist language that equated the threat of the Soviet Union with the 'threat' of the welfare state, against those who actively and deliberately sought to promote social equity. Said Friedman:

> The preservation and expansion of freedom are today threatened from two directions. The one threat is obvious and clear. It is the external threat coming from the evil men in the Kremlin who promise to bury us. The other threat is far more subtle. It is the internal threat coming from men of good intentions and good will who wish to reform us. Impatient with the slowness of persuasion and example to achieve the great social changes they envision, they are anxious to use the power of the state to achieve their ends and confident of their own ability to do so. Yet if they gained the power, they would fail to achieve their immediate aims and, in addition, would produce a collective state from which they would recoil in horror and of which they would be among the first victims. Concentrated power is not rendered harmless by the good intentions of those who create it.
>
> The two threats unfortunately reinforce one another. Even if we avoid a nuclear holocaust, the threat from the Kremlin requires us to devote a sizable fraction of our resources to our military defense. The importance of government as a buyer of so much of our output, and the sole buyer of the output of many firms and industries, already concentrates a dangerous amount of economic power in the hands of the political authorities, changes the environment in which business operates and the criteria relevant for business success, and in these and other ways endangers a free market. This danger we cannot avoid. But we needlessly intensify it by continuing the present widespread governmental intervention in areas unrelated to the military defense of the nation and by undertaking ever new government programs – from medical care for the aged to lunar exploration.
>
> As Adam Smith once said, 'there is much ruin in a nation'. Our basic structure of values and the interwoven network of free institutions will withstand much. I believe that we shall be able to preserve and extend freedom despite the size of the military programs and despite the economic powers already concentrated in Washington. But we shall be able to do so only if we awake to the threat that we face, only if we persuade our fellow men that free institutions offer a surer, if perhaps at times a slower, route to the ends they seek than the coercive power of the state.[5]

The notion of 'freedom' detached from reference to the hopes, goals and values of a political community (which includes the organs of government), is chimerical. Freedom is not the *goal* of a well-lived human life, but rather is a necessary *condition* for *a human life well-lived*. But what is a human life well-lived? As has been made clear by countless philosophers and thinkers from Aristotle on, freedom cannot be properly exercised apart from the political community that gives rise to the opportunities, options, resources, goals and values that make the exercise of freedom *meaningful*. Further, for there to be political community in any meaningful sense other exigent variables must come into view and be given relevance: concern for the welfare of others who are members of the community; a spirit of compromise; rules and laws; familial support; forbearance; fairness; the fulfillment of duties; and, perhaps most important, *trust*. Yes, the human rights that, for Friedman and many other libertarians who have looked to him as a guiding light, give freedom its importance (for the hallowing of freedom rests upon the dignity of persons as such) should never be abused by the state, just as they should never be abused by co-equal members of a state, i.e. by one's fellow citizens. No political liberal would disagree. But the state itself is the creation of a political community and has government as its regulator, fashioned out of mutual agreements, tacit and explicit, to preserve not only the peace and the commonweal, but to improve the opportunities for the exercise of freedom itself, construed as the 'pursuit of happiness' by the state's individual citizens (at least in the case of advanced democracies such as the United States, France, Germany and Britain, *inter alia*).

Human freedom is impotent when isolated from the types of constraints implied in the very idea of freedom and from the values that give rise to political community, which can exist only where members draw compromises and agree to make room for the various pursuits of others, just as J. S. Mill made clear in his 1859 masterpiece, *On Liberty*. Market fundamentalism's foundation is a pernicious and stubborn fallacy: it sees government as a dampener *simpliciter*, as the concentration of forces that *interfere* with the operations of markets and the lives of individuals. Such a notion is so discredited by the facts that its persistence seems indicative of a cognitive incapacity of some sort. Policies made with such a premise as a touchstone can only lead to trouble. This is not to say that government – which is, in large measure, but another tool – is perfect. *Far from it*. It sometimes makes *catastrophic* mistakes (and not merely when it comes to economic matters). But those mistakes no more mean that government 'is the problem' in some generalized sense than it is true that markets and individuals always perform for the common good, for markets, too, make catastrophic mistakes. The debate between market fundamentalists and liberals is, in fact, sophomoric and for that reason should be shunted aside, so that the proper mix of means and ends can be determined, given the stock of existing knowledge, given the present policy goals, and given the broader contexts that are extant. Libertarian slogans and reductionisms are like liberal slogans and reductionisms – useful for setting the stage of debate, but beyond that, troublesome.

As indicated, many of the proper values for a well-ordered and enduring political community are *other-regarding*, not merely self-regarding, as are the principal operating values of market participants – buyers and sellers, dealers and agents. Indeed, the capital-L Liberal state (United States, Canada, United Kingdom, and others in the West) must be concerned with the welfare of all the members of the political community, *equally*, precisely because the inherent or unalienable human rights of all of its citizens (a philosophical commitment embraced by both partisan political liberals and partisan political conservatives) requires that it be. Freedom, in the robust human sense sketched above, which is the only sense that matters, means little without the mechanisms of government imposing democratically-adopted and so democratically-sanctioned constraints and without rewarding incentives that make the exercise of human freedom not only possible but *secure*. Thus, as the philosopher Ronald Dworkin has put it, the 'sovereign virtue' of government is equal concern for all citizens, not merely the poor, or the rich, or the middle class. Equal *concern* does not mean efforts to create or guarantee equal outcomes (an ongoing but scurrilous conservative-libertarian charge against liberals and progressives), but only that the freedom of each citizen to pursue his or her happiness as determined by his or her own lights is not hampered or neutralized by morally illegitimate assaults on the exercise of their freedom, whether in the form of machinations of other citizens to deny that pursuit, or by negative externalities or harms produced by others where those suffering from the externalities or harms do not, alone, have the power to force reparation or create adequate disincentives against recurrence.

What Friedman did not seem to understand is what many market funda-mentalists and libertarian extremists continue to fail to understand, that is, free institutions include all of those institutions created by the free political commu-nity, for the sake of the political community, by means of the democratic action of its members. Such institutions are not limited to, as Friedman believed and as other libertarian extremists continue to believe, firms and markets, but include the various organs of governmental administration. Free institutions are so by virtue of the nature of the decisions and actions that give rise to them. When institu-tions are the result of public deliberation and uncoerced democratic action (both almost always imperfect), they are by their very natures free, for they are creations of free people by means of uncoerced assent. Thus, when Friedman wrote

> But we shall be able to do so only if we awake to the threat that we face, only if we per-suade our fellow men that free institutions offer a surer, if perhaps at times a slower, route to the ends they seek than the coercive power of the state

he was warning of a danger to our political community that proceeded from prem-ises that were fatally flawed. In a democracy all or at least most of our important institutions are the result of persuasion, however imperfect and, at times, ranco-rous. And such efforts at persuasion are an ongoing affair that will never end, if we are lucky. Such is the untidy nature of public deliberation, of democracy, of cultural politics, wherein there will always be pockets of citizens who bristle in the face of democratically-produced policies and decisions. And so it goes.

Equally fatally flawed is the notion that calls for 'justice' are calls for the use of government force *against* free people. For when Friedman asserted that those who call for more environmental protection or more medical care for the rural poor are those who are 'anxious to use the power of the state to achieve their ends and confident of their own ability to do so' – a claim, once again, asserted by contemporary libertarian extremists – he was flatly incorrect. The presumption is that 'government' (in the context of a democracy) is a power that can be marshalled against the people to short-circuit public deliberation and persuasion. It is true that in totalitarian or reactionary states this is a constant possibility (and, after the *Citizens United* decision in 2010, a growing possibility approaching from another vector – the vector of Friedman's preferred, free, nongovernmental institutions). But modern, Liberal, democratic states are not totalitarian or soaked-through with reactionary impulses. To obtain the aid of the 'power of the state' with respect to any change in civil society requires at least some effort at persuasion – through public protest, through lobbying, by making a sustained case in the various media, in arguments on the floors of legislatures, through white papers and books and lectures, through door to door canvassing, through satire, and so on. Those who are effective in their campaigns to change public policy cannot be accused of using the power of the state as a bludgeon to get their way. If they have been successful it is because they have persuaded enough people to see things their way (or – and here things get darker – they have been successful, at least for the moment, with their lies).

The extremist libertarian argument is, then, like so many ideological arguments. What is really an argument about the shape and degree of some form of action or policy is blown-up into a cosmological, Manichean clash between the powers of Good and the powers of Evil. Extremist libertarians make some good points, but they tend to quickly go off the rails into incoherent locutions of the sort Friedman gave us in *Capitalism and Freedom*. We can avoid this by understanding that all of government agencies and commissions, legislatures and judiciaries, firms and markets, are mechanisms, tools, not the preferred weapons of those who have convinced themselves that they are the soldiers and champions of 'The Light'. Just as the body cannot live without a brain, it cannot live without a heart or blood. The body is whole and works well only when its various organs are functioning as they should, individually and in coordination. In the context of political economy, the meaning of 'as they should' will be, perennially, a subject of reflection and debate. Civil society is constantly moving, constantly evolving and sometimes devolving, and constantly reinventing itself, in whole or in part (usually, in part). The roles and limits and utility of firms, governments and markets will therefore always be questioned and reconsidered. That is simply as it should be. Given that, the way forward is not to be found in the vilification of firms, markets or government, but rather through the use of public reason in determining where and which constraints should be eased, removed or, alternatively, tightened or made more robust, where and which incentives should be added or withdrawn, etc. In a Liberal state, public reason asks where the trade-offs should be, whether we are happy with the *status quo* (and should be), whether core values are being eroded by government or markets, and what should be done about it, through an endless process of deliberation, argument and persuasion. The trouble starts when we reify – or for all intents and purposes reify – markets or governments, and forget that their roles are functional, not the point of the game, and when we become, having taken on the role of defenders of one against the other, soldiers and 'Champions of The Light' over and against the 'Forces of Darkness'. This Manichean moment, this morality play, is the one in which politics in the United States has been stuck for the past several years. It threatens much – not only the economic achievements of the country but also the sororal and fraternal bonds that are required for its people to consider themselves members of the same political and moral community, with a common destiny. It threatens balkanization.

It should be clear, then, why the interests of the political community are far more expansive than the interests of markets and firms, and why the values that must be held by members of political communities cannot be the same as the operating principles of markets and firms, in which the participants' much more narrow objectives are to further their own financial interests, usually narrowly construed. What the late management guru Peter F. Drucker has told us I am happy to introduce here:

> I am for the free market. Even though it doesn't work too well, nothing else works at all. But I have serious reservations about capitalism as a system because it idolizes economics as the be-all and end-all of life ... It is one-dimensional. For example, I have often advised managers that a 20–1 salary ratio between senior executives and rank-and-file white collar workers is the limit beyond which they cannot go if they don't want resentment and falling morale to hit their companies.
>
> Today, I believe it is socially and morally unforgiveable when managers reap huge profits for themselves but fire workers. As societies, we will pay a heavy price for the contempt this generates among middle managers and workers. In short, whole dimensions of what it means to be a human being and treated as one are not incorporated into the economic calculus of capitalism. For such a myopic system to dominate other aspects of life is not good for any society.[6]

The wealth gap that currently exists in the United States (which attaches to Drucker's point about compensation) has indeed become worrisome. The ratio of salary and other compensation of senior executives to those of average workers in many American businesses is, today, far greater than 20 to 1. Indeed, it is now about 400:1 in the largest corporations. (Robert Reich, former US Labour Secretary, who is pro-capitalism and who is a tireless champion of economic justice, does an excellent job in educating the public about this in the 2011 documentary, 'Inequality for All', and economist Thomas Piketty addresses the roots and dangers of a widening wealth and income gap in his much acclaimed and award-winning book *Capital in the Twenty-First Century*). But while closely related to Wall Street culture, the wealth gap, which threatens the social fabric and might eventually lead to serious social unrest, cannot be placed at the feet of Wall Street alone. It is a much larger socio-economic problem, with many moving parts and a complicated history. It is not my intent here to suggest that bankers or brokers or portfolio managers should have their jobs disappear. Again, *to the contrary*, these jobs have important functions. But their levels of compensation invite curiosity, especially in an industry that is not at the centre of the real economy, but rather plays only an important supporting role on its behalf (and many argue that their levels of compensation amount to rent-seeking). The levels of compensation of these specialists (I would not call all of them *professionals*) is rooted in some of the dogmas listed above. Why should an investment banker make millions, while an airline pilot's compensation hovers in the high-five to low-six figures, should he or she be fortunate enough to get a job with one of the better airlines? Why should the banker make so much more than the seasoned nursing manager at a major metropolitan hospital, or an engineer who flies around the world testing the safety of bridges that are crossed by thousands (if not tens of thousands) of people on a daily basis? Because of market forces? Well, there is that, without a doubt, but there are also the powers that be, powers that pull the levers to make those forces what they are. Market forces are culturally rooted and result from people with agendas (and we *all* have agendas). They are as much the expression of qualitative considerations as they are quantitative expressions rooted in utility calculations. They are not dispassionate economic levers that 'naturally' set optimum price points. Market forces, like markets, are not natural kinds.

Neo-liberal economics has its answers, of course, and we all are well versed in them. But neo-liberal economics' answers are under rather severe pressure by those who think that they are out of touch with important variables – including non-market values – that have been shunted aside, as argued by those economists and graduate students of economics in the 'post-autistic' or 'real world' economics movement, a movement that challenges neo-classical economics' obsessions with mathematical models, inhumane logics, and conflation of explication with normative prescription.[7] 'Post-autistic economics' values such things as entrepreneurship, innovation, and efficiency, but it has created a new intellectual space that allows the sorts of questions about compensation that were just posed to be posed anew with intellectual respectability, despite derision from the guardians of the reigning economics orthodoxy. In what is called 'The Kansas City

Proposal' of August 2001, which was the result of a week-long discussion of the current state of economic thought, the following propositions were offered:

1. *A broader conception of human behaviour*: The definition of economic man as an autonomous rational optimizer is too narrow and does not allow for the roles of other determinants such as instinct, habit and gender, class and other social factors in shaping the economic psychology of social agents;

2. *Recognition of culture*: Economic activities, like all social phenomena, are necessarily embedded in culture, which includes all kinds of social, political and moral value-systems and institutions. These profoundly shape and guide human behaviour by imposing obligations, enabling and disabling particular choices, and creating social or communal identities, all of which may impact on economic behaviour;

3. *Consideration of history*: Economic reality is dynamic rather than static – and as economists we must investigate how and why things change over time and space. Realistic economic inquiry should focus on process rather than simply on ends;

4. *A new theory of knowledge*: The positive vs normative [or fact vs value] dichotomy that has traditionally been used in the social sciences is problematic. The fact-value distinction can be transcended by the recognition that the investigator's values are inescapably involved in scientific inquiry and in making scientific statements, whether consciously or not. This acknowledgement enables a more sophisticated assessment of knowledge claims;

5. *Empirical grounding*: More effort must be made to substantiate theoretical claims with empirical evidence. The tendency to privilege theoretical tenets in the teaching of economics without reference to empirical observation cultivates doubt about the realism of such explanation;

6. *Expanded methods*: Procedures such as participant observation, case studies and discourse analysis should be recognized as legitimate means of acquiring and analyzing data alongside econometrics and formal modelling. Observation of phenomena from different vantage points using various data-gathering techniques may offer new insights into phenomena and enhance our understanding of them;

7. *Interdisciplinary dialogue*: Economists should be aware of diverse schools of thought within economics, and should be aware of developments in other disciplines, particularly the social sciences.[8]

Exposing the dogmas referenced above meshes with the calls for a reconsideration of the economic thought contained in The Kansas City Proposal (and others like it). The reigning neo-liberal economic models have a lot to do with (i.e., help to enable) Wall Street's excesses, which manifest themselves with those models operating in the background. Challenging the dogmas and rethinking the reigning models will allow us to bring back to memory – *civic* memory, that is – the higher and grander purposes that Wall Street serves – bring back to memory the fact that, ultimately, Wall Street actors work for the teachers, bus drivers, municipal administrators, doctors, nurses, and cab drivers who entrust their often modest savings to it, either directly, as in the form of brokerage and bank accounts, or indirectly, via securitizations and derivative investments made through retirement plans and pension funds. But the pervasive assumption that one goes to Wall Street solely to make money interferes with this recollection, and this assumption is part of an ongoing feedback loop, a vicious circlethat maintains the *status quo*. The assumption fixes the eye on *taking*, on *extraction*, or on, as industry insiders sometimes call it, 'the kill'. Scandals, fraud, and breaches of fiduciary duty (the breaking of faith with clients and customers) are conceived and are born in the interstices of the dogmas and assumptions that have been operating for far too long.

Cynicism, Fatalism and Dogmatism: False Prognostications

To accept the cynics', fatalists' and dogmatists' views regarding reform is to accept a defeatist attitude about the power of people to effect change in their environments (including in their social institutions) and in themselves, and to effect such change voluntarily, without external coercion but rather because of changes in perspective, in ways of seeing. Pessimism about needed reforms, about the possibility of public *metanoia* (from the Greek, meaning 'transformation of the mind', about which I will be saying a good deal in due course) is nothing new. Pessimism pervaded policy discussions concerning curtailment of the use of tobacco products. 'Big tobacco' is now being squeezed to the point that its future, at least in the United States, is uncertain – and its grip on Europe and other parts of the world is beginning to weaken as well. Likewise, it had been assumed that women would never be granted suffrage or be welcome to participate in political life in any meaningful way, but women received the right to vote in the United States and throughout the West (through the strenuous efforts of Mary Wollstonecraft, Elizabeth Cady Stanton, and Susan B. Anthony, as well as supportive men, such as Gerrit Smithand Frederick Douglass). In the United States, a woman may soon be sworn in as head of state, a milestone in American history that, should it occur, will have lagged similar breakthroughs in other countries – Great Britain, Pakistan, Israel and Brazil, to name a few. And we can go on: workers' rights; a safety net that protects the average citizen from financial catastrophe; the right to legal counsel for the indigent; the election of an African American to the US presidency; the right, if disabled, to have accessible public accommodations; the right of gays and lesbians to be treated fairly and equally under the law, etc. All of these, for quite a long time, were thought unlikely, if not outright pie in the sky. Yet here we are.

So much for cynicism and fatalism, both based upon no more than intellectual inertia and the reification of a particular *status quo*. Things change. People change. It may take trauma, tragedy or crisis at times – in fact, it often does, to the great shame of our species – but things and people do change. So for those who are cynical or pessimistic about the prospects for Wall Street cultural reform, the preceding examples of once-thought unlikely *social* reforms may be enough to allow a reading of this book all the way through. In fact, for Wall Street culture, the handwriting is already on the wall – no pun intended. It is very unlikely that civil society will tolerate many more of the kinds of disruptions that were caused in the recent financial crisis of 2007/8, or those, such as the LIBOR rate-fixing and other scandals, uncovered subsequently. Governments have revamped Wall Street regulation to deal with many of the issues that gave rise to that crisis, and many (but not all) of Wall Street's weaknesses and corrupting influences have been exposed to daylight. Just as important, the crisis and the pain it has caused gave birth to a new level of awareness concerning Wall Street's narcissistic and rapacious culture. The Occupy movement, which foundered because of its lack of a coherent policy agenda and jejune assumptions about the mechanisms of political power, was just one expression of that awareness.

Gardens of Democracy

While planning this book I came across another, *The Gardens of Democracy: A New American Story of Citizenship, the Economy, and the Role of Government*, by Eric Liu and Nick Hanauer (hereafter, '*Gardens*'), a book that has been praised by many on both the political right and the political left as a balanced treatment of the current problems of consumerism, materialism, civic virtue (or its lack), and the reigning greed that suggests that capitalism is *per se* a perverse economic system. The authors are both self-described capitalists (Hanauer is actually a venture capitalist, a principal of the Seattle-based firm, Second Avenue Partners, and holds a degree not in finance but in *philosophy;* Eric Liu was a speechwriter and policy advisor in the Clinton administration and an executive at a noted technology company), so *Gardens* is not a rant against capitalism, just as it is not the usual fare that one will find in the business ethics literature, much of which is too dry, too rarified, or too professionalized to be of much use for broad public discourse – or, alas, even effective classroom discourse. To the contrary, it is a call for the restoration of important values that will help us recall just what capitalism and free markets are for. *Gardens* places a great deal of emphasis on the role of the citizen and on citizenship itself. To reform Wall Street, a process that will take years, that is precisely where the emphasis should be placed. Liu and Hanauer also authored *The True Patriot*, which is a call for Americans (and others) to rethink their notions of citizenship in view of the extant political polarization, as well as the dogmas and simplistic economic ideas referenced above. Liu has founded Citizenship University, in Seattle, Washington, where he has attempted to breathe new life into the meaning of citizenship, and he and those who work with him call for a rededication, a new pledge, to fulfil the obligations of citizenship:

> I pledge to be an active American
> to show up for others
> to govern myself
> to help govern my community
> I recommit myself to my country's creed
> to cherish liberty
> as a responsibility.
>
> I pledge to serve
> and to push my country:
> when right, to be kept right;
> when wrong, to be set right
> Wherever my ancestors and I were born,
> I claim America
> and I pledge to live like a citizen.[9]

I have a great deal of sympathy for what Liu and Hanauer are trying to do. My own thoughts about business ethics in general and the reform of Wall Street culture in particular were gelling well before the release of *Gardens*, and particularly since 2008, when I pitched the idea for a course in business ethics at Rutgers University titled 'Citizenship and Corporate Cultures' – a course I now teach. But finding and reading *Gardens* sealed my hunches about the sort of *metanoia* that is needed. It was my view then, as it is now, that the standard approaches to business ethics pedagogy (and *in situ* ethics training within corporations) have not been very effective in preventing many of the corporate scandals that we have seen in recent years.[10] To borrow a term from epidemiology, they have not generated the necessary 'herd immunity' to ward off the infectious greed and commercial myopia that lead to scandals, disruptions and loss of confidence in social institutions. Textbooks – topical narratives, amalgams of cases, theories, and law sandwiched between two covers – have their place and are useful, and I have my favorite textbooks for use in my own courses, but I have always had the sense that something important is missing. That something, I concluded, was an appeal to 'spirit', and most specifically the spirit of citizenship (but other communitarian 'spirits' as well). Such is an appeal to a *we* that is broader than the *we* of the shop floor or the executive suite. It is the *we* that provides us with our essential identities, the *we* that speaks to our *souls*. The textbooks and ethical monographs that focus on 'the rules of the game', agency, and the question of who is a fiduciary (etc.) are not enough to trigger important emotional *sentiments* rooted in the very identities of many students. Philosophical monographs and professional journal articles on a wide array of issues in business ethics have limited use in formal pedagogy, although they are of some use to the relatively small number of professors and business managers who have a taste for such literature. The notion of a *we*, the idea of solidarity in pursuit of a higher cause, has been eroded over the past fifty or so years, partly due to the politics of identity, the politics of recognition, the 'Gekkoization' of Wall Street, the rise of libertarianism *a la* Thatcher and Reagan and Friedman, and this erosion has been exacerbated by growing distrust of government and cynicism regarding social institutions. It has been hard to sustain the notion of a *we* and of civics in such an acid bath of negative ideas and scandalous events, eating into the ties that bind. But returning to the notion of a *we* will be key to any notion of sustainable reform, either of economic thought or of Wall Street's culture.

Many of the books written specifically about the causes of the recent financial crisis, or published as warnings preceding or subsequent to it, do not address the need for renewed solidarity. These books, though perfectly useful as far as they go, can be assigned, arguably, to the following categories: tell-alls (Andrew Ross Sorkin's *Too Big to Fail* and Frank Partnoy's *Infectious Greed: How Deceit and Risk Corrupted The Financial Markets*); risk alerts (Nassim Taleb's *The Black Swan*); calls for more and deeper thought about regulation (Randall S. Kroszner and Robert J. Schiller's *Reforming U.S. Financial Markets: Reflections Before and Beyond Dodd-Frank*) and Viral V. Acharya's (et. al) *Regulating Wall Street: The Dodd-Frank Act and the New Architecture of Global Finance*); I-told-you-so books (Nouriel Roubini's and Stephen Mihm's *Crisis Economics*); and crisis anthologies (Laurence B. Siegler's *Insights into the Global Financial Crisis* and, again, Roubini and Mihm's *Crisis Economics*). All of these books are worth reading, in whole or in part, depending upon one's level of interest or need, and there are many others that could be included in the above list according to the heuristic and admittedly imperfect typology employed. But these books don't go nearly as far to the heart of the problem of outrageous corporate conduct (or citizen amnesia) as I believe necessary. For that the call to a deeper and more pervasive *metanoia* is needed.

Psychology and The Spirits of the Sacred

In terms of market psychology, the often cited tulip mania bubble in the Netherlands, way back in the seventeenth century, tells us something that is not always the reason it is cited. That is, it is an archetype of market crises that *repeat*. The fact that they repeat means we do not yet have a handle on something important in our conceptions of the marketplace, although we have done a good deal to harness its excesses and to eliminate or at least mitigate various of its dangers (talk of new bubbles in real estate and equities is in the air even now, in 2014, despite the bubbles that we know all too well from our experience with the crisis of 2007/8). Those of us who have gotten a handle on the repetitions seize the opportunities instead of offering thought leadership, exploiting our knowledge of market psychology to our own benefit. Treating market psychology with circuit breakers can have salutary effects, but the underlying spirits that lead to them, most notably, but not only, the spirits of greed and fear (or perhaps I should say, of acquisition and aversion), are never addressed in any significant way in any of the otherwise very good books just referenced. There is some recent scholarship in empirical normative ethics (Daniel Kahneman's *Thinking Fast and Slow*, and Kwame Anthony Appiah's *Experiments in Ethics*, for example) that is beginning to fill some gaps, but these are not specifically concerned with *business* conduct. All of the 'crisis anatomies' and case instruction in the world will not be enough to check the end-runs of which *narrowly-construed* self-interest is capable. None of these books, for all their very valuable, takes on the challenge of checking rapacity and acquisitiveness *by calling upon other values and commitments* that are also *charged* with *emotional energy* – the commitment to (and a sense of ownership of) one's commonwealth and one's community, and the concern for one's reputation and standing in the eyes of others outside of the marketplace (in families, in religious communities, etc.). It is just assumed that the darker, primal impulses that lead to scandal and market excesses (let's call these primal animal spirits, to borrow and retrofit an appellation – i.e. 'animal spirits' – from Akerlof and Shiller – which *they* borrow from John Maynard Keynes's classic, *The General Theory of Employment, Interest, and Money*) can meet no countervailing emotional force that is powerful enough to check them.

But this conclusion seems premature. Sincere commitments to commonwealth, to community, the affective quality of *sororitas* and *fraternitas*, and a sense of pride in one's personal standing in the community of one's peers (let's call these 'the spirits of the sacred') can stand toe to toe with primal animal spirits. This is why *Gardens*, though short and in many ways simple (and in many ways well outside the typical business ethics or citizenship-theory literature) was and is so refreshing. It kindles the spirits of the sacred. It dares to take on market excesses by challenging readers to reflect upon their own claimed ideals and commitments to their political and even local communities, to democracy, to the natural world, and to life itself – including future life, the life of the unborn generations to follow. It is a book that dared to suggest that even within capitalism there is a cogent, reasonable, and necessary answer to the questions 'How much is enough?' and 'How far should we go?' – questions that the reigning economic ideology and dogmas tell us are pseudo-questions.

But, as Drucker noted, and largely though not entirely correctly, there is no mechanism within capitalism itself that permits such questions to be asked – *unless, that is, one rethinks the meaning of capitalism as necessarily containing within its own logics goals that lie beyond those logics* – and this, it seems to me, is not terribly difficult to do. Monistic thinking prevents us from appreciating the fact that there are *capitalisms*, not just capitalism (which exists nowhere), just as there are democracies, not just democracy (which, likewise, exists nowhere). The notion that GDP growth must be X, imports must not exceed Y, or profitability year on year must not be less than Z, are assumptions based upon monistic thinking, where X, Y and Z are reified, become natural kinds. There is a price to pay for such thinking. It takes the form of higher household debt with its attendant stress, of pressure on national governments to meet algorithmic expectations under the slogan '*It's the Economy Stupid!*', and human beings becoming the tail of the wagging dog of 'innovation' and 'progress'. Elections are assumed to be about 'pocket books' and 'purses' rather than values and sound policy, and this becomes an electoral feedback loop. The system wants predictability, but human beings should not oblige it with automaton-like predictability, for human beings are meant to grow, change, and swap existing values for new values and old goals for new goals based upon a wide variety of human considerations and variables. They should be 'irrational' in the sense that they may discount market logics – at least at times – and favor, instead, plans and choices that may in fact leave them financially diminished, economically worse off, and be enriched precisely thereby. To be human is to choose to value, at times, that which the market denigrates and to embrace goals that have no predictable relation to market logics. That is what makes humans beings (if not markets) *free*.

There can be too much of a good thing, even if that good thing is money, 'efficiency' and liquidity. Money, like calories, as Aristotle told us many centuries ago, is necessary for living a good life. Too many calories, unutilized toward constructive ends, can sicken and kill. Money is no different. Money, like markets, is a tool, a tool for growth and flourishing. Like blood in the body, it is best when it flows throughout the commonwealth, rather than when it forms and swells in occult pools – in bank accounts and equity holdings of the super-wealthy (who are decidedly not 'job creators', despite the rhetoric to the contrary). Money is a tool best placed into the hands that most need it or that can best employ it toward productive ends. I realize that there are a lot of assumptions woven into the preceding sentences, assumptions about 'need' and 'productive ends'. I will have to unpack and defend those assumptions, of course. For now, I hope it will suffice to say that the limits of economic and market logics stop at the shores of human values that derive from the spirits of the sacred – spirits rooted in the messiness and unpredictability of human growth, human values and human freedom (what I will call, alternatively, our 'positive animal spirits').

I don't want this notion of the spirits of the sacred to sound too ethereal. To the contrary, we see them at work every day. They are seen in the actions of a parent who quits a lucrative job to spend more time with a child; in a millionaire trader who gives up a trader's income to become an artist or to open a marginally profitable bed and breakfast or day camp; in a banker who decides to become a physician, or a rabbi, or a poet; in a new college graduate who passes up a lucrative offer by a Wall Street investment bank to become a high school science teacher. All employ, are motivated by, the spirits of the sacred to push back against machine-like market logics. The spirits of the sacred drive human beings toward engagement in non-commercial endeavors in search of community, family, meaning, friendship, fulfillment, nature, even God – even all of these at once. There is nothing mystical or unknowable about the spirits of the sacred. You and I know them very well indeed. And very few of us, upon reflection, would be any more inclined to include markets and commerce in our list of sacred commitments than we would be to include hammers and vaporizers on that list, for the latter are merely tools in the service of far more important human projects and goals. This is not to say that the spirits of the sacred cannot infuse our working and business lives, as philosopher and theologian Michael Novak has pointed out in his book *Business as a Calling: Work and the Examined Life* (1996), only that care must be taken not to forget their purposes and how they fit within a nexus of activities and values that weave our plans of life into something coherent, rather than a lading list of pecuniary activities and events on the road to the grave.

Regulation as Coercion?

Regulation is a form of coercion, and coercion is not enough to prevent ethical lapses in corporate and market conduct, though its the go-to remedy for policy makers. If it were, the many scandals and market crises of the past several decades would not have come to pass. So the idea that 'more regulation' will provide sufficient firebreaks is misguided. However, a few words about this are in order. First, it would be preposterous for anyone to claim that regulation is not needed to keep firms and markets in check. While there will always be debate over whether the *right* regulations are in place in order to prevent bad conduct and scandals, any suggestion that regulation (as well as practical protocols for enterprise risk management) is not the principal tool for keeping firms and complicated markets contained can only be called unserious – to put it mildly. I have spent over thirty years of my life dealing with regulation as a Wall Street insider – including the regulation of mutual funds, hedge funds, investment managers, investment banks, and private equity firms – and but for the regulations that constrain these businesses the investor abuses and systemic risks would have been far worse than they otherwise have been. Second, I do not mean to suggest that regulation is not itself constructive in shaping morals and ideals. The very fact that there is a law against (or a law that calls forth) certain behaviours informs us, obliquely, that our society or community holds certain values and ideals that it expects us, as individual members, to hold and to act upon, whether or not we recall or can recite passages of positive law. Thus, zoning laws that require us to keep our houses and lawns up to snuff and ordinances that require us to curb our dogs communicate values and ideals about the need to respect the sensibilities of our neighbours, and we develop habits of neighbourliness that reflect both what the law requires and the law's intent. Law shapes morals and ideals – or can – just as it imposes requirements that guide behavior. Law does not only instruct; it reflects. Thus, law is not *merely* coercion.

But reference to the law is, as mentioned, but an oblique way to talk about values and ideals. To talk about values and ideals we do well to take a more direct approach – to actually *talk* about them. We are better off answering questions such as *Who do we wish to be?* and *What sort of society do we wish to cultivate and pass on to our children?* through open conversation and debate as part of the activity of cultural politics and civic engagement. Reform in society, as with the adoption and amendment of laws, reflects conversion of the hearts and minds of its members. It always has and it always will. Reform of our commercial institutions is, likewise, an affair of hearts and minds. The heart prompts, the mind devises, things change. Looking to positive law (regulation) to answer the preceding questions is like looking to the owner's manual of a car to decide where you should go. The analogy is not perfect, but it should suffice to make the point. Law does indeed reflect back to us some ideals and goals valued by the political community, and we can often divine from the law just what those ideals and goals might be. But reliance on this static approach to teach and cultivate values is precarious. With countries driven by the often distant and automatic logics of markets, and undergirded by positive law, citizens themselves must actually deliberate and reflect upon the more fundamental questions concerning who they wish to be and what sort of society they wish to create. Beyond this, of course, we must remember an important insight provided by George Chapman in 1654: 'Ere he shall lose an eye for such a trifle ... For doing deeds of nature! I'm ashamed. The law is such an ass'.[11] The law is not always morally constructive, as so many libertarians, business executives, and civil rights activists are sure, rightly, to remind us (although for quite different reasons!). Indeed, the law is not only, at times, 'such an ass', but no more than the expression of powerful, self-serving interests whose concern about the commonwealth is slight at best. This point should not be gainsaid. So those who revere rather than respect the law should attenuate their commitment to fit the facts; the law is but another *tool* (there's that word again); it should not be an idol. It is the thinking citizen who is sovereign, or ought to be, not the law. In what follows there will be a call to citizen action, a call for citizens to reflect upon the two questions posed above – *Who do we wish to be?* and *What sort of society do we wish to instantiate and pass on to our children?* – with Wall Street culture placed squarely in the crosshairs.

That said, it is important to remember the civilizing role of regulation, and the erosion of respect for regulation and regulators that is often promulgated by ardent market libertarians. This erosion is captured very well by Noriel Roubini and Stephen Mihm, in this insightful and artful passage from their book, *Crisis Economics*:

> An old Latin phrase captures this most modern dilemma: *Quis custodiet ipsos custodies?* Or to paraphrase a little, "Who will regulate the regulators?" Who will ensure that those who are given the power to police society will perform their duties effectively and selflessly?
>
> It's not a new problem. Plato acknowledged this predicament in the *Republic*, though he was talking about a society's guardians or stewards, not its financial regulators. (Derivatives were still a long way off.) Plato's solution was an intriguing one: the guardians – and the people generally – would be told a "noble lie," or useful myth, that the guardians were more virtuous than other people. Convinced of their own goodness, they would scorn private gain and instead look out for the welfare of the republic. The illusion of virtue would be its own reward.
>
> This vision is apt to prompt snickers today, but it highlights an unsettling truth. Consider what happens if the guardians or regulators are ... derided as incompetent and corrupt. This is a different kind of lie, but we've been encouraged to believe it in our own time. Until very recently, regulators have been told they're chumps for not going to work in the private sector. They're fools who can't compete with the financial geniuses on Wall Street. Worse, they're an impediment and an obstacle to the brave new world of financial innovation.
>
> This lie, spread by fanatics of laissez-faire, deserves refutation.[12]

Civic and Corporate Soul-Making

There seems to be a general consensus that the recent financial crisis of 2007/8 *should not* have happened, implying that something or some things could have been done to prevent it. Few books get to what I take to be the heart of the matter, which has less to do with technical issues ('black swan' events, derivatives clearing houses, technical risk protocols, and enhanced capital requirements for banks, etc.) than with human *proclivities*. Human proclivities being the messy and slippery things that they are, involving such largely *non-quantifiable* variables as psychology, beliefs (including religious beliefs and beliefs about human nature) and, more generally, *affect* (broadly construed), they have scarcely been taken-up in the construction of remedies and prophylactics. Discussions about 'ethics' have been ubiquitous but painfully superficial, amounting to so many suggestions that 'people should behave themselves for their own good and for the common good', in life generally and in business specifically. But the construction 'people should behave themselves' is too vague, and that vagueness is one of the reasons that many people take a pessimistic view concerning the probable recurrence of what befell us in the recent financial crisis, not to mention the long string of scandals that preceded and succeeded it (not the least of which was, again, the LIBOR scandal, which was and is so monumental that policy makers have scarcely known what to do with it). Vague declarations that people should behave themselves do not get to the reasons that people often opt *not* to behave themselves. Without addressing the psychology, beliefs, and affect involved in human decision making, policy makers will never provide comprehensive solutions to wrongdoing in markets and business, and will continue to apply coercion and technocratic remedies. Because of this, I argue that both policy makers and corporate leaders should also be involved in civic and corporate *soul-making*. Civic and corporate soul-making require engagement with psychology, beliefs, and emotions.

There is the classic question, posed at the beginning of many introductory university ethics courses: *Why should I be good?* Perhaps an equally useful question is *Why should I not be good?* There are *existential reasons* that help to explain why it is that people shove aside moral obligations and even law, with all the consequences that may come with their violation. Human beings are extremely needy and dependent creatures, whether we are children or adults, and in many ways *especially* when we are adults. We need food, shelter, clothing, the respect of peers, self-respect, protection from dangers foreseen and unforeseen, self-confidence, companions and friends who are true and who will aid us in times of need and who make good times more rewarding and enjoyable, and a sense that life is meaningful and worth living. Let's call these things our existential needs. Permit me to place this in graphic form, in contrast to the stark notions that 'people should behave themselves' and the moral principles conjured up when that phrase is proffered:

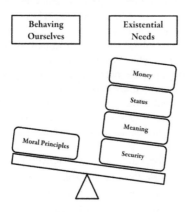

Figure I.1: Behaving Ourselves versus Existential Needs

It is easy to see which pressures can win the day, *especially during times of stress*. At the centre of all of these existential needs is our *existential sense* – that is, the sense of our temporariness, our vulnerability, and our mortality, and so whatever it is we wish to be in life, and whatever we wish to do in the time allotted we should pursue with little tolerance for obstacles. For many if not all of us, at least at times, moralisms and platitudes – which include fealty to abstract moral goods and principles – are seen as no more than obstacles that need to be 'negotiated'. In the face of existential needs, mere admonitions about 'behaving ourselves' and 'obeying the law', or philosophers' ruminations about 'categorical imperatives' and 'virtue' can ring hollow – *very* hollow. Each of us, day in and day out, is faced with having to grapple with our existential needs – a relentless, often agonistic, and sometimes exhausting engagement – and not a few of us are willing to take liberties, to effect gambits that, if successful, will reduce – or so we think – the existential anxieties that must be borne on a daily basis. In fact, we all do this at some time and in some place (and if we are honest, at some *times* and some *places*) over the course of our precarious and short lives.

Concerning some of the psychology that drives us to opt for reductions in our existential anxieties rather than 'behave ourselves', Robert Hoyk and Paul Hersey have this to say, with reference to the Stanley Milgram experiments (that were used to show the ways in which we can deaden our empathy for others due to obedience to authority (the Milgram experiments called for the subjects to inflict various levels of electric shocks on others at the direction of a supervisor, to see at what point the subjects' own moral commitments would cause them to cease (to disobey the supervisors), for fear of causing serious harm to the recipients of the electric shocks):

> In Milgram's experiment on obedience, the more anonymous the victim was, the easier it was for the subjects to deliver intense shocks. When no groans or protests were heard from the confederate in the next room, almost all of the subjects calmly delivered shocks to the highest level of intensity. If the confederate was seated in the same room as the subject, 40 percent of the subjects delivered shock to the highest level. If the subject was directed to manually press the confederate's hand onto a metal plate which delivered the shock, the obedience rate declined to 30 percent … In a world of international corporations, anonymity is the order of the day, imposed through the use of email, automated voicemail prompts, and videoconferencing. The larger the corporation, the more insulated executives are from their shareholders, employees, and customers.[13]

But there is something in the Milgram experiments that show why human beings not only may engage in morally questionable or reprehensible behavior where there is anonymity, but why we may do so in the face of vague and abstract moral rules or principles. 'Anonymous' at its (Latin) root means 'without a name'. In the Milgram experiments, it was known that the recipients of electric shocks were human, even if they were 'without a name'. The philosopher Jonathan Glover similarly points out how it was possible for bombers in World War II to drop their 'ordinance' (a conveniently banal euphemism for 'bombs', akin to others we use today, such as 'derivatives') on cities, without paralyzing moral qualms. *Distance*, which often attends anonymity, namelessness, can deaden moral commitment and moral feeling. But when faced with real existential needs, what is more 'anonymous' than a vague moral principle or a regulation? What chance do mere moral principles and laws have when human agents *with names* are faced with their incessant existential needs? Well, the answer is that most of us, most of the time, can balance our existential needs with our moral and legal duties. But there are those times when, faced with a crisis of one sort or another (and, for some, a crisis can mean missing the quarterly numbers or not getting the new product to market on time), the existential needs win out, and we sacrifice, or at least temporarily dampen, our moral sense.

The world of commerce/business is constantly placing people in crisis situations: the boss is demanding sex, and failure to give in means loss of a job; the CFO wants a large invoice from a supplier secreted by a staff accountant so that the profit and loss statement will look better for the period; a clever but flimsy argument is requested by an auditing client so that a more favorable transfer pricing regime can be effected; the loan officer at a bank is asked by the c-suite to look the other way when an applicant for a mortgage submits documents that are questionable but that allow the 'tick-the-box' approval process to move along; an executive is requested by a foreign government official to pay a bribe otherwise the official will stand in the way of a lucrative and long-term joint venture, etc. The candidates for 'crisis' are many, and often subjective. Unfortunately, much of the business ethics literature treats existential needs as merely the immoral impulses that normative ethics was invented to investigate and bridal. But this literature, in treating them in this two-dimensional way, misses a proper engagement with them, and so falls flat at the feet of just those agents it was written to inform. The late philosopher, Richard Rorty, got to the heart of this when he wrote the following in a somewhat famous essay (at least among certain academics), 'Justice as a Larger Loyalty':

> Let me begin by asking you to consider some thought experiments. Suppose that you are being pursued by the police and you go to your family home and ask them to hide you. You would expect that they would do so. It would be abnormal if they did not. Consider again the reverse situation. You know that one of your parents or one of your children is guilty of a sordid crime and nonetheless he or she asks for your protection, asks to be hidden from police inquiries. Many of us would be willing to perjure ourselves in order to supply such a child or parent with a false alibi. But if an innocent person would then be wrongly convicted as a result of our perjury, most of us would be torn by a conflict between loyalty and justice.
>
> Such a conflict will be felt, however, only to the extent that we can identify with the innocent person whom we have harmed. If the person is a neighbor the conflict will probably be intense. If a stranger, especially of a different race or class or nation, it may

be considerably weaker. There has to be *some* sense that the victim is one of us before we start being tormented by the question of whether we did the right thing when we committed perjury. So it might be equally appropriate to describe us as torn between conflicting loyalties – loyalty to our family and loyalty to some group large enough to include the victim of our perjury, rather than torn between loyalty and justice.

    Our loyalty to such larger groups will however weaken or perhaps vanish when things get really tough. Then people whom we once thought of as like ourselves will be excluded. Sharing food with impoverished people down the street is natural and right in normal times but perhaps not in a famine when doing so would amount to disloyalty to one's own family. The tougher things get, the more ties of loyalty to those near at hand tighten and those to everyone else slacken.[14]

For the angels among us, what to do in each clash between our existential needs and 'moral principle' is clear: Go Selfless. For the rest of us, these are 'crises' in both the etymological and emotional senses of the word; that is, they are weighty moments of decision in which whatever choice is made there will be significant *consequences* concerning our ability to move forward in our lives, as we construe 'forward'. What I like about Rorty's insight is that it doesn't sterilize the choices; it takes the question of what is to be done 'down into the streets', so to speak, where the grit and fallout and emotions of decisions are actually played out. What is to be done is not to be resolved by some algorithm that always provides the best pathway and the best impetus to right action, such as, for example, Immanuel Kant's categorical imperative (at least in its undigested form) purports to do. Rorty is telling us that the extent of our *identification* with the various stakeholders in our action or inaction is quite relevant if we are trying to create a corporate culture that honors and yields to important moral ideals and values.Let's call this identification the alignment of identities. The goal of the alignment of identities is to stimulate recollection of moral equivalence between the corporate actor and the client or customer. The choice before us is not merely between doing 'the moral thing' vs. 'the immoral thing'. It can also be profitably construed or framed as a choice between two competing moral commitments, two competing moral identities, for concern for the welfare of one's self and for one's kith and kin over and above concern for strangers in far flung places are both on the spectrum of moral options. Our lives are lived-out in a process of deciding what to do in the service of various moral options all along the moral spectrum at one end of which is complete selfishness, and at the other end of which is complete selflessness.

    When faced with crises in business we naturally, as in other settings, reflect on the litany of our Existential Needs, as listed above, or we at least have a strong intuition of them. We are often enticed to make the morally problematic choice (which may be, as well, the economically as well as financially problematic choice) because we believe that in doing so we are placed in a better position in view of those existential needs than if we opt to 'behave ourselves' for the sake of impersonal abstractions such as 'sound financial reporting' and 'fair and transparent markets' etc. This speaks to how we frame the choices before us, something discussed at length by Daniel Kahneman and Amos Tversky.[15] We reckon, often, that we can live with the fallout of not 'behaving ourselves', but cannot live with the fallout of failing to meet the preponderance of the demands imposed on us by our existential needs. With reference to the list of temptations sketched above, the accountant 'misfiles' the invoices allowing her firm to look as though it is in a stronger financial position than it is; the employee gives her boss sex, preserving her source of income, and thus, many of her options in life, not to mention her kid's tuition payments; the auditing firm tax partner writes the flimsy opinion, such that the client is happy, future fees are preserved, and his standing within his firm is preserved; the loan officer continues to rubber-stamp mortgage applications with limited due diligence, preserving his job and his bonus; and the executive pays the bribe to the government official, the modest amount of money demanded paving the way to a wide range of benefits to his firm and to his firm's joint venture partner. 'Moral principles be damned', each says – 'I have to look at myself in the mirror in the morning, and will be less happy with the person I see staring back at me (the person who is, among other things, provider for a family) unless I break some (nameless and faceless, i.e. anonymous) rules'. Notice that in saying this, each is claiming that he or she has taken a tenable *moral* position, for the care of the self and the attendance to one's own and one's own family's interests are part of a *moral* calculation. The matter comes down, at least in part, to a question of *loyalty*, not to the ethical vs. the unethical, as so much of the philosophical literature might simplistically frame the matter. Indeed, a key to heading off future scandals corporate crime is the alignment of identities, and the cultivating of a sense of loyalty to those who are 'anonymous'.

Gyges

The sorts of morally problematic decisions as those listed above might remind one of the turning of the collet on the Ring of Gyges, although with no guaranty of non-detection, but merely a *gamble* of non-detection. The Ring of Gyges allegory from Book 2 of Plato's *The Republic*, is almost always useful to rehearse when discussing corporate conduct. Here is an excerpt:

> Gyges was a shepherd in the service of the king of Lydia; there was a great storm, and an earthquake made an opening in the earth at the place where he was feeding his flock. Amazed at the sight, he descended into the opening, where, among other marvels, he beheld a hollow brazen horse, having doors, at which he stooping and looking in saw a dead body of stature, as appeared to him, more than human, and having nothing on but a gold ring; this he took from the finger of the dead and reascended. Now the shepherds met together, according to custom, that they might send their monthly report about the flocks to the king; into their assembly he came having the ring on

his finger, and as he was sitting among them he chanced to turn the collet of the ring inside his hand, when instantly he became invisible to the rest of the company and they began to speak of him as if he were no longer present ... Whereupon he contrived to be chosen one of the messengers who were sent to the court; where as soon as he arrived he seduced the queen, and with her help conspired against the king and slew him, and took the kingdom. Suppose now that there were two such magic rings, and the just put on one of them and the unjust the other; no man can be imagined to be of such an iron nature that he would stand fast in justice. No man would keep his hands off what was not his own when he could safely take what he liked out of the market ... For all men believe in their hearts that injustice is *far more profitable to the individual than justice*, and he who argues as I have been supposing, will say that they are right. If you could imagine any one obtaining this power of becoming invisible, and never doing any wrong or touching what was another's, he would be thought by the lookers-on to be a most wretched idiot, although they would praise him to one another's faces, and keep up appearances with one another from a fear that they too might suffer injustice.[16]

There is a good reason why certain texts are classics. They continue to speak to the human condition with as much insight as when they were first written. There are indeed times when 'injustice' (the hiding of the invoices, for example, i.e. misleading shareholders and creditors) seems 'far more profitable to the individual than justice', and many if not all of us have engaged in at least one such act of injustice in our lives, at times where we did not wish to see ourselves in the mirror as the 'wretched idiot' who placed 'behaving ourselves' over what we have taken to be vital interests, or 'moving forward'. This, I would argue, is as true of the legislators who pass the laws, as true of the commercial actors those laws are written to control, and it is true of the philosophy and business professors who hold forth (or pontificate) before their students about deontology and the principle of utility. To *not* turn the ring, at least on occasion, requires something more powerful than what is typically learned in university ethics classes. It is upon that 'something more powerful' that I will focus in this book. That 'something more powerful' is our larger civic commitments, our loyalty to something more than our team of co-workers and corporate bosses, and the *affect* that can be associated with such larger commitments.

What I have said so far assumes that most people are not utilitarian or deontological saints, and will not be consistently motivated by *mere* philosophical or theological abstractions. That assumption is far from problematic, but discussions of ethics in business tend to suggest that teaching what the right thing to do is will be sufficient to attain an ethical outcome (this is an assumption that dates back to Socrates – and also an assumption that has been criticized by his successors (for various reasons), including Aristotle). This is likely one of the key reasons that business ethics classes are not as effective as they might be. They tend to fail to use the prevalent knowledge of human psychology to address how employees and executives should engage morally problematic situations, as the weak, needy, yearning, vulnerable, and fearful creatures that they (we) are. The need to blend the discussion of business ethics with the sacred spirits of civic and communal commitment is acute. Any university course in business ethics or professional ethics that doesn't start with, or at least *get around to*, a discussion of the challenges of life, which are often intertwined with the challenges to ethical decision-making in business, is missing the mark. Any course that dawdles in ethical theory and that never touches the messy human impulses that drive us, that never touches upon a students' core identities as sons, daughters, parents, friends, lovers, Catholics, Muslims, patriots, etc., with affective commitments forcing them to balance and rebalance the importance of each of these in their daily lives, is not going to wind-up being very useful to many students – which is, perhaps, the reason that many MBA programs churn-out a good number of future and better equipped rogues who will plant the seeds for future headline-making scandals. Law matters and normative theory matters, but so do psychology and a larger treatment of the human condition that leads to the kinds of scandal that make headlines in our various newspapers. Ethics education and reflection in business, as elsewhere, must speak to the soul, the whole person, not merely to behavior or to the intellect.

Wall Street is not alone in needing a much more robust alignment of identities (the identities of the industry's operatives and identities of those it purports to serve). As Akerlof and Shiller remind us:

> If we wish to understand the functioning of the economy, and its animal spirits, we must also understand the economy's sinister side – the tendencies toward antisocial behavior and the crashes and failures that disrupt it at long intervals or in hidden places ... This is [most clear] in the area of securities [and financial services], which represent people's savings for the future.[17]

Of course, the bad acting that goes on is not limited to a single industry. Consider this quite conceivable litany, with scenarios inspired by actual cases in the business ethics literature and from my experience assisting client firms in times of crisis:

> Somewhere, right now, there are thousands of merchants' and traders' and bankers' thumbs on thousands of 'scales', causing patrons or customers to pay more than they should, and who are providing sub-standard services or goods.
>
> Somewhere, right now, there are thousands of stockbrokers, working in tall glass towers with handsome decors, plotting to cheat their clients out of their savings – and sometimes their life savings. For some it will amount to only a few dollars here and there, and for some it will amount to a sizable chunk of the principal investment. The brokers will explain it by telling their clients that they needed to 'rebalance their portfolios', or that it is 'time to get out of this sector' of companies and move into another sector, even when there is no good reason to do either.
>
> Somewhere, right now, accountants in businesses around the world are creating fictitious company bank accounts, over which they have sole signature authority, and

into which they will move small, unnoticeable amounts of money, to be collected at some future date – perhaps at retirement, perhaps when it is time to move to the next job. Perhaps it will be only a few thousand dollars, perhaps millions.

Somewhere, right now, some manufacturer and distributor of foods is rigging his sorting-and-filling machines to hold back twenty grams of product (perhaps baby food), while putting a label on the carton or jar that overstates the content weight – by twenty grams.

Somewhere, right now, perhaps, some employee of a computer manufacturer is trying to figure out how to hide some software code deep inside the mother board, so that he will be able to access from his own lap-top any computer he wishes, whenever he wishes, without the owner ever knowing.

Somewhere, right now, a food plant manager and a junior employee have discovered droplets of motor oil in a large sampling of jars of pasta sauce. The manager is deciding whether he should stop the canning machines and ignore his findings, since his annual bonus depends on avoiding such production glitches. He has decided that a little motor oil won't hurt anyone, and also to pay 5% of his bonus to the junior employee, as hush money.

Somewhere, right now, an executive, who had been having sex with his secretary (a single mother of two small children), is planning to go to work and fire her, because he can no longer live with *his* guilt.

Why do people do these things? Some would prefer to argue that those people sketched in the preceding litany are knaves, or suffer from what Aristotle called *akrasia* (weakness of the will), or are just, inexplicably, bad actors. Such conclusions strike me as simplistic. In the scenarios sketched the various agents are acting the way they are acting mostly out of loyalty – loyalty to themselves alone or to those who depend upon them for the money needed to continue to live a decent life, or to start to. That what they have done is wrong is more or less obvious to most of us, but preaching moral virtue and moral principles to them may not be enough to *motivate* them to act in accordance with their higher resolves concerning stealing, lying, self-compromise, and the like. They need to *feel* a sense of *loyalty* to others and to those outside of the small circle inside of which their loyalties are animated. Fortunately, the behaviors in these illustrations are exceptions to the rule. Most people in business would not engage in conduct such as what is depicted here, and certainly not habitually. But to reduce the problematic decisions sketched, to whatever degree they occur, the alignment of identities is what is required, for it is the plant manager seeing *himself* as the father opening a tainted jar of pasta sauce and serving it to *his* children that has the best chance of turning him toward the more responsible behaviour. *He must feel the impact of his decision through an act of moral imagination.*

I would not argue that acts of moral imagination are always sufficient, only that moral imagination is *insufficiently stressed* when addressing ethical breaches and in our efforts to head off scandal, whether in the classroom or in drafting corrective legislation. And getting commercial actors to employ their moral imaginations depends, in part, on whether the society in which they operate and upon which they depend is just, fair in offering certain basic opportunities and in providing certain basic protections so that there will be less temptation to draw the circle of loyalty close rather than extend its circumference far from its center, capturing clients, customers, and 'anonymous' stakeholders, even the putative non-living environment itself (as taken seriously by 'ESG' (Environmental, Social, and Governance) and '3BL' (or 'Triple Bottom Line') analyses. We should not fool ourselves into believing that ethical business conduct can operate in the midst of rife social injustice and in the absence of mechanisms that prevent utter impoverishment and personal collapse. Indeed, talk of alignment of identities and moral imagination (in the commercial context) in present-day Somalia or other failed states seems like an idle exercise. This book, and others like it, are but tinder in such places. Yet, we need not refer to such extreme cases. Rising inequality even in the developed world creates stresses that mitigate against ethical conduct in business.

Wrong Metaphors, Wrong Frames

It is foolish to think that we are immune to the temptations to do what most of our peers would find morally problematic, whatever moral compass we carry around inside of our heads. This is the darker truth that must be faced squarely if we are to get anywhere in our societal efforts to make sub-prime mortgage scandals and bad corporate actors more rare than they have been – in our efforts to change Wall Street culture. Additionally, it is worth remembering that virtue is not a constant in life. That is, our characters change throughout life, given various lived experiences and new insights and stresses, and so we may have moments of weakness even when we still consider ourselves upstanding persons, for the most part. One of the reasons that we give ourselves passes in business (or in government, or in any other organizational context) to do things that we won't do in our private lives, to others to whom we owe a duty of loyalty or at least respect, is because of the dynamic model that frames our view of the workplace and that holds us there. Stated otherwise, *how* we see determines our course, and often our fates. *How* people tend to see their engagements as officers and employees in the commercial sphere goes something like this:

> We *take* from the commercial (or institutional) world. We *bring* to home and hearth what we take. We repeat the cycle.

In this model, or metaphorical frame, the world of commerce is a teat that we suck or a mine to plunder. It puts out; we take in. And, at the end of it all, hopefully sated if not fattened, we retire. Thus, the commercial world, the world of institutions that we call employers, is a place to *take* rather than to *give*, to *extract* from rather than to *serve*, and that which stands in our way of acquisition must be shunted aside, or *neutralized*. This framing is one of *aggressive acquisition, strategizing*, and even *scheming*. We ask the college graduate three months out, 'Did you *get* a job yet?' This seems innocent enough, but the language we use carries perspectives on the world that are not always conscious or obvious.

Beyond the general framing of acquisitiveness we have, in business, various metaphors that operate both consciously and subconsciously. One such metaphor is the war metaphor. It is no wonder that Sun Tzu's book *The Art of War* is, purportedly, very popular among executives and other managers. Lawrence G. McDonald recounts in his book, *A Colossal Failure of Common Sense: The Inside Story of the Collapse of Lehman Brothers*, how Richard Fuld, CEO of Lehman Brothers, liked 'war similes' and that he referred to his staff as his 'troops'.[18] When business activity is framed as *warfare*, then what enters in are a host of other metaphors and tropes that *shape the thinking* of the individual actor or agent for whom those metaphors and tropes resonate. If it holds that 'business is like war' then the means and methods of warfare *seem* to have some relevance to business conduct. The warlike character of economic competition is accurately depicted in films such as *The Wolf of Wall Street*, the original *Wall Street, Boiler Room, Glenngary Glen Ross*, and *Michael Clayton*. In war 'one does what one must'. This speaks, as well, to the phallic nature of the acquisitive business model, a model that valorizes aggression, notions of conquest and zero sum outcomes. Not too far from the waging of actual war, one may think of Shakespeare's Macbeth: 'I dare do all that may become a man'. And what is it that 'becomes a man' better than vanquishing his enemies, besting his opponents in the game of acquisition?[19]

Table I.1: Problematic Commercial Metaphors/Frames

Problematic Commercial Metaphors/Frames
War
Kill
Hunt
Games

Well, it may be quickening (and very *male*) to understand business using the tropes of warfare, but the alert, critical mind looks for bad analogies, i.e. the ways in which business is *not* like war. But the business-as-warfare frame is very popular and, I hold, is one of the root causes of some of the corporate scandals that we have seen in recent years. In fact, for many, it is the 'root metaphor' of business, to borrow a phrase from the philosopher Stephen Pepper (writing on a subject, however, decidedly unrelated to business conduct). We will come back to this framing of business-as-warfare several times in this book, both with respect to the financial services industry, as well as beyond it. Also, the dynamic between the personal realm and the commercial realm, which construes the world of commerce as though it is merely a field full of bounty for the *taking*, or a teat for the sucking, creates in us attitudes toward business and commerce that lead us to see them as little more than *our* field of plunder. To use another metaphor, they are our 'hunting grounds' (another analogy that gets employed is that of *the hunter* whose duty it is to bring home a *kill*). The idea of 'keeping what you kill' – meaning that you take the largest share possible of the revenue for which you are responsible – is common parlance on Wall Street, in view of its dominant commission-based system of compensation. Too few executives and managers (as well as others employed in businesses) ever give thought to the duty of stewardship that he or she also, arguably, has. This duty of stewardship is what the business ethicist Kenneth Goodpaster discusses, from various different perspectives, in his useful book, *Conscience and Corporate Culture*.[20]

The Split Self

Human beings are malleable and, as well, psychological contortionists. When we believe that there is a good reason to do so we can cut ourselves into two halves (or into more pieces than that at times), seeing ourselves as having one set of obligations in our personal lives and a completely different set of obligations in our corporate or business lives. An extreme version of this is the fictional character Tony Soprano, who is a concerned and committed husband and father in one 'dimension' of his life and a ruthless mobster in another 'dimension' of his life. Arguably, it was also true of Jeff Skilling and Andrew Fastow of Enron, as well as John Rigas of Adelphia, as well as of a long list of others involved in corporate scandals over the past century. In our private lives, we are to nurture and encourage and create bonds of genuine *trust*; but in the commercial world we find people who, instead, seem as though they are at war or on the hunt, and must *win* or *bag their prey*, even if it means breaching trust and violating norms that they would never violate in their personal lives (the game metaphor, a metaphor of winning, is another that gets employed; it is a metaphor that carries with it (ordinarily) a zero sum mentality, for in most games (in the common sense of the word) there is a winner and a loser. Yet, this malleability has its positive side. Because we are so malleable we can be reshaped in our thinking (can achieve a *metanoia*) about the world and our place in it, and operate pursuant to new frames, to a new conceptual scheme. *Metanoia*, of course, is one thing. The process of achieving *metanoia* is another thing. The process is what I call *soul-making*, as I will discuss in the following pages.

Business people should not feel obliged to leave their consciences and value commitments at home just because they work in the service of some institution, even if that institution is a large and powerful one. Whether one believes it or not, possibilities for legitimate income abound, if one is flexible and creative enough to see and pursue them, so selling one's soul, 'breaking bad' in some Faustian bargain, is not worth the cost in the long run, unless one is prepared to sacrifice important parts of one's self on the altars of pecuniary acquisition, or unless one is willing to violate duties of loyalty, breaking faith with one's compatriots, one's family, and one's friends. Some people do and are, of course. There are people who are even secretly nihilistic about moral matters. The point of this book is that whether or not they get away with it in this sense depends upon whether one takes loyalty to self as trumping larger loyalties. The invocation of animal spirits, rather than mere normative ethics that is committed to one form of calculation or algorithm or another, can lead to quite a different conclusion about what 'getting away with it' means. From the point of view of, for example, civic virtue or personal spirituality, there is no 'getting away with it', for from these perspectives ethics is concerned with loyalty, trust, and stewardship. That said, we will, alas, always have our hardened rogues and knaves – people who scoff at notions such as stewardship and civic virtue; we must not be Pollyannaish about the prospects for total alignment of identities, about the prospects for a commercial culture that has rid itself of bad actors and bad behaviour. For these, the jail cell and the steep fine (or their prospects) are the only tools that seem to dissuade. And so it goes.

A Return to Spiritual Values

I have just used the word 'spirituality'. According to Peter F. Drucker,

> Society needs a return to spiritual values – not to offset the material but to make it fully productive. However remote its realization for the great mass of mankind, there is today the promise of material abundance or at least of material sufficiency. [We need a] return to spiritual values ... the deepest experience that the *Thou* and the *I* are one, which all higher religions share. In an age of terror, of persecution, and of mass murder, such as ours, the hard shell of moral callousness may be necessary to survival. Without it we might yield to paralyzing despair. But moral numbness is also a terrible disease of mind and soul, and a terrible danger.[21]

You will notice that Drucker drew a distinction between the necessary callous that helps protect the psyche from collapse in the face of the horrors of the age (a touch of Stoicism, a recognition that we lack the power to solve all woes, and woes there will be), on the one hand, and the numbness that can endanger much, if not all, on the other. Drucker understood that the world of commerce is sometimes a difficult world of stress and strivings, and so one must not wilt in the face of its challenges. But numbness is the road to sociopathology. One winds up on that road, often, by small steps.

What Drucker is calling 'spiritual values' can be read as 'ideals'. Ideals matter and they matter crucially. We only think they don't because actions rooted in their operation within us cannot be seen, as journal entries, assembly lines, and cargo containers are seen. But their absence certainly has real-world effects, real-world effects that register in the trillions of dollars. Indeed, we witnessed, during the recent financial crisis, trillions of dollars of wealth drained from the world's economies and capital markets. That draining of wealth has had devastating repercussions that still reverberate. In the United States the unemployment rate breached 8 percent. In Spain it is still 24 percent with youth unemployment approaching 54 percent (as of September 2014), leading to the claim that in Spain, as in other European countries, there will be a lost generation of workers which will have chronic financial and existential challenges, with many having to leave the country to find work and establish their lives far away from family and friends. The crisis, which was caused by a variety of factors and not just the banking and securities industries, has zeroed-out life savings, thrown people into drug and alcohol abuse or addiction, resulted in suicides in various countries,[22] and has financially set-back certain ethnic minorities for decades.[23] In the United States, the wealth gap between blacks and whites widened from 12:1 (pre-crisis) to 20:1 (post-crisis). That is an astounding change for the worse, further beleaguering an already historically oppressed and beset population. Because of the financial crisis charitable giving slowed to a trickle, international aid programs had their budgets slashed, millions of people lost their jobs (sometimes with devastating consequences), and whole communities, towns and cities will require many years to reclaim the vigour that they once had. All of that carnage is, surely, morally relevant, and has a great deal to do with what Drucker was calling 'spiritual values'. The view that the world simply needs to hurry-up and get beyond the effects of the crisis is myopic, for the world needs also to make sure that the conditions that led to the crisis won't be extant in the future, and those conditions rest, to a significant extent, inside of our souls (in The Other Wall Street), not out in the world measured and probed by economists.

But many are suggesting that in our rush to return to the *status quo ante*, the handwriting of the next crisis is already on the wall, as are, perhaps, the next bubbles. In the United States and elsewhere, students are continuing to borrow staggering amounts of money to pay for college and university tuitions, the US personal savings rate is still anemic (only 4.6 percent, compared to the mostly double-digit savings rates of most of the past fifty years; but according to the Organization for Economic Cooperation and Development (the 'OECD'), the net savings rate is only 2.4%),[24] the shopping malls remain full, and the Federal Reserve, through various stages of what it has called 'quantitative easing', has expanded its balance sheet (that is, expanded the supply of liquidity in the economic system, with its fiat currency) to the tune of tens of billions of dollars per month, in order to replace the liquidity in the bond and housing markets that dried-up since the troubles of Fannie-Mae and Freddie-Mac began, and to support asset values.[25] The Dow Jones Industrial Average, in the last days of 2014, reached an all-time high (punching through 18,000, as compared to its low of 6,547.05 in March of 2009, the midst of the wreckage of the crisis and of 'The Great Recession' that ended, at least technically, in the summer of that year), largely because of quantitative easing, which forced 'homeless money' into the equity markets.Home prices are up substantially from the worst levels of the financial crisis. Onward and upward. Some of this is, of course, good news. But new bubbles are born in such periods of premature relief and myopic exuberance.

Without real change in how we think about money, wealth, markets, and commerce, the next financial crisis may be only a few short years away, even with the legislative measures, such as Dodd-Frank in the United States, that were put in place to address many of the issues that led to the market meltdown and The Great Recession of 2007/8.

Affective *and* Intellectual Commitment to Something Larger

An important antidote to destructive ethical behaviour in commercial life is believing in or commitment to (being loyal to) something larger than markets or, for that matter, yourself. That is the point that Drucker was making, at least in part. The thing that you might believe in needn't be what you encounter as you pass through a narthex or enter a sanctuary. It could be, simply, your country. A sense of civic responsibility and commitment is an aid to doing the right thing, since at least one of your commitments is to the larger society, comprised of people to whom you *feel* some kindred spirit. This commitment – the commitment to something larger than yourself, to some circle of persons larger than your immediate one – also provides you with the emotional wherewithal to stand up to requests to engage in illegal or improper commercial behaviour. This is because your identity is strongly tethered to and shaped by your larger commitments, and so betraying those larger commitments becomes a betrayal of yourself. Of course, your family may also be a larger commitment and, there are times when our larger commitments come into agonizing conflict, as dramatized by Rorty – the sort of conflict felt by a just whistle-blower when she must decide between staying quiet so that she can go on feeding her family, and an act for the sake of strangers in her community that will almost surely end her career. I do not pretend that there is a fixed algorithm for deciding, as some others might suggest there is. I do not pretend that you will not pay a price at times for making the choice that will allow you to maintain your integrity and remain true to your ideals. I do not pretend to tell you that there is no price to pay for larger loyalties. *There is*. My hope is that the readers of this book, some of whom will be students, will be more prepared, after reading it, to pay that price. If that is the case, I will consider the book a success. Of course, for the most part I shall never know. The labour of any writer (or teacher) is, in part, an act of faith.

1 HUMAN BEINGS AND MARKETS

In a shady corner of the great market at Mexico City, was an old Indian named Pota-lamo. He had twenty strings of onions hanging in front of him. An American from Chicago came up and said: "How much for a string of onions?" "Ten cents," said Pota-lamo. "How much for two strings?" "Twenty cents," was the reply. "How much for three strings?" "Thirty cents," was the answer. "Not much reduction in that," said the American. "Would you take twenty-five cents?" "No," said the Indian. "How much for the whole twenty strings?," said the American. "I would not sell you my twenty strings," replied the Indian. "Why not? said the American. "Aren't you here to sell your onions?" "No," replied the Indian. "I am here to live my life. I love this market place. I love the crowds and the red serapes. I love the sunlight and the waving palmettos. I love to have Pedro and Luis come by and say: 'Buenos Dias', and light cigarettes and talk about the babies and the crops. I love to see my friends. That is my life. For that I sit here all day and sell my twenty strings of onions. But if I sell all my onions to one customer, then is my day ended. I have lost my life that I love – and that I will not do."and that I will not do."

E. T. Seton
The Gospel of the Red Man: An Indian Bible[1]

Government-imposed artificial limits such as trading halts and short-sale bans merely delay (or prevent) traders from finding mutually acceptable equilibrium prices ... [G] overnment regulations only serve to increase the very market volatility, uncertainty, and fear they were supposedly intended to "correct."

Although I am not a trader, I benefit from efficient capital markets that allow investors to freely allocate their resources to maximize their profits. For me, efficient trading markets mean a better life in the form of cheaper food, exciting new consumer products (such as the iPad), and life-extending innovations created by medical device manufacturers (such as improved MRI scanners). If the widespread adoption of computer-assisted trading means that regulators are less able to hamper such markets, then I consider that a feature, not a bug.

Or to paraphrase Kent Brockman from *The Simpsons*, "I, for one, welcome our new robotic trading overlords!"

Paul Hsieh
'A Defense of High Frequency Trading'[2]

Remembrance, Re-membering, Recollection

Marriages and families get into trouble when those who constitute them forget what they (the marriages and families) are. The same is true of institutions. This *forgetfulness* happens when functions and short-term goals eclipse missions, long-term goals and visions, or when the pursuit of a single goal (profit) eclipses all other goals (what ethicist John Goodpaster calls 'teleopathy', from the Greek *telos*, meaning goal or objective, and *pathos*, referring to, in this case, sickness or disease, as in *pathology*). In a marriage, the daily routines of parting in the morning, working for eight or ten hours apart, returning home for a few hours of private interaction, and all the functional stuff that comes in between, can blind a couple so that neither partner sees what brought them together in the first place or, in many cases, just why they should stay together. The result can be a zombie marriage – all the moving parts working, but to no mutually-agreed upon and quickening purposes. More generally, families that think family life will take care of itself – that cousins do not need to ring-up cousins, or uncles do not need to ring-up nephews or nieces – will be a family that is doomed to drift apart. Marriages and families need constant tending, constant *remembrances*, in order to beat back the entropic and centrifugal forces that constantly seek to break the bonds that keep them together. Those forces can turn family into *society*, the latter being the broadest and thinnest aggregation of individuals, each seeking his or her own ends. The activity that remembrance entails is captured in the word itself – remembrance is about re-member-*ing*, about reuniting the parts that must work in harmony if the body is to function well.

Firms and markets exist to serve human purposes, just as marriages and families do. The cycles of scandal that we witness time and again in the commercial world in general and on Wall Street in particular may correspond to or be brought about by cycles of commercial *amnesia*, where the functions of firms and markets dominate the foreground, and the purposes of both recede deeply into the background and so out of conscious consideration. When the scandal comes, we can see clearly that something has gone wrong, but we don't often hear or read in the accompanying media reports that the problem is not merely bad regulation or bad actors, but also includes blindness and forgetfulness. Usually, to say that the malefactors in the scandal are 'misguided' is also to say that they are *forgetful*, assuming that they had a proper understanding of the nature and purpose of business in society to begin with. Of course, some never did, the result of tutelage at the feet of the wrong mentors, or instruction within a business education machine that has become as notorious (fair or not) for churning out rogues as it has become known for churning out star and yeoman managers, entrepreneurs, and executives.

Despite various attacks and critiques, from both the right and the left, on this dangerous habit of mind and culture, we still live in an age of dualisms and reductionisms. Moreover, we live in a 'bottom line' world. Much of what is said about markets today, whether by market fundamentalists or by leftists, whether by politicians or commercial agents, seems to presuppose that markets are something sealed off from the rest of life, the rest of life being things like family, religion, and the arts. This is based upon a misconstrued conception of markets, and it goes hand in hand with the bureaucratization that Max Weber wrote about in the early years of the twentieth century, and the dualisms that John Dewey warned us about somewhat later. Markets – whether for onions or for equities – are an expression of and are in the service of human needs, and they exist to further human flourishing. While their operations are *functionally* sealed-off – just as a surgeon's technical considerations are functionally sealed-off from the rest of the pubic (and her patient) – markets themselves operate (or I should say are *permitted* to operate) for the sake of the larger goal of general social welfare. Conversely, family life, religions and the arts are not self-sealed and *sui generis* domains, although many who spend most of their time focused on these areas of human life often forget that the market is not The Other that they too often think it is. In order for them to function, families, religions, and the arts need services, materials and ideas, and the market is the place to which they go to acquire them. These services, materials and ideas are ultimately provided by persons who are themselves in need of other services, materials and ideas and who, themselves, have families, religious lives (at least often) and an appreciation for the arts of one kind or another – even if only kitsch.

Markets are efficient engines of social welfare. The locution 'social welfare' expresses more than the distribution of commodities, but rather it refers to the total well-being of a society (that is, its human members), which includes such things as environmental conditions, educational opportunities, opportunities for leisure, the pursuit of personal interests, freedom from crime and conflict, general wealth and purchasing power, and many other quality of life considerations that befit a proper human existence, transculturally and across political boundaries. There is an overlap between the things that, say, market libertarians consider to be social welfare, and the things that certain thinkers on the more or less pragmatic left consider to be social welfare, such as what has been developed by economist Amartya Sen and, as well, by philosopher Martha Nussbaum in their 'capabilities approach ', which focuses upon the conditions for human flourishing with reference to the ubiquitous capabilities of almost all human beings. The principal relevance of the capabilities approach to social welfare is its focus on what people are able *to do* and *to be*, rather than on happiness or wish-fulfillment in the abstract or the achievement of a certain economics status alone, such as where one is in relation to 'the poverty line'. In her book *Women and Human Development: The Capabilities Approach*, Nussbaum lists as our basic capabilities the following, which are worth rehearsing:

CENTRAL HUMAN FUNCTIONAL CAPABILITIES

Life: Being able to live to the end of a human life of normal length; not dying prematurely, or before one's life is so reduced as to be not worth living.

Bodily Health: Being able to have good health, including reproductive health; to be adequately nourished; to have adequate shelter.

Bodily Integrity: Being able to move freely from place to place; having one's bodily boundaries treated as sovereign, i.e. being able to be secure against assault, including sexual assault, child sexual abuse, and domestic violence; having opportunities for sexual satisfaction and for choice in matters of reproduction.

Senses, Imagination, and Thought: Being able to use the senses, to imagine, think, and reason – and to do these things in a, "truly human" way, a way informed and cultivated by an adequate education, including, but by no means limited to, literacy and basic mathematical and scientific training ...

Emotions: Being able to have attachments to things and people outside ourselves; to love those who love and care for us, to grieve at their absence; in general, to love, to grieve, to experience longing, gratitude, and justified anger. Not having one's emotional development blighted by overwhelming fear and anxiety, or by traumatic events of abuse or neglect ...

Practical Reason: Being able to form a conception of the good and to engage in critical reflection about the planning of one's life. (This entails protection for the liberty of conscience.)

Affiliation:

   A. Being able to live with and toward others, to recognize and show concern for other human beings, to engage in various forms of social interaction; to be able to imagine the situation of another and to have compassion for that situation; to have the capability for both justice and friendship ...

   B. Having the social bases of self-respect and non-humiliation; being able to be treated as a dignified being whose worth is equal to that of others. This entails, at a minimum, protections against discrimination on the basis of race, sex, sexual orientation, religion, caste, ethnicity, or national origin. In work, being able to work as a human being, exercising practical reason and entering into meaningful relationships of mutual recognition with other workers.

Other Species: Being able to live with concern for and in relation to animals, plants, and the world of nature.

Play: Being able to laugh, to play, to enjoy recreational activities.

Control Over One's Environment:

   A. Political. Being able to participate effectively in political choices that govern one's life; having the right of political participation, protections of free speech and association.

   B. Material. Being able to hold property (both land and movable goods), not just formally but in terms of real opportunity; and having property rights on an equal basis with others; having the right to seek employment on an equal basis with others; having the freedom from unwarranted search and seizure.[3]

This list of the capabilities (along with their brief descriptions) has been criticized for various shortcomings, but if Nussbaum's list of the basic capabilities is right, more or less (and I believe they are right, more or less), then it is clear that parsimonious notions of 'social welfare', 'economics', and 'well-being' won't do. Further, and perhaps more to the point, if Nussbaum's list is right, more or less, then it is clear that the notion that markets and markets alone are the best distributors of social welfare is *wildly inaccurate*. Markets have their role, but it is a limited one, though critically important. To think otherwise can lead us into that old bane called reductionism, wherein one takes all of the items on Nussbaum's list and links it to a 'necessary and sufficient' market function and market outcome. Play, then, becomes a function of market transactions – the markets produce play, by providing the 'materials' used in play; Affiliations become a function of the resources required for affiliation, which, under such reductionism, only the markets can effect; and so forth. But all reductionisms of this sort – whether in economics, religion, or art – are gross distortions of reality because they do little or no justice to the interpenetrations and the interlocking characteristics of all human activities.

Market fundamentalists and purists (those who tend to think that government regulation of markets should be very limited indeed), and those who are beguiled by them, are often guilty of such reductionism. They skate on very thin ice, although they tell a story about how that world works that is facially convincing. They like to use a few statements by Adam Smith as the foundation (or at least as a large section of the foundation) for their views. It is instructive to recall what it is that Smith actually said in his massive and monumental study, *An Inquiry into the Nature and Causes of the Wealth of Nations* (1776), often simply referred to as '*The Wealth of Nations*':

> But the annual revenue of every society is always precisely equal to the exchangeable value of the whole annual produce of its industry, or rather is precisely the same thing with that exchangeable value. As every individual, therefore, endeavours as much as he can, both to employ his *capital* in the support of domestic industry, and so to direct that industry that its produce may be of the greatest value; every individual necessarily labours to render the annual revenue of the society as great as he can. He generally, indeed, neither intends to promote the public interest, nor knows how much he is promoting it. By preferring the support of domestic to that of foreign industry, he intends only his own security; and by directing that industry in such a manner as its produce may be of the greatest value, he intends only his own gain; and he is in this, *as in many other cases*, led by an invisible hand to promote an end which was no part of his intention. *Nor is it always the worse for the society that it was no part of it*. By pursuing his own interest, he *frequently* promotes that of the society *more effectually than when he really intends to promote it*. I have never known much good done by those who affected *to trade for the public good*. It is an affectation, indeed, not very common among merchants, and very few words need be employed in dissuading them from it.[4]

Before I begin to discuss this passage, take note of the italicized words. I believe those words are significant, although they are often elided by market fundamentalists.

Let us note, to begin, that Smith uses the term 'invisible hand' only *once* in the entirety of *The Wealth of Nations*. I do not think that this renders the expression irrelevant, but market fundamentalists place far too much weight on this expression when defending markets against government regulation, taxation, or redirection – or even moral scruple. It is also noteworthy that Smith did not suggest that the phenomenon of the invisible hand is limited to commerce and economy. He suggests also that in other ways there are 'invisible hands' that seem to operate with similar salutary results for society. One could conjure any one of a number of ways in which this might be true. A woman praying, alone in her bedroom, for the health and safety of *her* family may have no thought for the families of her *neighbours*, but the mere act has social benefits, insofar as it reinforces within her the need to care for her own, which generates or hones greater sympathy for others who are equally concerned for their families, and this sympathy becomes a deepened *general* consensus concerning the need for strong and secure households. Smith allows such a conclusion as this when he tells us that it applies 'in many other cases', an allowance glossed over by market fundamentalists who see in it only justification for hermetically sealed markets and selfish pecuniary pursuits. The fundamental problem with those who abuse the invisible hand idea is that it is so very convenient to the invidiously selfish inclination, turning vicious and rank selfishness into a virtue. It corrodes real concern for others by making the welfare of The Other a byproduct of self-interested market pursuits, of a serendipitous emergent condition. Even for those who genuinely believe that the best path to a better society is the path of free market exchanges, there remains a moral hazard that one may actually come to believe that self-interest and social welfare are interchangeable notions, are the same thing because two sides of the same coin.

Smith also wanted to suggest that the gross revenues of society can be maximized best when each person is employing his capital and industry in the markets, where such a person 'intends his own gain' rather than attempting to promote the interests of 'society' as such. However, nothing that Smith said in the quoted passage in any way suggests that the markets will maximize social welfare, and certainly nothing in the passages suggests that it will be maximized in the way that social welfare is understood in the capabilities approach or in any similar, thicker conception of social welfare (say, Jeremy Bentham's, J.S. Mill's or John Rawls's). Smith only spoke of the maximizing of *revenues*, and that is what he meant by the promotion of 'the interests of the society more effectually'. And note the use of 'frequently' rather than 'always'. The richer and more accurate understanding of that in which social welfare consists requires the more or less free exchange that Smith was talking about, activities that do not *aim* at the public good, *as well as reflection on the public goals at which society aims and the values that society holds.* The idea of trading for the public good is, of course, often doomed to failure – and this is precisely why command economies fail miserably (as F.A. Hayek quite rightly expounded). 'Trading for the public good' is a misguided notion because no individual or institution in private, civil society can herself or itself know just what 'the public good' is or means, not any more than she or it can know what *your* or *my* good is.

The public good is not something divined *a priori*. It is, rather, a moving target, *discovered* through a blizzard of public transactions, 'ayes' and 'nays' in the marketplaces of products, services, and ideas, and it is an arrogation to attempt to 'trade for the public good' precisely because it is an act of hubris, and therefore, morally problematic, regardless of the sentiment that cloaks the platitude. Thoreau captured this well when, in *Walden*, he wrote: 'If I know for a certainty that a man was coming to my house with the conscious design of doing me good, I should run for my life'.[5] But it is equally problematic to assume that activities pursued for one's own gain must be pursued with monomaniacal *forgetfulness* that such gain means for the recipient of such gain the capacity to improve the commonwealth. Gain – ultimately, money wealth – is but a means to an end. Where that end is simply more gain the point is missed; it would be to mistake means for ends. It must be noted in the above passage that Smith did not have in mind the blind pursuit of gain, but the needs of the commonweal. Too many cite these few sentences from *The Wealth of Nations* to construct a facile and false argument that the pursuit of such gain must be monomaniacal, that intentionally to pursue wealth for oneself is intentionally to pursue the good for the commonweal. Were the formula for social welfare that simple, if it rested on egoism, it would have been ubiquitous many centuries ago.

Another way to understand Smith's comments is as follows: *The cord of the commonwealth that sustains and promotes all is only as strong as its weakest fibers.* To the extent each member takes care of his own needs, she will tend to lift from the shoulders of her neighbor the burden of taking care of her needs – nor can her neighbour know, except with respect to the most basic somatic requirements for living, just what her 'needs' are (refer to Nussbaum's list of the capabilities, above, with respect to the breadth of human needs). Her needs are met through her own decisions about what they actually are and how they might best be met. She engages in various transactions (not only mere exchanges of goods and services for currency or through barter), transactions of friendship, loyalty, service, and trust with a wide variety of people in her immediate and greater circle of friends and, ultimately, strangers. The excess of her economic exchanges is available to be taxed, saved/invested or donated to others whose marginal utility for that which is donated or otherwise given is greater, all else being equal.

Smith's notion was that the multiplication of this tendency throughout society would result in a population of more or less self-sustaining members, each addressing his own needs so that, in part, others will not be burdened with the task of addressing them; each able to offer excess gain (commodities, money, knowledge, etc.) to fund governments, help those in dire straits, and to take risks in new enterprises, whether commercial, political, or other. Top down economies don't work because, *inter alia*, the raw material needed – the excess acquired by individual members of society – is often inadequate in such economies; there is no excess gain for broader distribution where needed. So economic systems of command (or 'command economies') collapse due to economic anemia. They always have and they probably always will, wherever attempted.

Smith, as well, clearly understood that just as society needs the individual's productivity and creativity, the individual depends upon a stable and well-ordered society. He believed that a stable and well-ordered society is actually a protection for the interests of the individual. Though he did not believe that individuals should have as a sole aim the general needs of society he clearly understood the importance of the needs of those in society who are faring poorly, which is a general theme of his book, *A Theory of Moral Sentiments*:

> All men, even the most stupid and unthinking, abhor fraud, perfidy, and injustice, and delight to see them punished. But few men have reflected upon the necessity of justice to the existence of society, how obvious soever that necessity may appear to be[6]

This Smith is the Smith that few market fundamentalists quote, as they lecture government and fellow citizens about the 'invisible hand'. Love-talk and references to sympathy and to the welfare of others, as an immediate concern requiring direct action on the part of social institutions, goes missing among those who fetishize markets, but *A Theory of Moral Sentiments* is soaked-through with them.

That capitalism in its various forms generates enormous amounts of wealth cannot be gainsaid, even though its flaws are well known. But this does not mean that 'team capitalism wins!' ('capitalism' being used in its minimalist sense, i.e., *the blinkered* pursuit of private commercial and economic interests) and that a monomaniacal and forgetful view of private economic pursuits is justified. The market is not merely a self-referential machine, focusing on its own mechanisms to the exclusion of all other things and the desires of its most immediate masters, any more than an automobile engine can be construed as or divorced from the purposes of driving, which are myriad. The engine does not exist to serve its own purposes and any notion to the contrary can only be characterized as surreal. Who would conceive of, let alone build, such an engine? Like any tool, the market's purposes lie outside of itself. Yet, if one listens to market fundamentalists one will hear the surreal spouted without any awareness of the incompleteness of their arguments. Social welfare – exemplified in the upper-middle class novelist writing in her seaside home, the nurse who has achieved a professional award, the business person who funds scholarships for young people, the marine biologist who studies coelenterates (etc.) – is not merely the function of a machine called

'The Market' but of countless choices and decisions made each day, many of which have little to do with the buying or selling of things or services as narrowly construed by market fundamentalists. Social welfare is the result of an *ecology* of overlapping, interactive, and interlinked activities, deliberations, systems, plans, values and goals. The word 'ecology' is used because it refers to intricate, and often fragile, systems, networks, and transactions within systems and networks. Thus, the notion of 'market economy' might be replaced, with some significant payoff, by the notion of 'market ecology', which, perhaps, better explains the ways in which markets are always understood as one element in the creation and maintenance of human capabilities or, less preferably but more acceptable than the current conceptual scheme, strong and stable commonwealths.

In *Gardens*, Liu and Hanauer draw a distinction between what they call 'machinebrain' and 'gardenbrain' thinking – thus the 'Gardens' in the book's title. They use that metaphor throughout the book to show what they take to be wrong in both our politics and in our economic thinking. Here are some examples of their rather refreshingly simple and pragmatic perspective:

> We wrote this short book to offer a new way. We aim to reach not "moderates" or "centrists" who split the difference between left and right. We aim to reach those who think independently. That might mean those who claim no party affiliation, though it also includes many [who do]. It definitely means those who are uncomfortable being confined by narrow choices, old paradigms, and zero-sum outcomes.
> If you can hold these paired thoughts in your head, we wrote this book for you:
>
>> The federal government spends too much money. The wealthy should pay much more in taxes.
>>
>> Every American should have access to high-quality health care. We spend far too much on health care ... already.
>>
>> We need to eliminate our dependence on fossil fuels. We need to ensure our economy continues to grow.
>>
>> Unions are a crucially important part of our economy and society. Unions have become overly protectionist and are in need of enormous amounts of reform.
>>
>> We need strong government. We need strong citizens.
>
> Contemporary American political discourse sees these pairings as *either/or*. Independent-thinking Americans see them as *both-and* ... Our goal in these pages is to push past the one-dimensional, left-right choices of contemporary politics – between more government or less, selfishness and altruism, suffocating collectivism and market fundamentalism – and find orthogonal approaches to our challenges. The great challenge of this age ... is to rethink how we as citizens create change, how the economy truly works, and what government fundamentally is for. The great challenge of this age is to change how we *see*, and by so doing, improve our ability to adapt.[7]

Being aware of the importance and power of markets does not mean that we are obliged to fetishize them, or turn them into idols. The philosopher John Dewey developed a complete corpus of philosophical work largely around the notion that all of our institutions, industries, laws and even innovations and arts are best understood as *tools*, not as ends in themselves. They are tools that assist human beings in our efforts to create good lives, lives of richer experience, deeper relationships, increased security (broadly construed), and increased knowledge. Good lives require good communities, and to think otherwise is to live, as Drucker once warned we might, in 'a terrible danger'. To put this another way, the purpose of the market – any kind of market – is to serve human needs and interests. Markets, as tools, exist to make human beings better-off. When we start to think that our job, as humans, is to make *markets* better-off we have inverted all the relevant values, and are maintaining a perverse orientation toward others. It is precisely this perversion that causes or contributes to the cycles of scandal.

Keeping the Kleptomania Going

The financial services industry is, perhaps, unique among legal industries in that its oft-repeated *raison d'etre* is, simply, the maximization of profits. At its worst it gives rise to firms such as those depicted in the movies *Boiler Room* and *The Wolf of Wall Street*. (This does not mean that Wall Street is not concerned with innovations in its products and client-offerings. I have been involved with such innovations myself.) To that extent, Wall Street certainly seems to comprise the *forgetful*, most disconnected set of industries in the world. It may be described, quite tenably, as the red light district of the commercial world. On that point, in 2012, I wrote the following in an op-ed (*Newsday*, 19 March 2012):

> Why an industry thinks it exists matters a great deal. Everyone wants to make money. The people who become nurses, horticulturalists and airline pilots want to make money, too. But there tends to be an understanding among these professionals that money is not the endgame. They want to make a decent living, but they are about the work at hand – healing the sick, improving crop yields, transporting passengers safely and so on.
>
> Not so with Wall Street, which continues its reputation as a bastion of sophisticated, self-dealing kleptomaniacs. It is extremely good at separating clients from their money and convincing them that it is for their own good. An industry with such a mindset cannot be reformed through regulation alone. Regulation is coercion. Real reform for Wall Street means core cultural reform, and that will have to come from within. The Dodd-Frank Wall Street reform law of 2010 and similar regulations work to a degree, but also invite brilliant and cynical minds to find ways to keep the kleptomania going.
>
> The capital markets, though imperfect, are not inherently evil. They have improved the quality of life for billions of people. When their functions are properly respected, it is easy to see them as valuable generators of social welfare. When they are not, their core functions get occluded, and scandals, bubbles, meltdowns and "uncreative destruction" happen – and billions of people may get harmed.
>
> What's the route to reform? The bar of entry into the industry needs to be raised: New educational standards need to be implemented, including regular and required proficiency and business ethics training that teaches more than dos and don'ts; common fixtures, such as the commission system, must be scrapped; the sales men-

tality must be replaced by an ethic of service and care; research needs to be isolated – utterly – from sales; long-term investing must be rewarded, and short-term speculation dissuaded; and corporate managers' kowtowing to the expectations of traders and speculators must be punished rather than rewarded by shareholders.

Wall Street needs to enter the painful process of reinvention. Unfortunately, it's hard to see how this will happen without enlightened leadership from within, and new firms with new models of service that are willing to earn less in exchange for client trust, loyalty and stability[8]

In Chapter 5 I will have many more proposals for reform than those proffered in this op-ed – very specific, meat and potatoes proposals, for to speak in generalities is to be in danger of being perceived as trafficking in platitudes, in a manner not unlike the market fundamentalists. Of course, discussing ideals, the duties of citizenship, commitment to things bigger than markets and oneself is, of course, not to traffic in platitudes, or velleities, or desiderata. Such discussions are what can turn the tide, reduce scandal and malfeasance, shift the focus of Wall Street away from the mere pursuit of personal fortunes and compensation where the clients and customers are the *mere occasions* for such acquisition (that is, are merely objects to satisfy pecuniary desires), and toward a culture of care operating within a model of service. This can happen, as surely as slavery came to an end in the United States and apartheid fell in South Africa, as surely as women were eventually granted the right to vote, and as so many other sweeping reforms and changes have occurred – all of which seemed, for many decades, like impossibilities, pipe dreams. Indeed, while Wall Street has always had less than a stellar reputation, there were times, including relatively recently, during which the focus was on the needs of clients and customers who were thought of as the *point* of professional activity, not, as Greg Smith revealed in his book, *Why I Left Goldman Sachs*, as 'muppets'. The fiction is not that Wall Street's culture can be reformed, but that it *cannot* be. As John F. Kennedy put it in a commencement address at American University in 1963: 'Our problems are man-made, therefore they may be solved by man. And man can be as big as he wants. No problem of human destiny is beyond human beings'.[9]

'A Patina of Shit' and an Ethos of Defoliation

There is a kind of mesmerizing purity to Wall Street. There are few industries that overtly tout maximizing personal remuneration and firm profits as its sole purposes, its *raison d'etre*. There are few industries that labor under the assumption that they are entitled to participate, quite literally, in the goods or services they provide. Physicians do not claim that their patients owe them a few years of their lives because those physicians preserved their patients' health. Airline pilots do not pass their hats around the cabin when they deliver passengers to their destinations safely. They understand that their jobs are healing and piloting, respectively.

They do their jobs because they are their jobs. But Wall Street is different. Its culture is a culture of *entitlement* that has permitted it to continue to justify itself when all others condemn it. It believes that its proximity to other people's money confers upon it a right to participate in the wealth that it helps to create – that is, when it is not going about destroying it, as it did in the years leading up to the recent financial crisis. Wall Street has earned a reputation as, as I suggested, the red light district of the business world. Its clients and customers are seen, all too often, if not as 'muppets' then as 'Johns' seeking services that too many Wall Street bankers, brokers, analysts, and traders are more than ready to provide. Too harsh? The record speaks for itself, unfortunately. Protestations against such a characterization by insiders will merely be taken as delusional whimsy, as they fly in the face of a very sordid history, and the monthly recaps of the fines levied and the charges leveled against Wall Street insiders, both people and firms. If Wall Street operatives do not like these characterizations, they will have to earn better ones. For now, the culture of Wall Street remains a culture of greed, and greed, by definition, is a vice, for it is not merely the desire to earn a profit and one's keep, but rather it is the desire to acquire with no limits and no constraints, to take more than one is entitled to take after proper consideration of all of the important variables that simply ought to matter. As for the argument that Wall Street only takes what the market will bear, it is an argument that, to a significant degree, is specious. The market is often, after all, *rigged* – rigged by the kleptomaniacs themselves. That is no exaggeration, and there are numerous instances of just how rigged it is. For example, in 1999 the self-regulatory agency that had oversight responsibilities over Wall Street broker-dealers and the over-the-counter equity markets was found to be in violation of its own mandate by looking the other way when market makers colluded to maintain artificially wide spreads (something that eventually led to penny pricing on stock shares). The SEC wrote in its report on the matter:

> A primary focus of the investigation was whether the NASD [the National Association of Securities Dealers, renamed the Financial Industry Regulatory Authority (or "FINRA") in 2007] had adequately carried out its obligation under the Exchange Act to oversee the Nasdaq market and the conduct of its members. The investigation identified a number of serious deficiencies in the NASD's performance of its duties as a self-regulatory organization ("SRO"), especially as they relate to oversight of the Nasdaq market. The NASD failed over a period of time to conduct an appropriate inquiry into an anticompetitive pricing convention among Nasdaq market makers, even though the NASD knew of facts and circumstances evidencing such matters by 1990. In addition, the NASD failed to enforce vigorously significant rules applicable to its market maker members. These rules included the firm quote rule and the trade reporting rule, both of which are crucial to the fair operation of the Nasdaq market.[10]

One of the reasons for this turpitude, that likely cost individual investors and traders countless millions of dollars, is that the NASD was a revolving door to the industry, with senior executives and managers not wanting to offend the very firms (including market makers) they regulate, since they wanted to be employed by them one day – with a substantial increase in compensation (arguably, a form of regulatory capture). While FINRA instituted a revolving door prevention rule in 2011, that rule only precludes former FINRA senior executives, now employed in the industry itself, from making appearances before FINRA on behalf of clients, or from testifying as experts in FINRA cases.

In late 2014 the SEC brought an action against one of the industry's high-frequency trading ('HFT') firms for a scheme to manipulate the shares of equities at the end of the trading day (an infraction referred to as 'marking the close'):

> The Securities and Exchange Commission today sanctioned a New York City-based high frequency trading firm for placing a large number of aggressive, rapid-fire trades in the final two seconds of almost every trading day during a six-month period to manipulate the closing prices of thousands of NASDAQ-listed stocks. This marks the first high frequency trading manipulation case.
>
> An SEC investigation found that Athena Capital Research used an algorithm that was code-named Gravy to engage in a practice known as "marking the close" in which stocks are bought or sold near the close of trading to affect the closing price. The massive volumes of Athena's last-second trades allowed Athena to overwhelm the market's available liquidity and artificially push the market price – and therefore the closing price – in Athena's favor. Athena was acutely aware of the price impact of its algorithmic trading, calling it "owning the game" in internal e-mails.[11]
>
> Athena agreed to pay a $1 million penalty to settle the SEC's charges.

These are but two instances of the rigging of the game (and, as Michael Lewis argues in his book, *Flash Boys: A Wall Street Revolt*, HFT's harms are not limited to 'marking the close', but are rooted in pernicious efforts to front-run the market orders of millions of investors), and others will be discussed in the proposals for reform that I discuss in Chapter 6. The rigging has become so pervasive that it is understood as axiomatic. Often, even among Wall Streeters themselves, you will hear it said that Wall Street has pushed-out the individual investor. Direct access to exchanges, privileged allocations of new issues of securities, program/algorithmic trading, flash trading, interest-rate rigging, mortgage shenanigans, and the commission system of compensation are all part of the rigging.

Wall Street firms seem to be part of the workings of processes that extract valuable resources from the economy as much as they are crucial for injecting valuable resources into it. It helps to create hundreds of billions in new wealth, and then it destroys hundreds of billions of dollars of market value. Society itself becomes the focus of one big, cyclical 'trade'. This process of value creation and destruction may remind one of a monologue in the movie *Michael Clayton* rather than of Schumpeterian thought – a rather poetic, if dark, indictment of powerful institutions that front as noble commercial players but are complicit in the 'defoliation' of communities, cities, even nations. The movie tells a story centered around the life of a law firm 'fixer', Michael Clayton (played by George

Clooney), whose job it is to save the law firm's high profile clients from legal trouble of one variety or another, even if it means thwarting justice. Arthur Edens (played by Tom Wilkinson) decides that his own role as a powerful law partner who has for years defended an important client, U-North, from legal troubles concerning the deadly effects of one of its products, is no longer morally worthy or tenable. In fact, his work on behalf of U-North has corroded his sense of morality and humanity. In a moment of blinding moral clarity leading to an act of self-redemption, Edens decides to blow the whistle on U-North. He desperately needs to cleanse himself and reassert his humanity and reverence for life, even though this violates an important professional duty of loyalty to his client. There are examples of it in real life, though perhaps less artfully and less dramatically expressed (Karen Silkwood, Erin Brockovich, Greg Smithand Wendell Potter come to mind), so Edens' monologue is not mere fancy. In the movie's opening scene, Edens' voice is heard in the background, engaging Clayton, who was dispatched by their law firm, Kenner Bach & Ledeen, to reel-in Edens before he continues farther down the path on which he is treading, a path that could bring ruin to both the law firm and the client:

> Michael. Dear Michael. Of course it's you. Who else could they send? Who else could be trusted? And I know it's a long way and you're ready to go to work, all I'm saying is wait, just wait ... Two weeks ago, I came out of the building, okay, I'm running across Sixth Avenue, there's a car waiting, I got exactly 38 minutes to get to the airport and I'm dictating. There's this panicked associate sprinting along beside me, scribbling in a notepad and suddenly she starts screaming and I realize we're standing in the middle of the street, the lights change and there's this wall of traffic, serious traffic spinning towards us and I freeze. I can't move. And I'm suddenly consumed with the overwhelming sensation that I'm covered with some sort of film. And it's in my hair, my face. It's like a glaze, like a coating. At first I thought, my God, I know what this is, this is some sort of amniotic, embryonic fluid. I'm drenched in afterbirth. I've bridged the chrysalis. I've been reborn. But then the traffic, this stampede, the cars, the trucks, the horns, the screaming and I'm thinking, no, no, no, reset, this is not rebirth. This is some kind of giddy illusion of renewal that happens in the final moment before death. And then I realize no, no, no, this is completely wrong because I look back at the building and I had the most stunning moment of clarity. I, I, I realized, Michael, that I had emerged not through the doors of Kenner Bach & Ledeen, not through the portals of our vast and powerful law firm, but from the asshole of an organism whose sole function is to excrete the poison, the ammo, the defoliant necessary for other larger more powerful organisms to destroy the miracle of humanity and that I had been coated in this patina of shit for the best part of my life. The scent of it and the stain of it will in all likelihood take the rest of my life to undo. And you know what I did? I took a deep cleansing breath and I set that notion aside. I tabled it. I said to myself as clear as this may be, as potent a feeling as this, as true a thing as I believe that I have witnessed today, it must wait, it must stand the test of time, and Michael, the time is now [edited from original screenplay for clarity].[12]

The fictional Arthur Edens had *re-collected* and *re-member-ed* himself, not in a way dissimilar to the real Greg Smith's or real Wendell Potter's re-collection and re-member-ing. In Potter's confessional book, *Deadly Spin*, he begins by telling us about his moment of redemption:

> [']My name is Wendell Potter and for twenty years, I worked as a senior executive at health insurance companies, and I saw how they confuse their customers and dump the sick – all so they can satisfy their Wall Street investors'.
>
> That is how I introduced myself to the U.S. Senate Commerce, Science, and Transportation Committee on June 24, 2009. The committee's chair, Senator Jay Rockefeller (D-W. Va.), had asked me to testify as part of his investigation into health insurance company practices that for years had been swelling the ranks of the uninsured and the underinsured in the United States.
>
> I explained how insurance companies make promises they have no intention of keeping, how they flout regulations designed to protect consumers, and how they make it nearly impossible to understand – or even obtain – information needed by consumers.
>
> I described how for-profit insurance companies, in their constant quest to meet Wall Street's profit expectations, routinely cancel the coverage of policyholders who get sick, and how they 'purge' small businesses when their employees' medical claims exceed what underwriters expected.
>
> I knew that as soon as I said those words my life would change forever. It did – but in ways I never could have imagined. I had quit my job as head of public relations at CIGNA – a job that had paid me deep into six figures – because I could no longer serve in good conscience as a spokesman for an industry whose routine practices amount to a death sentence for thousands of Americans every year.
>
> I did not intend to go public as a critic of the industry. But it gradually became clear to me that the industry's duplicitous PR strategy was going to manipulate public opinion and likely shape health care reform in ways that would benefit insurance company executives and their Wall Street masters far more than most other Americans.[13]

Edens's re-collection and re-member-ing involved coming to terms with some truths about himself, painful truths, truths that involved a sense of self-revulsion, a sense that he was coated by a film of excrement. Edens spoke in general terms as being involved with aiding and abetting the creation of 'the defoliant necessary for other, larger, more powerful organisms to destroy the miracle of humanity'. He wasn't simply referring to U-North, which was producing literal toxins and then going to extreme measures to cover up that fact; he was referring to the 'shitty' work of using the law against justice itself, against life itself, so that 'other larger more powerful organisms' can survive and thrive. Greg Smith's book is about how 'larger, more powerful organisms' use the mechanisms of capitalism against those whom the mechanisms of capitalism are supposed to serve. In both cases, what are revealed are perversions. Neither Greg Smith nor Wendell Potter said, explicitly, that they felt as though they were coated with a 'patina of shit', but they may as well have.

It is not hyperbole to say that what Greg Smith discovered in his career on Wall Street was that too many firms were, likewise, churning out 'defoliants'. The foliage that was and is under threat and subject to constant attack are life savings, retirements, economic well-being, the financial resources needed to expand social welfare, and intergenerational wealth transfers. These translate into general well-being for individuals, communities, and nations. The defoliants take the form of outright lies and fraud, half-truths, obfuscations, doublespeak, outrageous fees and commissions, misinformation, and disingenuous claims (about concern for 'free markets' or 'liquidity', among others). One of the results was a global economic crisis the likes of which, in many respects, the world has never seen. Peoples' lives were turned upside down: retirement plans, after decades of wearisome work, were ruined (partly because of panicked selling, directly triggered by the crisis and the harms of which were just as real as the crisis itself); millions of people around the globe lost their jobs or businesses; marriages and families dissolved under the strain of financial loss; the sick lost their health insurance due to unemployment; charitable giving dried up for years, along with research and development into things too varied to name; and a generation of young people lost hope that they will be able to have anything close to the quality of life their parents enjoyed. Trillions of dollars of market wealth evaporated, and were it not for the robust and (at least often) concerted actions of a handful of governments and central banks around the globe the story could have ended much more badly than it did. The damage Wall Street has done, and of which it is still quite capable of doing, is a *species* of the defoliation that Arthur Edens was denouncing. The 'defoliation' was described in *The Financial Crisis Inquiry Report*.[14] Here is just a portion of the devastation – the defoliation – it describes:

> The recession officially began in December 2007. By many measures, its effects on the job market were the worst on record, as reflected in the speed and breadth of the falloff in jobs, the rise of the ranks of underemployed workers, and the long stretches of time that millions of Americans were and still are surviving without work. The economy shed 3.6 million jobs in 2008 – the largest annual plunge since record keeping began in 1940. By December 2009, the United States had lost another 4.7 million jobs. Through November 2010, the economy had regained nearly 1 million jobs, putting only a small dent in the declines.
>
> The underemployment rate – the total of unemployed workers who are actively looking for jobs, those with part-time work who would prefer full-time jobs, and those who need jobs but say they are too discouraged to search – increased from 8.8% in December 2007 to 13.7% in December 2008, reaching 17.4% in October 2009. This was the highest level since calculations for that labor category were first made in 1994. As of November 2010, the underemployment rate stood at 17%. The average length of time individuals spent unemployed spiked from 9.4 weeks in June 2008 to 18.2 weeks in June 2009, and 25.5 weeks in June 2010. Fifty-nine percent of all job seekers, according to the most recent government statistics, searched for work for at least 15 weeks.

The labor market is daunting across the board, but it is especially grim among African American workers, whose jobless rate is 16.0%, about 6 percentage points above the national average; workers between the ages of 16 and 19 years old, at 24.6%; and Hispanics, at 13.2%. And the impact has been especially severe in certain professions: unemployment in construction, for instance, climbed to an average of 19.1% in 2009, and averaged 20.6% during the first 11 months of 2010.

Real gross domestic product, the nation's measure of economic output adjusted for inflation, fell at an annual rate of 4% in the third quarter of 2008 and 6.8% in the fourth quarter. After falling again in the first half of 2009 and then modestly growing in the second half, average GDP for the year was 2.6% lower than in 2008, the biggest drop since 1946.[15]

Culture Matters

Such 'defoliation' is the result, at least in large part, of a failure to recall the purposes of markets, commerce, and business. This failure of recollection is a failure that gets baked into market institutions themselves, from industrial corporations, to law firms, to Wall Street banks, brokerages, and investment management firms. That is, it is a failure that gets baked into corporate *cultures*. Edward B. Tyler, a cultural anthropologist working and writing in the nineteenth century, told us that culture is 'that complex whole which includes knowledge, belief, art, law, morals, custom, and any other capabilities and habits acquired by man as a member of society'.[16] I take this to be as good a definition of culture as any. Of course, when we speak of corporate cultures, as 'sub-cultures', some of the components of this definition either recede or drop out. In business, for example, 'art' (*simpliciter*) drops out (although commercial creativity is quite creative at times). Culture at the level of firms are indeed 'complexes' that include, for sure:

Knowledge: The firm must use specialized knowledge in the production of goods and services;

Belief: The firm must operate so that it can navigate by means of settled opinions and facts concerning the nature of its products and services, but also about the entire commercial environment in which it operates;

Law: The firm's activities are constrained by rules;

Morals: Those de facto guides to actions that attend the constraints of law but have (usually, though not always) less severe forms of sanction for violation;

Customs: Unreflective habits of operation;

Capabilities: The internal potential/power to achieve goals and express itself in ways not always obvious; and

Habits: Similar to customers, but at a more granular level, the patterns of operation that are part and parcel of custom.

To talk about corporate culture is to talk about each of these components, which have expression in the world but which are fathered and nurtured *in the mind*, which is where culture actually resides. To talk about changes in corporate culture is to talk about effecting an alteration in one or more of these components, which means talking about *metanoia*. To talk about change in Wall Street's culture is, then, also to talk about effecting cultural *metanoia*.

Metanoia

I have used the word *metanoia* several times in the preceding pages. The word *metanoia* is the transliteration of the ancient Greek μετάνο. The word has critical importance in the Christian religion, with cognates in Buddhism. While problematically translated into English as 'repentance' throughout the Christian scriptures, its real meaning is more like 'complete mental and attitudinal transformation'. In the Christian tradition, the call to *metanoia* is the call to become, effectively, a new person, with a new mind. This is not reducible to merely 'changing one's mind' or 'sorrow over past mistakes'. It is a change in the way one *sees* and *understands*.

But we need not think of the word *metanoia* as only applicable to religious contexts or religious purposes. *Metanoia* happens in what is often referred to as the 'secular' world as well. Often, it comes about because of new insights into the way the world works, or *can* work, and what those insights imply concerning the transformation of our physical and social environments, or even of our political community. For example, the scientific age brought about a *metanoia* concerning how we might assess and bend the physical world to human purposes, and ended the belief, mostly, that human beings were fated to be the playthings of chance and circumstance.

Metanoia can be forged by social visionaries who lead their contemporaries to change their habits and attitudes: John Brown at Harper's Ferry, whose vigorous stance against slavery led him to the gallows; William Wilberforce, in Britain, in his long and arduous push to end slavery in the British Empire; Susan B. Anthony and Mary Wollstonecraft, who forced men and women alike to see the then-prevailing status of women as nothing other than the result of degradation and the denial of women's full humanity; John Dewey and Paulo Freire in education, who abjured the notion that children are mere passive receptacles of instruction, but rather are active participants in the educational process, among many other examples. *Metanoia* can happen in scientific exploration (such as in our understanding of the causes of disease, or of the fundamental structure of the material world, as in quantum physics); in sexuality (as in the acceptance of gay marriage and the bursting of the binary notion of gender); in the development of the self (the American ideals of individualism, as in Ralph Waldo Emerson, Henry David Thoreau, and Thomas Paine); and in government (in the notion that the power of monarchy can be constrained, as provided in the *Magna*

Carta, or in the postulate or proposition that human beings have inalienable rights). In philosophy, John Locke revolutionized thought about government when he published his *Two Treatises on Government* (1689), which contained a rebuke of the notion that kings rule by divine right, and an argument concerning self-ownership and the nature of property. Thomas Hobbes did the same when he told us a story about civilized society, how it is only possible through a substantial renunciation of our 'natural' right to use force against our neighbors, or when he helped to lay the foundation for what Mark Lilla called 'The Great Separation', i.e., the separation of the sphere of politics from the authority of the church. The Prophet Muhammad, the founder of Islam, transformed the Arabian Peninsula (and many places well beyond it), squelching the raging blood feuds and rank injustices that were common in his world with his message of a God who calls for submission, justice and charity. And *metanoia* can happen in business, as has been the case time and again: Henry Ford's decision to raise worker wages so that a new market for the products the workers themselves created could be established (the new market being the workers themselves); shifts in management theory, as those ushered in directly or indirectly by Frederick Taylor, Max Weber, Mary P. Follett and Peter F. Drucker; and the democratization of creativity and innovation, as is the mainstay of Google, Apple, Facebook, Twitter and other extremely innovative firms. *Metanoia* is the word I use for these changes because they concern changes not in practices and habits only, but in ways of seeing that can change, almost totally, how one understands the world and/or what is possible in it. When properly understood, one can see that it is *metanoia* that has led to many of the changes that have made life better for millions upon millions of people. What makes *metanoia* possible are the human capacities for learning, for the employment of imagination (moral and other), and human malleability. These capacities do not get turned-off like a light switch because one has entered the world of commerce or capital markets.

I said at the outset that this book would not be a call for more regulation or for the typical remedies that are offered up by the managerial classes. By now it should be clear that this book is a meditation on the possibilities of *metanoia* regarding the way we understand capitalism and capital markets themselves. To achieve *metanoia*, at least often, people must be shoved out of their comfort zones and thought ruts. This is often achieved by reframing the object under consideration. Reframing, *a la* George Lakoff, Daniel Kahneman and other thinkers, is a powerful tool of and for change. Reframing entails a reorientation and a reconceptualization of the metaphors and clusters of concepts that guide our actions inside and outside of the fields of commerce, and that rest upon as well as shape our systems of belief. Reframing allows us to take the same set of facts that are at play and approach them through a new scheme of inquiry and engagement.

The Self-Centred Model and The Ministerial Model

Here are sets of phrases:

Table 1.1: The Self-Centred Model

Column A1 – Objectives	Column B1 – Plan or Remedy
I need a job.	I must go out and *get* job.
I need more money.	I must go out and *get* (*make*) more money.
I need to improve my standard of living.	I must *acquire* more economic goods.
We need more profits.	We must bring in more revenue and cut expenses.
We have made our firm successful.	We have achieved the goal of a profitable business.

Now consider these pairings:

Table 1.2: The Ministerial Model

Column A2 – Objectives	Column B2 – Plan or Remedy
I need to find a way to contribute to society while earning a living.	I must hone talents and skills that will make me useful to society.
More money would be useful to my efforts to serve others and my own needs.	I must see how my talents and skills can be put to more remunerative uses, or how I might need to develop new ones.
I need to be in a better position to serve.	I must develop the ways in which I am useful to others.
We need to be more efficient and retain more earnings.	We must find better ways to create customers and to meet customers' needs and goals.

Here are some of the key words and senses of use from Columns A1 and B1: 'need' (for oneself or one's organization), 'increase' (for oneself or one's organization), 'made' (for oneself or one's organization), 'get', 'bring' (to oneself or one's organization), and 'achieved' (for oneself or one's organization).

Here are some of the key words and senses of use in Columns A2 and B2: 'need', 'useful', 'serve', 'create', 'inquire', 'develop', 'customer', all with the sense of being directed toward advancing the interests, needs, and desires of others, often through the development of one's self or one's organization, while recognizing the need to meet one's own needs and goals.

Let's take A1 and B1 as representing one type of individual and one type of business firm, while A2 and B2 represent another type. Call A1 and B1 'The Self-Centred Model' and A2 and B2 'The Ministerial Model'. Now, these are, in a loose sense, 'ideal types', to borrow an expression from Max Weber. Most people and businesses exhibit a mixture of the key words and senses of use expressed in both sets of columns, but there are businesses that do seemingly operate closer to the opposite ends of the spectrum than others, to be sure. In many ways, as many management experts already know, there is nothing new in what I have sketched: A2 and B2, or The Ministerial Model, in the business context, sketch out the organization that is keenly aware of what the customer or client wants and positions itself accordingly. In the famous words of Bob Dylan, 'It might be the Devil, or it might be the Lord, but You're gonna have to serve somebody'.[17]

Actually, it may be neither the Devil, nor the Lord; it may simply be yourself or your customers and clients. But, indeed, 'you're gonna have to serve somebody'. Dylan's binaries remind us to keep an eye on just who and what we are serving. So, given Dylan's cue, we need not look at The Self-Centred Model and The Ministerial Model as sketching a choice between the service of nobody and the service of many others, respectively. No, both models address service. The difference between the models is the recipient or recipients, the beneficiary or beneficiaries, of the services we render.

The Ministerial Model ('ministerial' simply means the service of others, which is why it is used in the religious context) calls for people (individuals, directors, executives, employees) to be *outwardly focused*, committed to satisfying needs beyond their organizations and beyond themselves. This is the way that many if not most highly innovative and highly successful business leaders think, as was discussed succinctly in a 2011 article by William W. George, a Professor of Management Practice at Harvard Business School:

> Leaders can avoid [the various pitfalls of leadership] by devoting themselves to personal development that cultivates their inner compass, or True North. This requires *reframing* their leadership from being *heroes* to being *servants of the people they lead*. This process requires thought and introspection because many people get into leadership roles in response to their ego needs. It enables them to transition from seeking external gratification to finding internal satisfaction by making meaningful contributions through their leadership.[18]

People who remain devotees to or adherents of The Self-Centred Model (perhaps the most stark case depicted in film in recent years is that of Jordan Belfort, the so-called 'Wolf of Wall Street') lead firms that fixate on themselves, which often leads to a loss of market share and that because of a loss of customer trust and loyalty. The important thing to be grasped here is that *where* a person or business is on the spectrum the poles of which are self-centred thinking and ministerial thinking has a lot to do with culture and, as we know, culture is mostly in the mind, i.e., it is replicated by minds, although the expressions are external, in the world (on the shop floor, in the office suite, in the trading room). The Self-Centred Model reflects a mindset of *acquisition, seizure, taking*, while The Ministerial Model reflects a mindset of usefulness and service. Yes, there are serious implications concerning the long-term prospects of the business, but there are also serious implications concerning the prospects for scandal, business disruptions and negative externalities. Management experts gravitate to The Ministerial Model not because it is the most facially ethical model to adopt, but because it works better for the long-term prospects of the firm. That is, they gravitate toward The Ministerial Model for both strategic and prudential reasons, understanding that those strategic and prudential reasons are supervened by ethical ones. What good managers operate from is genuine concern for others (in the case of the firm, customers and clients who want better products or services, as well as stakeholders in a circle of concern beyond customers and clients).

Perspective Matters

As I hope has now become clear, how we conceptualize and frame things can make a huge difference. Markets are too often framed as fields to plunder or to exploit, as discussed earlier. A more sober and academic definition of a market is as follows: 'An actual or nominal place where forces of demand and supply operate, and where buyers and sellers interact (directly or through intermediaries) to trade goods, services, or contracts or instruments, for money or barter. Markets include mechanisms or means for (1) determining price of the traded item (2) communicating the price information (3) facilitating deals and transactions, and (4) effecting distribution. The market for a particular item is made up of existing and potential customers who need it and have the ability and willingness to pay for it'.[19] To move away from the notion that markets exist to be plundered, we need only keep in mind this simple definition, for in it we find, once again, the word 'customer'. And who or what is a 'customer' according to the same source? A customer is '[a] party that receives or consumes products (goods or services) and has the ability to choose between different products and suppliers'. In a nutshell, people or institutions to which you and your firm can provide goods and services, in a competitive environment in which other firms believe they can provide better goods and services, or provide them in a better manner, or both. But Peter Drucker was right to focus, as well, on the rather glaring etymology of the word 'customer'. A real customer is one who makes a habit of returning to receive the goods and/or services on offer. This is why Drucker wrote that the purpose of a business is to make a customer:

> Asked what a business is, the typical businessman is likely to answer, "An organization to make a profit." The typical economist is likely to give the same answer. This answer is not only false, it is irrelevant ... In fact, the concept is worse than irrelevant: it does harm. It is a major cause of misunderstanding of the nature of profit in our society and of the deep-seated hostility to profit, which are the most dangerous diseases of any industrial society ... To know what a business is, we have to start with its purpose. *Its purpose must lie outside of the business itself.* In fact, it must be in society since business enterprise is an organ of society. There is only one valid definition of business purpose: "to create a customer".[20]

What a business hopes to cultivate where one sees a market for a particular good or service that it thinks it can deliver better than other businesses is a relationship wherein the business can remain confident of repeat orders of goods or services by purchasers (who, pleased with what they have received, recommend such goods or services to others), and wherein the purchaser of such goods or services can remain confident that it/she/he will be able to rely on consistent satisfaction with each successive purchase. Such a relationship can stand a few shocks and disappointments along the way, an occasional 'Edsel', if you will – even an occasional scandal. Why? It is because the firm-customer relationship is built upon *trust*. Trust is what, in large part, creates the conditions for longevity, since it makes it difficult for the pathogens of *anomie* to take hold, as Francis Fukuyama expounds in his book *Trust: The Social Virtues and the Creation of Prosperity*. Trust is probably the single most important element in the success of any business, because it is rooted in an existential fact: the world, for human beings as for other creatures, is a dangerous place, and so it is in our interests to surround ourselves with people and things (including institutions) that do not contribute to the dangers.

And this is why Wall Street has such a sorry reputation. Ask the average person if he or she thinks that trust is pervasive in the financial services industry, and it would be fair to predict that the response is going to be a knowing smile if not an outright guffaw. Wall Street, generally speaking, does not operate according to The Ministerial Model (although this is the model its regulators *wish* for), but rather pursuant to The Self-Centred Model – the model that gives us Jordan Belfort, insider trading scandals (such as at SAC Capital), and HFT. And it is the Self-Centred Model that is *celebrated*, not only on Wall Street itself, but 'on' The Other Wall Street, which I will be discussing later. The poor understanding of the nature of the business enterprise in general arises because of myopia and an impoverished notion of self-interest. Indeed, it is not the manager or executive concerned with such things as trust and service who are the problem, although these may be the first to be shown the door at many Wall Street firms. Such managers and executives are not the uninformed ones. The managers and executives who think businesses are run for the benefit of shareholders and the executive class, or, commensurately, run to maximize profits in the short run, it is these persons who operate from deficits in their reasoning. This is not to say that businesses can't survive managements with a very noticeable bias in favor of The Self-Centred Model. Goldman Sachs comes to mind here, given recent press since the beginnings of the financial crisis in 2007/8. It would be foolish to think that a certain level of self-interestedness can't or won't be tolerated by customers, so long as those customers continue to get what they want or need, and so long as they can trust the firms that service their interests not to self-deal and unjustly enrich themselves at their expense; so long as the customers are the centre of the firm's business activities, and are not mere means to the firm's ends. But over time self-centred cultures, such as many on Wall Street, erode an organization from the inside. Over time, customers, feeling that the prospects for abuse are too pronounced, sever ties. One or two Edsels, one or two scandals, can be endured. Nobody, after all, is perfect. But where it is clear that a wholesale culture of self-centredness is extant, customers move elsewhere, based upon a simple risk calculation.

One of the things that it is important to grasp is the importance of *perception* and *conception*. This is because how we *perceive* and *conceive* makes a great deal of difference concerning outcomes in certain and sometimes critical situations. To make the point, I will introduce a pictorial representation that I use with my students on the first day of class in the business ethics courses that I teach at Rutgers University and Molloy College. I show them this:

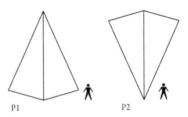

Figure 1.1: Pyramids illustrating perception and conception

I point out to my students that both shapes are pyramids (well, as I myself am the artist, both are at least *intended* to be pyramids). They usually assent to this assertion, at which time I rehearse that the shape is the same in every respect, other than its orientation in space and its placement on the ground. Both, I rehearse, are pyramids – one is not less of a pyramid than the other. 'Now', I ask them, 'which do you suppose is more stable, P1 or P2?' They tell me P1. 'Which appears to be unstable, that is, which is perched precariously, assuming both P1 and P2 are, somehow, set on the ground?' They tell me that P2 is. Finally I ask, 'If you were the little person standing next to P2, and assuming P2 is made out of the same stuff as the pyramids in Giza (stone), how would you feel?' 'Very concerned', they tell me, 'since P2 could very well fall on me'. 'Yet', I continue, 'you agree that both are pyramids. Suppose you are a client of a financial services firm and your friend is the client of another financial services firm. Let's say that P1 represents a financial services firm that is seeking more and better ways to service client needs, and P2 represents a financial services firm with a corporate culture that leads to the aggressive pursuit of short-run profits above all else. It stands to reason that, *ceteris paribus*, you want to be the client of P1, does it not?'

More than this, I tell my students that both P1 and P2 need to be profitable, and both need to run their businesses well if they will be and stay profitable. The difference is the perspective that management and employees have as to the nature and purpose of the business. Most of the time, this won't matter much. In both firms, paper clips need to be bought, water coolers filled, and utility bills paid. In both firms, sales (income) need to be generated, payroll needs to be processed, and innovation (of some sort) must be a mainstay. But the firm that stresses short-term profits will reveal much about itself when it is facing real *stress* in the marketplace or when it faces *crises*. The instability in firm P2 is the result of the perspective that management and employees have on the business, that is, on it *raison d'etre*. In a firm that seeks only the most profit in the shortest span of time, corners will be cut, quality will be sacrificed, trust will be eroded, and expenditures for innovation may be marginalized – or worse. Here, I will suggest, are the perspectives and attendant commitments that operate in each case:

Table 1.3: Primary concerns and commitments of Firms P1 and P2

Firm P1	Firm P2
Primary Concern: Interest of the client	Primary concern: Profit maximization and personal remuneration
Time Horizon: Long	Time Horizon: Short
Service Orientation, External: Toward Clients' Goals	Service Orientation, Internal: Toward Firm's Goals
Response to Acute Stress and Crisis: Direct response with eye to preserving and enhancing the long-term prospects of the firm	Response to Acute Stress and Crisis: Deflection, denial, concealment of exposure, blame of others
Key example: Johnson & Johnson during the cyanide-laced Tylenol crisis in the 1980s	Key example: Enron, following exposures that its financial disclosures were fraudulent and that its business was based upon gimmicks and sham transactions

Beliefs

Our perspectives, whether in or concerning business or other endeavours or matters, are shaped by or derive from our *beliefs*, including background beliefs about our society or organization, and including metaphysical beliefs about the nature of reality itself (which factors in much more than we sometimes realize). One of the reasons that it has been so hard to curb Wall Street's excesses, to shift its *modus operandi* and its culture from The Self-Centred Model to The Ministerial Model, is that many inside and outside of Wall Street think that Wall Street has got something right about the nature of things – that the universe and society only deliver what we need when we aggressively extract it from others, whether those others are employers, clients, or customers. In that regard – and this cannot be stressed too much – Wall Street is a reflection of Main Street, not its antithesis, as so often suggested by pundits and the media. The wolves of Wall Street exist because they come from among the wolves of Main Street.

That beliefs (social, economic, political etc.) are important in ethics was highlighted by the philosopher Jonathan Glover, and I will quote him at length here from his book *Humanity*:

> A belief is not held in isolation, but is part of a system. [Philosopher] Frank Ramsey said that a belief is 'a map of neighbouring space by which we steer'. Our beliefs about the world hang together, like a mental map of a city too large to be fully known. Some parts of the mental map are sharp and detailed, others are hazy. There may be vagueness or mistakes about how some regions join up, and some parts of the map may be inconsistent with others; but, despite these defects, the map does not show a series of isolated streets, but a system of streets.
>
> All our beliefs have links to neighbouring ones. I believe the pills the doctor prescribes will cure my illness. This is bound up with my beliefs that the doctor is competent and knows the current evidence. My expectations of the medicine are vulnerable to changes in these other beliefs. More generally, if I abandon my present belief in scientific medicine, or my expectation that evidence from the past is a fairly reliable guide to the future, my confidence in the pills will also be undermined. This confidence rests on beliefs bound up with other parts of my whole system ...
>
> One model of a system of beliefs is a kind of wire frame sometimes used as a children's toy. The frame is made of many bits of rigid wire. The joints where the bits of wire meet can be adjusted to different angles. You can choose the shape of any bit of the frame, provided you allow the rest of the frame to bend and twist to accommodate it. *The belief you want to preserve at all costs is the bit you hold rigid, letting this determine the shape of the rest of the frame. Systems do not only contain beliefs about what the world is like and about what is desirable.*
>
> Some beliefs are about the acceptability of other ones, and are used to adjudicate between them. They could be called structural beliefs. They are like the load-bearing walls of a house. When a structural belief is given up, there are likely to be changes throughout the system. Some structural beliefs are about plausibility. For instance, it is sometimes held that, where two beliefs are both compatible with the evidence, the simpler explanation should be treated as more plausible. Appeals to authority are a different kind of structural belief.[21]

Wall Street rests upon or operates pursuant to a set of structural beliefs that make it very difficult for the shift from The Self-Centred Model to The Ministerial Model to occur. Since, as I pointed out earlier, it is a place where one goes to make money *über alles* (that is the principal motivator for a career in the financial services industry, and it is a motivator that reproduces itself from generation to generation), the structural beliefs of Wall Street must be, as Glover argues, tied into a larger set of structural beliefs – beliefs about the nature of society, of human beings, of the self, and must even be tied into a cosmology. For an industry that beckons one to the pursuit of personal wealth above almost every other commercial consideration must contain within itself, among its various high-level operatives and leaders, a certain social philosophy and a certain kind of psychology. I would argue that this social philosophy and psychology are, essentially, Hobbesian. It is a view that we all, as individuals, stand over and against our compatriots and neighbours as potential, if not as actual, rivals and threats. Underneath this view is a heated, bubbling reservoir of enmity. The only way, then, to assure one's own survival and well-being, on this view, is to amass the requisite amount of resources (force) to 'win' in contests between one's self and another, or between one's self the organs and institutions of society, more generally. This is Wall Street's social philosophy and so it ought not to surprise us that its players do not want government mechanisms or egalitarian ideologies to get in the way, for they are attempts to, on such a view, insert chimera and velleities into the actual and unvarnished and phallic) world of competition for security and even what Jean-Jacques Rousseau referred to as *amour-propre*, the love of self that depends on the esteem in which others hold you. There are threats not only to one's pecuniary wealth, but there are threats to the social self, as Richard Wilkinson and Kate Pickett discuss in their book, *The Spirit Level*.[22] Of course, this is not in any way peculiar to Wall Street. It is extant in commercial settings in general, in sport, and in interpersonal relations at more granular levels of society. But it is hard to deny that it is particularly prominent on Wall Street.

The irony, of course, is that the very Hobbesian concerns and conclusions that motivate Wall Street's traders, bankers and brokers to action – the desire to amass the requisite amount of force (read, wealth) to 'win' in contests with others – creates a feedback loop that prevents the formation and maintenance of the very laws, policies and institutions that would make unnecessary the cultivation of 'the Hobbesian hero within'. It is the social philosophy (and social psychology) of Wall Street that must be exposed and critiqued, at much deeper levels than offered by most contemporary commentators, if we are to get a handle on its *anomic* culture. The capital markets reflect who we are as human beings. They are constructed within the framework of our desires, beliefs, understanding and, perhaps most important, our fears. Our fears are what make Jordan Belfort's 'keen insight' sound like the acme of sensibleness and the rallying cry for the avoidance of victimization: 'Let me tell you something. There's no nobility in poverty. I've been a poor man, and I've been a rich man. And I choose rich every fucking time'.[23] Because this resonates with many (Who, after all, wants to live a life of deprivation and powerlessness?) many are drawn to think that the people most driven to avoid poverty, the people most enamoured with wealth and most willing to do whatever it takes to acquire it, have keener vision about the nature of things than the rest of us – are like 'wolves' in that they share a primal sense with the predatory *animal* who 'survives', albeit at the expense of its prey. Indeed, Wall Street's ethos in constructed from such primal instincts. But high civilization is not. High civilization is the result of emergence from the muck and mire of primal drives, and that is in many ways why Wall Street remains out of sync with larger civilizational goals and the larger social welfare goals of the political community whose first duty is *mutual* care and concern.

No, there is no 'nobility' in poverty *per se*; but neither is there 'nobility' in wealth *per se*. In a larger sense, as Marshall Sahlins has put it, 'poverty is not a certain small amount of goods, nor is it just a relation between means and ends; above all it is a relation between people. Poverty is social status. As such, it is the invention of civilization. It has grown with civilization, at once as an invidious distinction between classes and more importantly as a tributary relation'.[24] If it was nobility that Jordan Belfort was looking for, he missed it by a thousand miles. For 'ignoble' does not even begin to capture what his wealth enabled him to become. Nor, for that matter, was he truly wealthy. Wealth is not the accumulation of money and possessions in absolute terms. It is a relation between what one has and what one desires. The bottomless pit of desire for more money and more possessions indicates insatiability, and insatiability is not wealth but a state of lack – which is, ironically, how many people understand poverty.

It does no good to say, simplistically, that Wall Street is motivated by greed. For greed is not the *cause* of Wall Street's troubling culture, but only a symptom that itself grows out of a set of beliefs about much bigger things. In the case of Wall Street, it may very well be that its pervasive greed (the relentless pursuit of more than one is entitled to or more than propriety allows) rests on the very fears that social egalitarians, so often seen as Wall Street's enemies, have been trying to address for the past hundred and fifty years, both in Europe and in the United States. Clearly, it would be naive to conclude that *all* greed is driven by such fear, for there are those among us who seem to be vicious by nature, and so no assurances that they would never go without the basics required for a decent life would dissuade them from their hyper-acquisitiveness, knavery, and animality. But I think most people on Wall Street (and Main Street) are basically decent, and that many of them operate under a set of structural beliefs and a dominant social philosophy and social psychology that compel them to continue in behaviours that erode the trust of clients and the trust of the citizenry in society's commercial institutions (more generally), lead to scandal, and cause cycles of wealth destruction.

The right shift in perspective can lead to a proper relationship between people and markets, can lead to a view that markets are, first and foremost, tools for the creation of social welfare and not first and foremost tools for the creation of vast personal wealth, and not the habitats for 'wolves' and other predators to 'bag' their 'kills' and 'win' the 'game' of acquisition, and prevail in pecuniary 'wars'. Nothing about such a shift suggests that profit and gain must go by the boards, for profit and gain are among the logical expedients in the way of commerce. Rather, it would create the proper understanding of what profit and gain are for. This would seem to require a shift in both the way Wall Street sees itself and in the way Main Street (where The Other Wall Street may be found) understands the purpose of commerce and economy.

2 RECENT SCANDALS AND THE CULTURES THAT CREATED THEM

NEWSCASTER: Two former SAC portfolio managers were named yesterday, prosecutors alleging what many have speculated for years, insider trading at Stevie Cohen's SAC Capital.

NARRATOR: The arrests were a big shock, but not a surprise to many traders on Wall Street.

CHARLES GASPARINO, Fox Business Network: Listen, if you walked up to a typical Wall Street trader and you say, "Hey, is there insider trading at SAC Capital going on?" after the guy falls on the floor dying of laughter, will get up and say, "Yes," OK?

MARTIN SMITH, Correspondent: He dies of laughter because it's a naive question?

CHARLES GASPARINO: It's a naive question. I mean, that's their reputation.

M. Smith and N. Verbitsky
'To Catch a Trader'[1]

In what follows I will discuss two Wall Street scandals: the insider trading scandal at SAC Capital Management (hereafter, 'SAC'), which came to resolution in 2014 (well, mostly), and the scandal involving sell-side research, which erupted in the early 2000s. The common threads of these scandals is the desire for advantage over one's competitors and the teleopathic pursuit of such advantage. The SAC scandal is the most recent, so I will begin with it.

Insider Trading at SAC

Steven A. Cohen has been in the news for quite a while. Beginning his career in the 1980s at the Wall Street broker-dealer Gruntal & Co., Cohen rose, through his successful investment acumen and drive, to be one of the most successful hedge fund managers in history, often mentioned with George Soros, Michael Steinhardt, and Julian Robertson. Beyond that, but certainly not unassociated with it, he has been in the media because of his lavish lifestyle, his large and impressive art collection, and his success at catalyzing the careers of investment fund managers (one of which set up a hedge fund in Stamford, Connecticut, of which I was for several years the Chief Compliance Officer).

Hedge funds in general have had a good deal of bad press over the years. They are associated with murky and dangerous financial schemes, black box trading, outrageous market speculation, dizzying amounts of leverage, and large systemic risks. While some of this bad press is deserved (one need only think of Long-Term Capital Management, which has become a poster child for the potential for hedge-fund-manufactured systemic risk), much of it isn't. Before we delve more deeply into a discussion of what went wrong at SAC, it might be worthwhile to review just what a hedge fund is and how a manager of a hedge fund operates. There is a lot of mystification concerning hedge funds, but much of it is unwarranted. They are rather, in their basic operations, relatively simple.

Anatomy of a Hedge Fund

A hedge fund is a company like any other company. Some companies make shoes, some make tennis rackets, some provide accounting services. Hedge funds invest and trade a variety of classes of assets, ranging from plain vanilla equity securities to commodities to derivatives (contracts or assets, such as options and futures, which derive their value from other assets). In some ways this is not very different from what individual investors do in their own brokerage accounts. Individual investors buy equities (stocks), fixed income instruments (such as bonds and certain preferred stocks), money market instruments (such as certificates of deposit and T-bills) and, in some cases, options and even hard assets like gold or copper, and they may employ different strategies in managing these assets in order to maximize returns and avoid losses.

But as private funds (that is, their shares are not sold to the general public indiscriminately), hedge funds differ from the brokerage accounts of individual investors in several ways. First, they are investment *pools*. That is, they take in money from a number of different investors (usually wealthy individuals or institutions) and that money is then pooled, allowing the hedge fund manager to invest in greater quantities of various assets and employ various strategies. Often, hedge funds will leverage the money that they receive. That is, they use the assets they own as collateral for loans that they use to buy even more assets, sometimes at multiples of their capital base. Again, in principle this is not very different from what an individual investor might do in his or her brokerage account, where he or she uses margin (loans from his or her broker, using existing assets in the account as collateral) to acquire more assets, in order to magnify returns (which can, unfortunately, magnify losses). Like individual investors (especially those persons who are sophisticated when it comes to investing), hedge funds employ different strategies and, contrary to what is often said of them, impose investment parameters and disciplines in the management of their investment portfolios.

Much has been made of the supposed 'fact' that hedge funds are unregulated. Hedge funds have always been regulated to some extent (even if obliquely), but what was usually meant by that claim is that hedge funds, unlike mutual funds which are generally tailored for smaller and less wealthy investors (that is, investors less able to afford losses as hedge fund investors are), do not go through the same rigorous registration process with the SEC that mutual funds go through. Mutual funds, which sell their shares to the public, are required to adhere to a list of portfolio and governance obligations and constraints, constraints that have to do with concentration of investment in single companies, the use of speculative instruments, exposures to certain industries, and the composition of fund boards. They are also required to file updating registration documents with the SEC, which reviews the content of those documents for clarity and adequacy of disclosures. In terms of governance, mutual funds have much more elaborate governance structures – separate boards of directors or trustees with very specific obligations, dedicated compliance officers, codes of ethics, and complex reporting obligations, all of which are required by law. Hedge funds, as such, have far less onerous obligations and constraints, although the amount of money they invest on behalf of their shareholders is substantial, sometimes hundreds of millions or even billions of dollars.

All of this said, *prudence* dictates certain restrictions and constraints. Hedge fund managers risk much when they are too brash when it comes to portfolio investments. While not hampered by the sorts of cookie-cutter constraints imposed by the SEC on mutual funds, it should not be concluded from that alone that hedge fund managers may do whatever they please. The due diligence process imposed on hedge funds by investors (which is now the subject of several books), especially by pension funds and other institutions that invest in them, have become increasingly rigorous, and before many hedge funds receive any money from such investors they are required to answer a host of question and provide all pertinent operating, compliance, and valuation documentation (and often, more than that) to demonstrate that the hedge fund and the manager will manage the fund's assets properly, are properly organized, and have paid attention to important business and risk details. Also, hedge fund investors monitor their investments closely and are less forgiving when losses mount, and so many hedge funds dissolve not too long after the commencement of their operations if investor expectations are not met, largely due to redemptions (withdrawal by investors of their money):

> Most hedge funds fail: their average life span is about five years. Out of an estimated seventy-two hundred hedge funds in existence at the end of 2010, seven hundred and seventy-five failed or closed in 2011, as did eight hundred and seventy-three in 2012, and nine hundred and four in 2013. This implies that, within three years, around a third of all funds disappeared. The over-all number did not decrease, however, because hope springs eternal, and new funds are constantly being launched.[2]

And what are those hopes? That the managers provide what is known as 'uncorrelated returns' in a consistent manner, and earn positive (or relatively positive) returns despite broader market conditions. That essentially means that hedge fund managers are expected to achieve significant returns that are not correlated with broad market indices. Since they have fewer constraints, they are expected to do better than mutual fund managers who operate with significant constraints. This expectation exists primarily because investors in hedge funds give up a substantial chunk of total return on investment to the hedge fund managers, from ten to twenty percent per annum typically (subject to certain conditions), and in the case of SAC, as much as fifty percent per annum. In addition to that, hedge fund managers often charge a flat fee – fifty basis points or one half of one percent, to as much as three percent per annum. The relative safety of hedge fund investing, given all of this due diligence, is attested to by the hundreds of billions of dollars invested in them and other private funds, such as private equity and venture funds.

Further, in recent years, the activities of hedge funds have been increasingly regulated, more or less through the regulation of their managers. An abortive attempt was made to regulate hedge fund managers in 2005. The SEC's attempt at that time failed because the agency lacked the authority to impose on hedge fund managers an obligation to register with the SEC as investment advisers. It was not until the passage of Dodd-Frank that most hedge fund managers were required to register with the SEC, and many were later required to register with the Commodity Futures Trading Commission ('CFTC') as 'commodity pool operators'. Internationally, even more regulation is in place, such as in the European Union's Alternative Investment Fund Managers Directive, or 'AIFMD'. Still, the fact that hedge fund managers are now required to register with the SEC does not mean that hedge funds themselves are required to register (in the way that mutual funds are). Even post Dodd-Frank, hedge funds are still free to buy and sell the same broad range of assets, with the same frequencies as was the case prior to Dodd-Frank, and using as much leverage as their investors will allow.

Yet, the registration of hedge fund managers does impose certain governance and compliance constraints on hedge funds, and has imposed on hedge fund managers a number of operational considerations that simply did not exist prior to Dodd-Frank. Hedge fund managers are required to have rather substantial compliance programs in place in order for the managers to comply with applicable bodies of regulation, including, but not limited to, the Investment Advisers Act of 1940 (as amended over the years). They are also required, like other registered investment advisers, to have formal compliance policies and procedures as well as knowledgeable compliance officers who are responsible for implementing a compliance program based upon those policies and procedures. Further, hedge fund managers are required to have written codes of ethics, and to make sure they are distributed throughout the firm. Also, hedge fund managers have requirements to file detailed fund-level information with the SEC, the CFTC, the Federal Reserve (in some cases), and, depending upon their activities in other countries, with regulators in those other countries (such as prescribed by AIFMD).

But, as indicated, it isn't only the government that imposes constraints on hedge funds and hedge fund managers. Many investors in hedge funds are institutional investors (pension funds, other hedge funds, municipalities, and large corporations), investors themselves keep a sharp eye on the managers and the funds to make sure that they are living up to the requirements imposed in the hedge funds' governing documents, running annual background checks on officers and principals of the investment advisers that manage the funds, and imposing annual due diligence and requalification requirements. They review the use of leverage, industry concentration of investments, the evenness or unevenness of returns (which can be an indication of fraud or administrative problems), conflicts of interest, the background and sophistication of the professionals, and many other variables. Institutional hedge fund investors seek the greatest amount of transparency that the law permits, and they expect answers when questions are put, under threat of redemption and 'negative chatter' among the investor class. So while there is a public perception that hedge fund managers operate as lawless yahoos on the frontier of the investment world, this is largely a caricature.

Yes, hedge funds fail, but that is to be expected given the high demands placed upon them by their investors. Failure is not scandalous in and of itself, although the media may portray it as such. Part of the media portrayals of hedge funds and hedge fund managers have to do with a general lack of sympathy for or understanding of hedge funds and their managers (the scrutiny of the tax imposed on carried interest is one example). It is, of course, an industry in which only the wealthy have any truck. It is not my goal here to alter that perception, to some degree fomented by populist or egalitarian commitments, *but it is important to point out that good public policy does not emerge from inadequate understanding or caricatures.* And while the culture and the mentality at many hedge funds are similar to what one finds on the 'sell side' of the business (aggressive, phallic, and sometimes even *adolescent*), hedge funds, because of their accountability to investors, are relatively remarkably free of scandal. Indeed, hedge funds are awash in people who have come from large financial institutions and who bring a great deal of professionalism to hedge fund organizations, although there are exceptions. In the report published by the Financial Crisis Inquiry Commission, in 2010, there was no consensus that hedge funds played a significant role in the most recent financial crisis – neither with the crumbling values of mortgage-backed securities, nor the tumbling of real estate values. In fact, hedge funds were some of the principal *losers* during the crisis, since many were holders of the toxic securities and derivatives at the center of the crisis.[3]

One of the important things to remember about hedge funds is that their investors expect more than typical market returns. This is critical in considering what happened at SAC. For the expectation of such outsized returns, so to speak, places pressure on hedge fund managers to perform – or die. The pressure makes its way down – sometimes quite aggressively – to individual traders and portfolio managers, who feel the need to get those outsized returns by any means necessary, which in the case of some meant by means of illegally used inside information.

Insider Trading

For years there has been a debate about whether insider trading should be illegal. United States regulators differed with certain non-US regulators who thought that insider trading was essentially a victimless 'crime' at worst, and in fact should probably not be raised to the level of criminality at all. For example, columnist David Gleason recently wrote, in an opinion piece in South Africa's *Business Daily*:

> As for genuine insider trading, where an individual obtains information not available to anyone else, and uses it to his advantage, I consider that a perfectly normal element in the market. It is part of the complex, hidden process through which the market makes a price.
>
> In all the outrage about insider trading I have yet to see the authorities parading anyone who has been damaged by an inside trade. Where are those who have been injured?
>
> They don't exist. Classical insider trading is used only once. Immediately it is used, the information becomes public. Someone bought or sold inexplicably or unusually. The market is alerted. It quickly unravels what caused this. But who was damaged and where is this person?
>
> Criminalising insider trading is an example of regulation advanced energetically by those who take it upon themselves, like avenging crusaders, to put right a wrong that doesn't exist.
>
> Insider trading is a crime without a victim.
>
> If I have information which tells me that I can make money by buying or selling a counter, and make use of it, what have I done that damages anyone? The buyer or seller was in the market anyway. I haven't advanced any trumped up scheme. I have simply offered to buy or sell. If, later, someone claims he wouldn't have bought or sold had he known what I knew, how can he really prove that? Why should I believe him? Why should anyone, for that matter? Perhaps he's just saying it to get out of a deal, or to make additional moolah.
>
> Raj Rajaratnam, a self-made hedge fund billionaire, famously got an 11-year sentence and $150m fine for conspiring to engage in insider trading and fraud in the US.
>
> He bribed execs to spy for him and used the information to trade.
>
> I would have thought industrial espionage (and fraud) more appropriate charges.
>
> There is probably an argument that old-fashioned morals stand against using inside information for personal gain – but it isn't criminal (yet) to behave amorally.[4]

There are not a few people who share the sentiments expressed by Gleason, and this may be the reason why insider trading allegations and cases are not more rare. There are some who argue on utilitarian grounds that the benefits of insider trading (e.g., added liquidity in the markets) outweigh the alleged unfairness of trading on privileged information. In fact, scholars Peter-Jan Engelen and Luc

Van Liedekerke explicate how many of the arguments against insider trading hold little water.[5] Even if one does find fault with insider trading, some argue, it is hard to understand why it should be *criminalized*. But while some of Gleason's and others' observations seem to make some sense facially, a more careful analysis shows just why insider trading is not quite victimless – just as bribing a foreign official is not actually victimless, even if there are substantial short-term benefits from a utilitarian point of view. US securities laws concerning insider trading rest upon the conclusion that insider trading violates principles of fairness that permit securities markets to be perceived as safe for investors of all types:

> 'Insider trading' is a term that most investors have heard and usually associate with illegal conduct. But the term actually includes both legal and illegal conduct. The legal version is when corporate insiders – officers, directors, and employees – buy and sell stock in their own companies. When corporate insiders trade in their own securities, they must report their trades to the SEC ...
>
> Illegal insider trading refers generally to buying or selling a security, in breach of a fiduciary duty or other relationship of trust and confidence, while in possession of material, nonpublic information about the security. Insider trading violations may also include "tipping" such information, securities trading by the person "tipped," and securities trading by those who misappropriate such information ...
>
> Because insider trading undermines investor confidence in the fairness and integrity of the securities markets, the SEC has treated the detection and prosecution of insider trading violations as one of its enforcement priorities.[6]

The SEC's view of insider trading is echoed by Engelen and Liedekerke:

> The remaining argument that occurs regularly in the literature is the effect that legalized insider trading would have on general market morality. In several publications, [Patricia] Werhane [a noted business ethicist] ... goes back to Adam Smith in order to clarify the need for a basic market morality, carried by values like fairness in competition, or a form of self-interest that is restrained by reason as necessary conditions for a free market. The problem about insider trading then becomes that the practice is connected to a "Boeskyian greed culture" [a reference to the notorious insider trader of the 1980s, Ivan Boesky] (Werhane 1989) that undermines market morality and, if it takes the upper hand, destroys the market itself. It is very hard to argue with this type of general argument, and on the whole we are rather sympathetic to it.[7]

The notion of 'general market morality' entails the notion of market *culture*, and so of institutional culture, and ultimately of personal ethics, which entails certain moral principles, such as that one should not reap where one has not sown. As we turn to the 2013 Justice Department indictment involving SAC, it is important to keep these things in mind, because in many ways what was going on at SAC was going on despite the constraints imposed on the firm by law and by SAC's various investors – i.e., those who invested in SAC's various hedge funds.

My objective here is not to address the legality of insider trading. In the United States, the legality of insider trading is settled – insider trading is illegal.

I wish to, instead, review the motives and culture that seem to have led to SAC's regulatory and public relations woes and, ultimately, to the indictment. That is, why would and how could an astoundingly successful hedge fund firm need to play it over the line in the first place? How could SAC, knowing for years that it was being closely observed by just about everyone, from Main Street to Capitol Hill, from Hong Kong to Mexico City, have opened itself up to the accusation that it was 'a veritable magnet of market cheaters' and make itself a huge target for aggressive government intervention?[8] It is too simplistic to say that the answer is 'greed', although that is frequently at work on Wall Street and was clearly at work as a driver of the decisions of the defendants in the SAC case. As I have been saying, the element of *forgetfulness* – forgetfulness of the public mandate that is given to private commercial actors, forgetfulness of civic obligations and forgetfulness of basic moral principles concerning fairness – is a part of the story as well. Of course, forgetfulness assumes that one at one time already *knew* something that has been forgotten. This, indeed, is the other part of the story of SAC's insider trading problems and of similar problems that have led to the implosion of many other firms. Let me unpack this. But as I do, bear in mind that I am fully aware that what I am about to say will sound somewhat naive in view of the realities of Wall Street culture. But those 'realities' are precisely the ones that need to be gotten rid of, so the charge of naiveté would beg the question.

What are the realities that serve as the guiding principles of so much of Wall Street, and that led to the demise of SAC? My analysis is subjective, but based upon the government's conclusions and the media reports I think the following sums up what went wrong. First, there was a cult of personality at SAC, just like there is and has been a cult of personality at other very successful firms – Jamie Dimon at Chase, Sandy Weill at Citigroup, Jeff Skilling at Enron, Jack Welsh at GE, Bill Gross at Pimco, Steve Jobs at Apple etc. (I do not intend to draw any moral equivalence between any of the people on this short list, only to provide examples of business leaders with outsized personas and a commensurate ability to influence subordinates, peers, and even those charged with supervising *them* (such as boards of directors and, sometimes, regulators). The cult of personality creates in subordinates an inordinate concern to please the 'cult leader', and to subordinate one's own views to his or her demands. Second, there was an internally-propagated certitude about the way 'business really gets done' which rested upon a scofflaw conception of what business is. Third, there was a self-centered culture. Fourth, there was a failure to inculcate and then to communicate high ethical standards across the organization. Fifth, risk was limited to concerns about portfolios, while the enterprise risks caused by the firm's aggressive culture were marginalized, if not utterly dismissed.

The government's indictment asserted that the defendants in the SAC case

> At various times between in or about 1999 through at least in or about 2010 obtained material, non-public information ("Inside Information") relating to publicly-traded companies and traded on that Inside Information in order to (i) increase the return

on investment in the SAC Hedge Fund; and (ii) increase fees received by the [defend-ants] and committed the insider trading scheme through the acts of, among others, numerous portfolio managers ... and research analysts ... who engaged in a pattern of obtaining Inside Information from dozens of publicly-traded companies across mul-tiple industry sectors. Employees of [SAC and certain affiliated companies] traded on Inside Information themselves and, at times, recommended trades to the SAC Owner based on Inside Information.[9]

The indictment also discusses the fact that what SAC was after was an 'edge' in the market. Every business seeks to cultivate some way of securing its place in the marketplace, some way of distinguishing itself among its competitors. But the 'edge' that the indictment indicates that SAC sought was not merely some-thing that would help distinguish it within the field of fair play, among its money management competitors. According to the indictment, it (and certain of its employees) sought to do so outside of the limits of the law:

> At bottom the encouragement by the [defendants] to pursue aggressively an informa-tion "edge" overwhelmed limited SAC compliance systems. Further, the relentless pursuit of an information "edge" fostered a business culture within SAC in which there was no meaningful commitment to ensure that such "edge" came from legiti-mate research and not Inside Information. The predictable and foreseeable result, as charged herein, was systematic insider trading by the [defendants] resulting in hundreds of millions of dollars of illegal profits and avoided losses at the expense of members of the investing public.[10]

The Wall Street Research Scandal

Let's turn to the Wall Street research scandal. In the early 2000s, a brash New York Attorney General, Eliot Spitzer, took on Wall Street, and set his sights on Wall Street research reports in particular.

For many years, knowledgeable Wall Street operatives knew that research reports (in-depth reports on public companies prepared by broker-dealer research analysts) were compromised by the investment bankers and sales desks of the firms whose monikers and logos went on the finished reports. Very few research reports dared to contain a recommendation to sell a company's stock or criticize senior management or other operational details of the company (in 2002, only about two percent of Wall Street sell-side research reports contained sell recommendations). Why? Because the same firms that issued the analysts' reports were also the investment bankers to the companies that were the subjects of the reports. The job of an investment banker is to make sure that her client is as able as possible to tap the public markets for capital, and that required that the markets maintain a favorable opinion of the banker's client company. If you are an investment banker, the last thing you want to see is a research report published by your own firm, written on another floor by another team of employees (research analysts), that contains negative information about your client, or recommending that people *sell* the client's stock just when you, as an investment banker, are trying to convince people to *buy* it. The tension between investment banking departments and research departments was palpable, and many managements of broker-dealers arranged things so that research analysts were placed under the thumbs of the investment banking department, to the point that before the issuance of a research report the investment banking department had to 'bless' it. Certain bankers simply coopted research analysts by paying them handsomely to toe the line and write only favourable reports about client companies.

As *The New York Times* reported at the time:

> The use of research analysts by investment bankers to secure underwriting [investment banking] business on Wall Street is no secret. Nor is the fact that they [the research analysts] have been paid rich sums. Frank P. Quattrone, Credit Suisse First Boston's former head technology banker, had a staff of research analysts who reported to him. Jack B. Grubman, the telecommunications analyst at Salomon Smith Barney, earned $15 million a year for writing glowing research reports for top banking clients like WorldCom.[11]

Research analysts, who were supposed to be, essentially, Wall Street's paid 'scholars', reporting honestly on the strengths and weaknesses of thousands of companies so that investors the world over would be better able to assess them, were so corrupted by the culture that was driven by investment banking departments ('Thou shalt not write anything negative about an investment banking client') that some reports (we will never really know just how many) were misleading or quasi-fraudulent, if not outright fraudulent, in terms of substantive content. It did not take too long before the SEC (who was a late-comer to reform, outshined by Spitzer), the New York Stock Exchange, and the NASD (now FINRA) joined forces with this brash New York Attorney General, to expose the fraud that had taken hold, forced a settlement with the leading offenders (the so-called 'Global Settlement', which encompassed ten of the largest Wall Street firms), forcing them to pay in fines and restitution of some $1.4 billion.

One of the larger offenders was Jack Grubman, an analyst with Salomon Smith Barney. The SEC forced Grubman to pay a total of $15 million to settle their charges against him. The regulators charged that Grubman, who was the lead analyst at Salomon Smith Barney in the telecommunications (telecom) sector and deep in the weeds with the firm's investment banking department's efforts to cultivate business in that sector, 'issued fraudulent, misleading, and otherwise flawed research reports'. They charged Grubman with aiding and abetted Salomon Smith Barney's violations of the federal securities laws and with violating industry rules as well as New York State law.

The Global Settlement, of course, cast a net much wider than one that would only capture a single bad actor. As mentioned, ten firms were part of the settlement, and these served as examples for the rest of the securities industry. The ten firms were Bear, Stearns & Co. Inc. (Bear Stearns), Credit Suisse First Boston LLC (CSFB), Goldman, Sachs & Co. (Goldman), Lehman Brothers Inc. (Lehman), J.P. Morgan

Securities Inc. (J.P. Morgan), Merrill Lynch, Pierce, Fenner & Smith Incorporated (Merrill Lynch), Morgan Stanley & Co. Incorporated (Morgan Stanley), Citigroup Global Markets Inc., f/k/a Salomon Smith Barney Inc. (SSB), UBS Warburg LLC (UBS Warburg), and U.S. Bancorp Piper Jaffray Inc. (Piper Jaffray). The two individuals who were nabbed were Jack Grubman and Henry Blodget. What follows is the SEC's statement of summary concerning the settlement, in substantive part:

> Under the terms of the firm settlements, an injunction will be entered against each of the firms, enjoining it from violating the statutes and rules that it is alleged to have violated. Additional terms of the firm settlements include:
>
> Monetary Relief – Firms will pay disgorgement and civil penalties totaling $875 million, including Merrill Lynch's previous payment of $100 million in connection with its prior settlement with the states. The civil penalties in these actions are among the highest – and the civil penalty against SSB [Salomon Smith Barney , Jack Grubman's firm] is the highest ever imposed in civil securities enforcement actions. Pursuant to the settlements, the firms may not seek to treat the civil penalties as tax deductible or eligible for reimbursement under their insurance policies. Under the settlement agreements, half of the $775 million payment by the firms other than Merrill Lynch will be paid in resolution of actions brought by the SEC, NYSE and NASD, and will be put into funds to benefit customers of the firms (the "Distribution Funds"). The remainder of the funds will be paid to the states...
>
> Structural Reforms – The firms will separate research and investment banking, including physical separation, completely separate reporting lines, separate legal and compliance staffs, and separate budgeting processes. Analysts' compensation cannot be based directly or indirectly upon investment banking revenues or input from investment banking personnel. Investment bankers cannot evaluate analysts...
>
> Enhanced Disclosures – Each firm will include a disclosure on the first page of each research report stating that it "does and seeks to do business with companies covered in its research reports. As a result, investors should be aware that the firm may have a conflict of interest that could affect the objectivity of this report"...
>
> Independent Research – For a five-year period, each of the firms will be required to contract with no fewer than three independent research firms and will make available the independent research to the firm's customers ... Payments for independent research will total $432.5 million.
>
> Investor Education – Seven firms will make payments totaling $80 million for investor education. The SEC, NYSE and NASD have authorized that $52.5 million of these funds be put into an Investor Education Fund to support programs designed to equip investors with the knowledge and skills necessary to make informed investment decisions. The remaining $27.5 million will be paid to state securities regulators and will be used by them for investor education purposes...
>
> Voluntary Initiative Regarding Initial Public Offerings – The firms have collectively entered into a voluntary agreement restricting allocations of securities in 'hot' Initial Public Offerings (IPOs) – offerings that begin trading in the aftermarket at a premium – to certain company executive officers and directors, a practice known as 'spinning'[12]

How Did This Happen? The Tyranny of Goals

What noted business ethicist Kenneth Goodpaster has called teleopathy others call 'the tyranny of goals', and it was this tyranny of goals (in the cases of both SAC and the named broker-dealers, the goal was fees) that would lead to the trouble in which SAC and the broker-dealers sanctioned for misleading or fraudulent research found themselves. The pursuit of the illicit 'edge' (rather than that advantage over competitors gained within the field of fair and legal play) is the result of the relentless and myopic pursuit of outsized returns – at almost any cost. Robert Hoyk and Paul Hersey, in their very useful book *The Ethical Executive – Becoming Aware of the Root Causes of Unethical Behavior: 45 Psychological Traps that Every One of Us Falls Prey To*, put it this way:

> We can be inspired by our goals to succeed, to climb the corporate ladder, to achieve status and recognition – but our goals can also drive us. Goals can become all important. We can move too fast, take short cuts, do anything to reach our goals. "Ends are used to justify means." We're more apt to cheat and lie when we're striving for an important goal and we encounter major roadblocks that stand in the way of achieving that goal ... In 1967, B.F. Goodrich landed a contract with the U.S. government to provide brakes for fighter planes. A scandal ensued when "a tight schedule produced shortcuts in quality control. Competition for the work led to underestimation of the time required to complete it which, in turn, led to 'pressure' on supervisors to pass defective equipment as sound." ... In this well-known business scandal, B.F. Goodrich supervisors were driven to complete a contract within an unrealistic time frame. When roadblocks to completion got in the way (defective equipment) they continued to push for closure – taking an unethical and potentially disastrous shortcut.[13]

Many business scandals are the result of relentless pressure to achieve short-run profit or revenue goals. Of Angelo Mozilo, former CEO of Countrywide Financial, journalist Bethany McLean (who was, now famously, the first to raise suspicions about Enron's financial position) writes: 'No, Mozilo's fatal flaws were different. One was a desperate hunger to be No. 1, which led Countrywide into a race to the bottom as the mortgage market spiraled out of control'.[14] Some may point to SAC as a special case, but there are very few special cases. SAC's woes are quite typical – the result of that corporate-cultural infection called the tyranny of goals (and, as in the case of Mozilo's Countrywide Financial, the cult of personality). The same pressures that led to SAC's indictment led to other corporate scandals of recent years: Enron (fraudulent accounting); Arthur Andersen (internal conflicts of interest between its consulting and auditing business, and complicity in the Enron scandal); WorldCom (falsified financial statements); Parmalat (falsified financial statements); Barclays and other banks (Libor manipulation); Sunbeam (accounting scandal, under aggressive CEO 'Chinsaw' Al Dunlap); Carrian Group (accounting fraud); Countrywide Financial (aggressive peddling of sub-prime mortgages), Ford (covering-up tire blowouts on its Explorer model); and many others. In a famous case from the 1990s that I teach every year in my business ethics class, a defense contractor, Bath Iron Works sought an 'edge' over its competitors by contemplating the use of a competitor's proposal which fell into Bath's possession because of an error by representatives of the government. The same competitive pressures are at work right now in businesses all around the world. Sounding off in the backs of the minds of their executives and managers, as though on a loop, is: *Why not? Why not do what needs to be done to vanquish our foes? Why worry about high standards when nobody else is? Why not play the 'game' to 'win'?* Like a dust storm casts pebbles against a window, these questions pelt the instrumental, means-ends reasoning of countless business leaders – constantly. They are questions that can only be addressed with the proper effect and success if the corporate culture, which is set at the top of the organization, provides countervailing ethical pressures that will allow the organization's executives, managers and other employees to make decisions that will keep the organization clear of scandal.

Scandal. It is a word with an interesting etymology. It refers to a 'shock' to the sensibilities of those who look on. To shock the public, customers, and the organs of government is not something that a business wants to do. 'Shock' does not mean amazement after a stellar quarter or a dazzling but unexpected new product. In the case of scandal, 'shock' refers to *a state of heightened repugnance.* The immediate demand of shock is a battery of activities to repair and reverse the damage, if at all possible. Scandal, which creates shock, is something analogous to a ship taking a torpedo broadside. Without immediate damage control and repair, the ship – and all its crew – may sink beneath the unremitting waves of commerce.

Scandal costs a great deal of money, because damage control and reparation cost a great deal of money. Just the legal fees and fines alone that were accrued by JPMorgan Chase in view of its direct and indirect involvement in the sub-prime mortgage debacle, and its trading losses associated with 'The London Whale' debacle, had a very significant impact on its financial position. Additionally, these scandals led to the need to add additional operational checks and balances that themselves cost a great deal of money. In the case of JPMorgan Chase, the total tab would be in the billions of dollars.[15]

All too often scandal leads to *massive costs* (including opportunity costs). They are occasions for the dissipation of hard won revenue that is the result of many hours (perhaps tens of thousands of hours) of employee time and the undermining of, perhaps, many months or even years of organizational planning. Those who set an organization up for scandal, because of self-dealing or self-centered behaviors, are disrespecting other employees' honest activities and diligence. People who cause scandal betray their firms and the employees and stakeholders whom they are supposed to serve.

As Warren Buffett told his son, 'It takes 20 years to build a reputation and five minutes to ruin it. If you think about that, you'll do things differently'.[16] Then why didn't firms, such as SAC and the referenced broker-dealers, do things differently? Precisely because they didn't *think*. They suffered from *forgetfulness*. They failed to *re-member*. Like sexual arousal or fear, there is something about the tyranny of goals that interferes with our ability to *think* and to *re-member*. When all that matters is the 'edge', when all that matters is the outsized investment return, and when all that matters is profit and personal remuneration, the recollection that is necessary for real thinking is subdued. Warren Buffett is known for the long game, for taking the long-term view. He has been pilloried and mocked for years for his 'buy and hold strategy', but Buffett understands that the managements of the companies in which his Berkshire Hathaway invests need time to implement their plans, and along the way, and because of various processes associated with that implementation, short-term operating results may be poor. But while market traders, whose horizons are a day or sometimes a minute, see any crumb of negative or positive news as a valid reason to move billions of dollars of capital from one set of hands to another, long-gamers (true investors) keep their eyes on fundamentals, on trends, and on managements. There is a need for traders in the world, but the trader's *mentality* must be kept in its place, permitted to be expressed only in view and in the context of other exigent organizational considerations. When the trader mentality becomes a *management philosophy*, the probability of scandal increases sharply. Business firms are not trades, they are going concerns – actually, collections of going concerns (Ronald Coase viewed the firm as, itself, a market, while other theorists, such as Amitai Etzioni, view the firm as an economic community), and their existence depends upon more than short-term considerations. The trader mentality and the manager mentality are very different:

> When managers are seduced by the siren song of unfathomable riches, largely unfettered by the notion of serving the interests of the corporation's long-term owners, they are easily tempted to focus on driving the stock price higher. When earnings growth goals are unrealistically high and the investment community brooks no interruptions in a regular progression of growth, the temptation to run the business around the numbers becomes overwhelming. To meet "the numbers," important long-term initiatives may be the first cost to be cut, with downsizing (artfully renamed as "right-sizing") next in line; then financial standards are pushed to the limit; finally, earnings become so illusory and subjective that credibility is lost. What can all too easily follow is the severe damage to the corporation's reputation and then its business, happening right under the noses of our traditional gatekeepers ...
>
> The truth is that most business measurements are inherently short-term in nature. Far more durable qualities drive a corporation's success over the long term. While they cannot be measured, such traits as character, integrity, enthusiasm, conviction, and passion are every bit as important to a firm's success as precise measurements. Human beings

are the prime instruments for implementing a corporation's strategy. Other things being equal (of course, they never are), if those who serve the corporation are inspired, motivate, cooperative, diligent, ethical, and creative, the stock-holders will be well served ...

Yet recent years have shown us that when ambitious chief executives set aggressive financial objectives, they place the achievement of those objectives above all else – above proper accounting principles and sound balance sheets, even above their corporate character.[17]

From what we can determine from the SAC indictment and the reporting around it, SAC was managed as though it was a trade rather than a real business. A trader's mentality permeated the firm – that is, a mentality that privileged very short-term results over long-term results. SAC was not (or so it appears) seen as a place to make a life and to contribute to the future success of an organization, it was seen as a place where one could make a lot of money for oneself, and make it fast. Those most senior in the firm believed that the firm itself would be the beneficiary of this self-serving ethos, a misguided and misinterpreted notion of *laissez-faire* – 'Get out of the way of the traders, let them aggressively pursue their gains in the financial markets, and the firm will be the winner'. Fair enough, as far as such a notion goes. But this is too often, as we have seen over the years – from the demise of Kidder Peabody to the demise of Barings to the demise (of sorts - it has transformed itself into a family office, using the name Point72 Asset Management) of SAC – a precarious if not disastrous *management philosophy*.

The Wall Street research scandal was, essentially, a massive fraud on the public. One of the reasons why the major regulators were so embarrassed by Spitzer's findings is that what was going on for years was more or less obvious to all. The coopting of research departments by the investment bankers was well known, and the lack of rules of accountability that would compel analysts to published honest opinions was a glaring hole in the management of conflicts of interest.

In considering how such things as insider trading scandals and fraudulent research reports happen, we must consider another variable. In part, it is an 'Emperor's New Clothes' phenomenon, and it leads to a kind of coopting and self-censoring. The obvious can become dubious to the perceiver because of powerful political, career, and status pressures *not to see what is in plain sight*. Some years ago, I asked a derivatives trader why it was that credit default swaps were not deemed insurance contracts or policies, and so regulated by state insurance commissions, when they have all of the indicia of an insurance contract or policy, or, in the case of naked credit default swaps, were not further regulated by state gaming commissioners (who regulate casinos), when naked credit default swaps have all the indicia of gambling bets. He told me, with rather superior affectation, that I didn't understand the distinctions, otherwise I wouldn't be making such comparisons. This, of course, was B.S. – and I told him so, though I did not know, at the time, that my questions were the same questions raised by Brooksley

Born, once head of the CFTC, just a few years earlier. As John Lachester points out in his recent book, *How to Speak Money: What the Money People Say – And What It Really Means,* the 'money people' of Wall Street make good use – as do not a few academics – of the 'Emperor's New Clothes' phenomenon. If Wall Street can shame the public (and not a few regulators) for 'being ignorant' of its sophistication and 'superior knowledge' then the public (and not a few regulators) is silenced, and requested to stand back in awe of the princes of finance and economy who 'know how the world really works'.

Citizens should not continue to be so easily cowed, even though a degree of knowledge of how the industry works is a prerequisite for reasonable criticism. Yet again and again, whether it is the latest rage to invest in emerging markets, or in 'dot-coms', or in new-fangled products, the duping goes on. Fortunately, journalism has soldiered-up (Bethany McLean, Gillian Tett, Joe Nocera, Gretchen Morgensen, and Chrystia Freeland jump to mind), and is now a fair match for the obfuscations, double-talk, and outright lies. Yet, the public must become more wary of hype. As pointed out by the Financial Crisis Inquiry Commission:

> THESE CONCLUSIONS must be viewed in the context of human nature and individual and societal responsibility. First, to pin this crisis on mortal flaws like greed and hubris would be simplistic. It was the failure to account for human weakness that is relevant to this crisis.
>
> Second, we clearly believe the crisis was a result of human mistakes, misjudgments, and misdeeds that resulted in systemic failures for which our nation has paid dearly. As you read this report, you will see that specific firms and individuals acted irresponsibly. Yet a crisis of this magnitude cannot be the work of a few bad actors, and such was not the case here. At the same time, the breadth of this crisis does not mean that "everyone is at fault"; many firms and individuals did not participate in the excesses that spawned disaster.
>
> We do place special responsibility with the public leaders charged with protecting our financial system, those entrusted to run our regulatory agencies, and the chief executives of companies whose failures drove us to crisis. These individuals sought and accepted positions of significant responsibility and obligation. Tone at the top does matter and, in this instance, we were let down. No one said "no."
>
> But as a nation, we must also accept responsibility for what we permitted to occur. Collectively, but certainly not unanimously, we acquiesced to or embraced a system, a set of policies and actions, that gave rise to our present predicament.[18]

I will have more to say about what we 'permitted to occur' in the chapters that follow. For to assume that Wall Street reform is a task to be undertaken by Wall Street alone is a grave mistake.

3 CORPORATE SOULCRAFT

Americans are overreachers; overreaching is the most admirable and most American of the many American excesses. But in the first half of the nineteenth century, many Americans felt they were reaching for the wrong star. Before and since, there have been episodes of anxiety that something – some sphere of life, perhaps the citizenry itself–was getting out of control, and taking on a pace and style of life, and a dimension of character, that was unworthy of citizens of a city on a hill.

George F. Will
Statecraft as Soulcraft: What Government Does[1]

In the Introduction I referenced Eric Liu's and Nick Hanauer's short but timely and insightful book, *The Gardens of Democracy*, a book that punches above its weight. In *Gardens* Liu and Hanauer try to take the reader on an exploration of a middle path between what they believe are certain false choices of our age – e.g., the false choice between socialism and *laissez-faire* capitalism, for one. Here is some of what Liu and Hanauer have to say using their distinction between "machinebrain" and "gardenbrain" modes of thought:

> In its time, Darwin's theory of evolution was corrupted into a powerful ideology of Social Darwinism, which treated the weak and marginalized as presumptively unfit for survival (and government aid). Later, Taylorism and "scientific management" led government leaders to believe they could engineer their way to desired social outcomes. In our own time, the belief that markets follow the equilibrium dynamics of physics has had its own awful results. Consider that policymakers did not foresee or forestall the crash of 2008 because their dominant economic model had [that is, their collection of economic beliefs], as Alan Greenspan [the then Chairman of the Federal Reserve] later admitted, "a flaw" – namely, that it didn't contemplate human irrationality. This is not just about economics or politics; it's about imagination and our ability to conceive of new ways of conceiving of things. It is about our ability to adapt and evolve in the face of changing circumstances and the consequences of our actions. History shows that civilizations tend eventually to get stuck in the patterns that had brought them success. They can either stay stuck and decay, or get unstuck and thrive. We posit in these pages that this country has for too long been stuck in a mode of seeing and thinking called Machinebrain. We argue that the time has come for a new mode of public imagination that we call Gardenbrain. Machinebrain sees

the world and democracy as a series of mechanisms – clocks and gears, perpetual motion machines, balances and counterbalances. Machinebrain requires you to conceive of the economy as perfectly efficient and automatically self-correcting. Machinebrain presupposes stability and predictability, and only grudgingly admits the need for correction. Even the word commonly used for such correction – "regulation" – is mechanical in origin and regrettable in connotation. Gardenbrain sees the world and democracy as an entwined set of ecosystems – sinks and sources of trust and social capital, webs of economic growth, networks of behavioral contagion. Gardenbrain forces you to conceive of the economy as man-made and effective only if well constructed and well cared-for. Gardenbrain presupposes instability and unpredictability, and thus expects a continuous need for seeding, feeding, and weeding ever-changing systems. To be a gardener is not to let nature take its course; it is to tend. It is to accept responsibility for nurturing the good growth and killing the bad. Tending and regulating thus signify the same work, but tending frames the work as presumptively necessary and beneficial rather than as something to be suffered.[2]

Liu and Hanauer have an approach to some of the sicknesses of our time – sicknesses that have deep roots in our business cultures – that might be part of the cure that is needed to keep businesses, especially large corporations with broad markets into which they sell on a more stable path to growth and profits. That said, *Gardens* does not merely focus on what corporations should do to fix themselves, it also focuses on what we as individual citizens must do to become the kinds of people who will be part of the solution, since we are all – or almost all – employees and/or contractors to businesses of all sorts. What we are, Liu and Hanauer would insist, our business culture will be – or become. If we are aware of what is really important in life, concerned about those around us (whether communities or individuals), so will our commercial organizations be. In other words, train the citizens and corporate conduct will follow.

George F. Will, the American conservative writer and commentator, urges us to recognize the limitations and insufficiencies of government coercion. (Liu and Hanauer, who are not political conservatives, have a similar point of view when they criticize overreliance on regulation.) Says Will, 'My thesis is that the most important task confronting Americans as a polity is, in part, a philosopher's task. The task is to reclaim for politics a properly great and stately jurisdiction. It is to rescue politics from the stale, false notion that government is always and only an instrument of coercion, making disagreeable (even when necessary) excisions from freedom, which is understood as Hobbes understood it, as "the silence of the law".'[3] I agree with Will's thesis. I also think that a philosopher's task might be, as well, the task of helping to reclaim commerce as the important pillar of civilization that it is, and to inform commercial actors (especially executives and other managers) that commerce is ruled by and connected to something larger than itself. These reclamations will require us to put aside some very unhelpful ways of thinking that tend to reproduce themselves on both the political right

and the political left. It will also require constructed occasions for recollection –
recollection (re-collection) of the various values that are sometimes forgotten as
we press, sometimes monomaniacally, towards commercial goals.

The latest round of efforts to reform what is commonly referred to as 'Corporate America' will not, of themselves, accomplish these goals of reclamation
and recollection. Such efforts at reform are missing important components, rely-
ing primarily on coercion. Coercion is often overcome through the gaming of
the system and technical loopholes, or new, cleverly devised contrivances. The
reduction of excess risk-taking and of the number of scandals requires what the
theologians call a *metanoia*, as I discussed earlier. As one informed commentator
put it, in respect of problems of corporate governance, 'Corporate governance
is really a state of mind. Whether it be pre-Sarbanes, during Sarbanes or post-
Sarbanes, the fact of the matter is, without the right state of mind, what we're
creating is just more hurdles for people who are committed to gaming the system
to jump over. We're not fixing the system'.[4] Sarbanes-Oxley, passed after the scandals that took place in the opening years of this century, with all of its coercive
elements, has not succeeded as expected. In the midst of the collapse of vener-
able financial services firms and the credit crisis of 2008, Jim Cramer, the former
hedge fund manager and current host of CNBC's popular show *Mad Money*,
blared, in his inimitable manner, 'It's all fiction! ... How can we have these levels
of fiction in financials after Sarbanes-Oxley? How do people get away with this?
How do they live with themselves?'[5]

Dodd-Frank, which became effective in 2010, was some 2,300 pages long.
There isn't *a single word* in the bill that calls for training and education, within
financial services firms, that might be useful as a tool to align the interests of
directors, executives, managers and employees with the interests of the commonweal. (This follows from Senator Christopher Dodd's declaration, 'I can't
legislate integrity'.[6]) This may seem like a quite understandable omission, until
you step back and ask the question: *If not government then what will serve as
the catalyst to align those often competing interests? The markets?* If you conclude
that such an alignment is not needed, then what you may also be concluding is
that commercial activity is activity that is beyond the pale of worry as regards
the commonweal and commonwealth, except in those limited ways that Milton
Friedman suggested some decades ago – the interests are aligned in virtue of
the virtue of commercial activity itself, for it is that activity that provides the
machinery for economic growth. Counseled Friedman, the only interests that
the commercial sphere is bound to consider, as long as it plays within the law or
the 'rules of the game', are its own, and by doing so all benefit optimally.

There are many who have heaped scorn on Friedman for this conclusion. I
used to be one of those people. My view, now, is not so much that it is wrong, but
rather that it goes too far. It suffers from, as Ralph Waldo Emerson might have

put it, a 'violence of direction'. One can readily agree that commercial enterprises should do what they do best – generate goods, services and exchanges of both. We Americans, like our counterparts in other developed countries, are fortunate to live in a country with such a vibrant commercial life, notwithstanding the attendant problems and pathologies. Our entrepreneurship and zest for innovation remain astounding, one of the hallmarks of American civilization. They have led to better building techniques, better emergency services, better medicines, better roads, better cars, better channels of information, and so on. We must not be too quick to scorn ourselves for the excesses that are committed in commerce, and I will not do so in these pages. (I am not one of those academics whom F.A. Hayek criticized for their 'disdain for the commercial', nor am I one of those philosophers who, following Aristotle, hold the activities of the market (of *chrematistika*) in general contempt, as though somehow real life is only possible when one's back is turned, in moral and intellectual self-congratulation and smugness, to the marketplace. What I will do, however, is add one more voice to those who have debunked the notion that commerce can operate without lifting its head or looking over its shoulder from time to time to make sure that its operations are not at odds with the larger goals of the commonweal and commonwealth – long-term prosperity, long-term security, a concerned and informed citizenship, the avoidance of painful fiscal and monetary shocks, and the improvement of social institutions in general, and of individual characters in particular.

These certainly are not, as the libertarians are right to tell us, the *primary* concerns of commercial activity. However, commercial activity – more accurately, its active executive agents – cannot forget about them entirely, because no significant activity in the social space can without causing significant disruptions or damage. This may be a high-minded prescription for the average worker, who is more concerned with ways to make a better microchip or better potato chip rather than wholesale stewardship of their industries (as is, for the most part, appropriate), but it cannot be seen as too high-minded for the executive class, which is the class in which most of the scandals of recent years were incubated. A quick survey will prove that point. Given that, it should be easy to see that the damage done in corporate suites has a direct impact on those who have never seen one, and most likely never will. The executive suites of America must be seen as places where well-considered decisions are made, must be seen as places of *trust*. As Peter Drucker wrote in his magnum opus, *Management*, with his characteristic insight, 'Organizations are no longer built on force. They are increasingly built on trust'.[7]

Drucker then goes on, several pages later, to relate a story about a meeting that he and his father had with the famous economist Joseph Schumpeter. Drucker's father (Adolph, an old friend of Schumpeter) puts the question:

> 'Joseph, do you still talk about what you want to be remembered for?' Schumpeter broke out in a loud laughter, and even I laughed. For Schumpeter was notorious for having said, when he was thirty or so and had published the first two of his great economic

books, that what he really wanted to be remembered for was to have been 'Europe's greatest lover of beautiful women, and Europe's greatest horseman – and perhaps also as the world's greatest economist'. Schumpeter said, 'Yes, this question is still important to me, but I now answer it differently. I want to be remembered as having been the teacher who converted half a dozen brilliant students into first-rate economists'.

He must have seen an amazed look on my father's face because he continued, 'You know, Adolph, I have now reached the age where I know that being remembered for books and theories is not enough. One does not make a difference unless it is a difference in the lives of people'. One reason my father had gone to see Schumpeter was that it was known that he was very sick and would not live long. Schumpeter died five days after we had visited him.

I have never forgotten that conversation. I have learned from it three things. First, one has to ask oneself what one wants to be remembered for. Second, that should change as one gets older. It should change both with one's own maturity and with the changes in the world. Finally, one thing worth being remembered for is the difference one makes in the lives of people.[8]

There are a number of things that one can take away from what Drucker wrote. The one less obvious thing is the idea that that for which one wants to be remembered, in business, need not be the obvious goal of profit or even singular innovations. One might analogize what Drucker is telling, in relating his father's exchange with Schumpeter: Organizations (and even whole societies) have life cycles, no less so than individuals. In his youth, Schumpeter wanted notoriety and even fame, desires not uncommon among young men. In later years, he realized that these things are not enough. Just as Schumpeter moved into stages of his life in which hedonic pleasures were no longer as satisfying as they once were, corporations led by mature executives understand that their legacies may be more about what their careers have given to others than what they gained for themselves. At the moment, too many American corporations, whether on Wall Street or Main Street, appear to be in the adolescence of their understanding of themselves – that is to say their executives are (although many European executives *seem* to be a little farther along on the maturity curve). To analogize to gardening, they see their institutions as *annuals* when those institutions have everything it takes to get and keep customers, *perennially*. A shift of perspective refocuses a life. No doubt, when Schumpeter determined that he wanted to be remembered for helping to educate eager young minds, his priorities and his behaviour followed. Schumpeter could not have conducted himself for the purpose of vainglory if he had an authentic, internal transformation, which it appears he had.

Corporate America needs an internal transformation as well, and neither management programs (which train executives), nor humanities departments in even the best universities have, for the most part, come up with very effective ways to help bring that about. I suspect that one reason for this is the typical compartmentalization of thought that obtains in the educational process. The easy fallback position is coercion. The call for coercion is the call for the application of the 'brute' force of the state, rather than a call to a higher self, a better society through active citizen deliberation about what is important. The calls for 'more regulation' are the politician's typical response to bad corporate behaviour. But bad corporate behaviour, if only killed at the site of expression, and not throughout the 'body', will only live on to infect and sicken again. New regulation can stop certain types of behaviour outright, but the desire to reap where one has not sown, a desire that drives too much of Corporate America, pushes the voracious in its ranks to seek out ever new ways to express their voracity. Close one door, and the wolves will enter through another.

Lessons, apparently, don't stick, and as one generation of business people passes the baton to the next, the old lessons must be learned over again, and sometimes the hard way, which is by repetition of error. The lessons about bubbles, whether in real estate, stocks, or gold, won't long guide our thinking, neither will the lessons about corporate and executive voracity and rapacity. As we rock in our rocking chairs, one day hence, we will watch our and our neighbours' children repeat the mistakes of our generation if we don't endeavour to do more than corral their actions through law and the fear of penalty. The next generation of 'geniuses' are now being born, are now graduating from elite schools around the world, and if part of their education did not entail a review of the dangers of reaping where one has not sown, of myopic analysis, of corporate hubris, they will be part of the future downfall of this or that institution, with, perhaps, painful 'collateral damage' spread across the economy. We will most likely stand, immobile, as, at their hands, the next bubble inflates, while 'sophisticated observers' stand ready to lop off the heads of anyone who warns of 'irrational exuberance', anyone who might suggest that, for the good of all, it is time to insert the safety pin of sound policy or, to use another metaphor, to take away the punch bowl. Even now, libertarians, who like most true believers in some theory of politics, economy or metaphysics, would set the world up for endless cycles of unsustainable expansions and socially painful contractions, and who will, like sirens, cheer on this next generation of 'geniuses', are ready to tell the rest of us that the old standards of valuation, the old wisdom concerning corporate governance and risk, are outdated. Why, the system can handle more debt than ever imagined, or more liquidity, or more risk – or so they will continue to tell us. When you express your common sense trepidation, they will gleefully inform you of the quaintness of your perspective, and bid you Adieu.

Coercion does not only fall short as a tool when it is government that is wielding that tool (through law); it also falls short when it comes to managing organizations from within. Codes of ethics and compliance policies are good management tools that inform employees concerning what an organization expects of them. They are not necessarily good tools, however, for informing employees about *why* certain behaviours (and even attitudes) are expected. These tools tell employees that there will be personal consequences if they step out of line. They do not explain the overarching public policy *benefits* that are at stake. In fact, they often are not the least concerned with such efforts at employee education (corporate *paideia*), since all that is sought is general compliance. But if general compliance is what is sought, then the best way to effect that outcome is through a proper combination of education and coercion. When employees are informed about why the rules of the road are written as they are, they become *de facto*, if not *de jure*, participants in the management processes of the firm, because they are better equipped to manage *themselves*, removing the full burden from the formal managers of the firm. When directors, executives, managers and employees *regulate themselves*, all sorts of risks are attenuated – including the risk of scandal, as discussed in the previous chapter. This is the approach that I will call, following Will, Appiah and others, *corporate soul-making*.

Corporate soul-making entails initiation, among corporate officers, into certain values and habits of mind. In the military, for example, general officers are not just soldiers. They have significant, even vast, authority and power, and because of that they have been initiated, over years of training and experience, into the virtues and principles established by generations of predecessors. They must have one eye on the martial mission, the other on their civilian masters, and they must look over their shoulders from time to time in order to recall the values of the society and political communities that they serve, and in order to recall the virtues that keep soldiers from becoming bestial. Likewise, senior executives of public companies are not mere supervisors. They, too, have vast power and authority, in many cases. Given the power and reach of large public companies, their executives must be initiated into the habit of considering the implications of corporate decisions and activities beyond the immediate impact on close stakeholders, and to recall the embeddedness of their organizations into the fabric of civil society. This initiation process is what I am calling corporate soulcraft or soul-making. It is an initiation process that is, however, largely non-existent in too many centres of commercial activity, and especially Wall Street.

The larger aim of corporate soul-making extends beyond officers, and includes all employees. The objective of corporate soul-making is to create a *corporate conscience* in all employees, but especially in executives, managers, directors and those others who are in a position to place the franchise at significant risk. The corporate conscience is an internal set of brakes and alarms that are activated by consideration of large moral and policy commitments. It is fed by a better understanding of the relationship between the commercial self and the citizen self, between the objectives of corporate growth and return on capital, and the aspirations of the commonweal.

The reform of Wall Street (of the banks, brokerage firms, and other financial and investment firms) requires, ultimately the reform of the *citizenry*. That is, the engines of business and commerce have to be reattached to that from which they have been torn away for far too long – the common good that is, or should be, the guiding light for the ship of state. To proffer a call of that magnitude much of what I write here will seem sermonic. But I know of no other way to make the case that needs to be made without calling forth from in those engaged in business, especially as executives and other managers, their sense of themselves as connected to something larger and more important than jobs, careers and remuneration. Such a calling forth does not ask that executives and other employees carry about the business ethics equivalent of a Book of Hours, or engage in sustained supererogatory activity (at the expense of the corporate mission), but only the preparedness to do what may have to be done at some time(s) in their working lives – to say 'No' to powerful interests, which are, in this case, the interests that, for the moment, sustain them. They must be willing to say 'No', and mean it.

Some, especially academic philosophers, may be tempted to boil down what follows to something conceptually recognizable – 'McClean is simply a virtue theorist', or 'McClean is laying out a civic republican approach to corporate conduct', etc. Some may suggest that I have not considered enough Marx or Hayek, while others may claim that I am calling for some sort of affective, feel-good commitment to fill-in the gap where coercion fails. There would be some truth in all of these criticisms, and I have heard many of them before in debates and conversations with colleagues, clients and friends. I am prepared to let the chips fall where they may, for something more than the usual fare must be served up to head off the next waves of scandals. I have concluded that the old fix cannot be relied upon, that we need something affective to beat back our primal animal spirits. Reason and positive law are not enough. The spirits of community – stigmatization, deep shame, the guilt of betrayal – are the spirits I will be eliciting as aids. We have been too reticent to employ them. We must now put that reticence aside, and assign corporate knaves the same social and penal *fate* that we assign to violent criminals, for they are often far more destructive. Some of the worst predators on the commonweal do not wear bandanas and baggy jeans, but rather thousand dollar suits and five hundred dollar wingtips. Their personas of wholesomeness and reliability give them access to some of our most important treasures, when in fact they should be let nowhere near them. The transformation of our corporate cultures, and especially the culture of Wall Street, will not be a painless and neat task. Some cultural furniture (and 'bones') will need to be broken. Better that than the social upheavals that may well come along if we don't do the work that needs to be done.

I am often asked by my business ethics students, 'Who are you to say that executives shouldn't make an unlimited amount of money?' My response to them usually goes something like this: 'I am nobody in particular, and the answer to the question you pose is not merely mathematical or algorithmic but rather it is largely *cultural*. When enough of us find certain levels of executive compensation (or other forms of corporate excess) absurd, things will begin to change, for the sentiment will begin to invade the inner spaces of the executives suites in ways that it does not presently. My job, as I see it, is to try to persuade more and more people that it is time for change, just as there are others trying to persuade more and more people that all business is about is *laissez-faire* "market-based compensation", as though CEOs' pay packages were really based on fully informed and fully rational market forces. If I have my druthers, it will be because a tipping point will have been reached, and there will be a "new normal", and we will do with that new normal what we always do with a new normal – we will come to think that it is the way it has *always* been, and recoil in shock to find out later what preceded it'. The slow erosion of our social constraints, in and outside of business, has led us to shrug our shoulders at the most egregious conduct, conduct which has become our current normal. Because human beings are conservative by nature, we take the status quo to be a sort of natural kind. It is hard to shake us out of this way of thinking. The good news is that when we are so shaken, the improved status quo enjoys an equivalent status. And so it goes.

If my tone sounds a tad too melodramatic, it is only because of the precarious place in which we found ourselves, as a country, over the past seven years or so. When the full weight of where we were finally hit me, I was standing in an open-air, multi-level parking lot at Rutgers, in Newark, New Jersey, one day in late September, 2008, heading to teach class. It was a very pleasant day, but one could feel the autumn air begin to arrive in the late afternoons – around the time I would arrive to campus. I had just been thinking about the state of affairs – the credit crisis, the financial markets, Nouriel Roubini's dire predictions of terrible unemployment, the travail of the auto industry, worries over energy, and the many scandals that were erupting. I put down my briefcase, and just stood there in the quiet, and this is the thought that ran through my mind: *Will this be the last year of the life that I have always known, a life of possibilities and hopes? Will we get through this?* As it turned out, many people did not get through it, and we are, in 2015, not completely out of the woods.

The Nobel Prize winning economist Joseph Stiglitz writes in his recent book, *Freefall: America, Free Markets, and the Sinking of the World Economy*:

> It is said that a near-death experience forces one to reevaluate priorities and values. The global economy has just had a near-death experience. The crisis exposed not only flaws in the prevailing economic model but also flaws in our society. Too many people had taken advantage of others. A sense of trust had been broken. Almost every day has brought stories of bad behavior by those in the financial sector – Ponzi schemes, insider trading, predatory lending, and a host of credit card schemes to extract as much from the hapless user as possible. This book has focused, though, not on those who broke the law, but the legions of those who, within the law, had originated, packaged and repackaged, and sold toxic products and engaged in such reckless behavior that they threatened to bring down the entire financial and economic system. The system was saved, but at a cost that is still hard to believe.[9]

It is the twenty-first century, as in the nineteenth, 'many Americans are feeling that we are reaching for the wrong star'. We are having new 'episodes of anxiety that something – some sphere of life, perhaps the citizenry itself–is getting out of control, and taking on a pace and style of life, and a dimension of character, that is unworthy of citizens of a city on a hill' (recalling the earlier quote from George Will). If we do not insist upon reform in and of how we think about the capital markets, about commerce, and about business enterprise, we will run the risk that we, or our children, will witness the death rattle of America's potential for continued greatness. Those of us who understand, more or less, some of the intricate details of the past few years have a special obligation – especially if we are educators. To borrow some prose from the writer James Baldwin, if we – those of us who grasp the meaning of what we have just been through – do not falter in our duty now, we may be able, handful that we are, to achieve our country and change the history of the world. Any such sweeping attempt at transformation must aim at souls.

Education has a critical role to play. To put it starkly, with a few exceptions we are not educating our future business leaders so that they will be in the best position to avoid both outright debauchery, on the one hand, and the too-slick-by-half knavery to which Stiglitz is referring, on the other hand. There are many reasons for this, but I will suggest two, for now. First, management programs in business schools do not tend to take themselves to be truly 'professional' programs, providing accreditation as 'professional managers' in the sense that law schools and medical schools do (though they do teach various types of proficiency that are hard to come by outside of the academy). That is, they tend to resist the notion that there is a common set of dispositions and rules of conduct (as in medicine or law) that apply to all managers across the board. It is true that one need not go through an MBA program to be a manager. Many executives and other managers come up through the ranks and are trained on the job, narrowly focused on their spheres of responsibility, and perform well for their employers, in all technical respects. That is thought, by most, to be enough (which, as I will argue, is an ongoing problem). Second, the training of managers in MBA programs is focused upon the narrow interests of business enterprise itself. This creates a certain kind of tunnel vision approach to commercial understanding from which it is hard to pry students free.

Concerning the first reason, that management education is not seen as professional education, a 2010 article in the *Harvard Business Review*, titled 'No, Management is Not a Profession', by veteran management educator Richard Barker, states the case (in part) thusly:

> Management educators need to resist the siren song of professionalism. Functional and technical knowledge is an important component of business school curricula, but it is not the essence of management or the substance of business leadership. Nor

is it what makes a business school like Harvard or Stanford great. Business schools do not uniquely certify managers, enabling them to practice. Nor do they regulate the conduct of those managers according to a professional code of practice. What they do is provide learning environments that consolidate, share, and build business experience, that accelerate personal development and growth, and that help equip managers to deal with their diverse working environments. Business schools are not professional schools. They are incubators for business leadership.[10]

Incubators for business leadership? What Barker is describing, essentially, is what is commonly referred to as '*vocational*' education – and that is not said with any sort of condescension regarding 'vocational' skills. But it does not do justice to the complexities and responsibilities of the type of management roles that, specifically, those leaving business schools will seek, and that many will obtain. The arguable mission of a vocational school is to 'provide learning environments that consolidate, share, and build ... experience, that accelerate personal development and growth, and that help equip [students] to deal with their diverse [future] working environments'. I sympathize with Barker's focus on the *sine qua nons* of management education as those things that best define it – which are, after all, what *sine qua nons* help to do. To try to professionalize it in the sense in which Barker, and many other educators, think the study of management *cannot* be can be construed as trying to take something whose application is incredibly diffuse (car companies, pharmaceutical companies, waste disposal firms, and even universities, etc.) and treat it as though its application is narrow (the human body or the law).

Also, what Barker may be missing is that even vocations have codes and rules that guide behaviour, which is why it does not seem like a category error to refer to licensed carpenters and masons as 'professionals', and unlicensed ones as 'handymen'. Carpenters and masons have their codes as well, and code violations brand them as second or third rate, even though sloppy or second rate work might not preclude their use of the titles 'carpenter' and 'mason'. There are correct ways to pour foundations, correct ways to nail shingles, correct ways to raise a fieldstone wall, and correct ways to transplant a human heart, and in doing these the voices of past practitioners will ring in the ears and nudge the practical conscience when the temptation to cut corners presents itself. We can quibble forever about whether the carpenters, the lawyers or the physicians are the 'true' 'professionals', yet one may be content with family resemblances rather than essentialist identifiers and hard definitions, and see the similarities between all of these spheres of practice as much as one sees the differences. That there are codes, stigma and penalties for infractions across each activity suggests something in common, and something that is very important. Perhaps in a certain sense business school trained managers are not 'professionals'. An MBA is not the bar of entry into business or management activity, as is the case with surgeons, for example, who must acquire the MD before commencing their practice. But so what? The whole point of all the texts used to teach students in business schools is to explicate proper and improper ways to conduct oneself in their commercial undertakings as managers – as financial officers, marketing officers, technology officers, etc. Of course, the fact is that managers come in classes – for better or for worse. There are business-school-trained managers, and managers who rise up through the ranks, or arrive in their positions via different channels. In no way should the two classes be equated because the naked commercial results may be the same, or because in many cases the non-business school trained manager has even more commercial or remunerative success. Being better as a manager means more than that. If it doesn't, why should anyone bother with business school at all? Education creates, or at least, as I will argue, *should* create a certain kind of manager – a manager that is in many important ways superior to those who have never set foot in a business school, or for that matter, in a college. I think the upshot of Barker's argument is that education does not do any such thing. If he is right, that may be one of the things that is wrong with the world of business, and especially finance. If business schools see their missions as training (*techne*) rather than education (*paideia*), they will churn out skilled workers rather than wise managers of the substantial resources of others and stewards of important knowledge that is important to the maintenance of the social order itself.

The point I am making here is a point similarly made by philosopher Greg Pence. Managers (and *management)* have come a long way. The bar has been raised during the twentieth century, during which management was elevated to a full-fledged field of study by such persons as Adolph Berle, Peter F. Drucker, Benjamin Graham, Mary P. Follett, Ronald Coase, Michael Porter and many others. That is to say, a *tradition* of good management and good management techniques has been established. Management has become a kind of knowledge as much as it is a set of varied practices. In effecting to undertake the establishment of new plants in a foreign country there are certain standard considerations that come right out of text books, and this is the case with many other types of business undertaking. While decision-making in various types of business require attention to the specific natures of those businesses, there are many overlapping considerations, considerations that are shared with other businesses. Management, as is the case with medicine, has established for itself a *moral* tradition (moral because there are standards of performance and practice insofar as there are effects and consequences on and for others):

> For example, medicine has a moral tradition that dates back at least to Hippocrates and Galen. This tradition sets out what a physician is supposed to do when a patient comes bleeding into the emergency room or a plague begins. Within this tradition, physicians' lives can achieve a certain unity or 'narrative.' They can look backwards (and forward) and see that their lives made (make) a difference. Moreover, medicine has its internal 'practices' which allow for intrinsic pleasure beyond its extrinsic rewards: the deft surgical hand, the perspicacious diagnosis of the esoteric disease, the esteem of a great teacher by students.[11]

This is true, as well, of Management (which I will now capitalize to set it apart from business managerial activity undertaken by the untrained), although Management, as a distinct subject of serious study and a form of knowledge, is newer than medicine, largely because of the complexities that have arisen in modern commercial life, under capitalism. There is a narrative unity that makes the study of Management cohere, and it is taught, or reproduced, in management programs, both graduate and, to some extent, undergraduate. So far as this is true, is it correct to say that teachers of Management 'need to resist the siren song of professionalism' as Richard Barker suggests? The diffuse application of management knowledge does not mean it is beyond the pale of professionalization, any more than the diverse employment of medical knowledge means that medicine is beyond the pale of professionalization, so long as one drops the rigid demand that the test for who is a 'professional' and for what counts as 'professionalism' pass all of the tests that distinguish the physician and the lawyer from taxi drivers. Once that is done, it is easy to see that Managers, i.e. those trained rigorously in the academy, are as well, 'professionals' according to the family resemblance test I proffer. There are certain things that *any* physician is supposed to know and do, and the same is true of Managers. As a kind of knowledge and sets of practices, 'Management' is held together by no more than, but no less than, a narrative thread that consists of technical skills, broad and deep reflection and deliberation, analysis, empirical observation, and attention to the specifics of the firm's activities and goals, as well as its customers, clients and other stakeholders. And why should that narrative thread not be, in part, composed of *generalized* and *internalized* standards of conduct?

Management is so prized in our civilization because of its important effects upon it. To not see this is myopia, pure and simple. Also, to fail to see the level of theory that is part of Management curricula also misses an important distinction between the Manager, who is supposed to know and understand this theory, and vocational technicians. I say this not to equivocate regarding my earlier claim that it is not terribly useful to draw hard lines between vocations and professions, but rather the point is that it is precisely because Managers are trained to think about *theories* of organization, of the corporation, of accountancy, of law (etc.) that adding ethical theory to the mix is certainly not beyond the pale, but well within it. If Managers are trained to understand the intricacies of the operations of their employees, their firms, their industries and their sectors, why not require them to, as well, understand the impact of business and commercial activity on various stakeholders, even that stakeholder seemingly most tenuously connected to the particular firm – society? The degree of care, it would seem, is connected to the level of potential impact. That is why the Securities and Exchange Commission (as agent for the public good), for example, has a higher set of standards for managers (executives) of public companies than for private companies. While it does not mandate that all engaged in the management of public companies actually be Managers, it is Managers who are best equipped to assume the full range of responsibilities, including fiduciary responsibilities, that others are generally not trained to assume.

Now onto the second reason that education has a critical role to play. The specializations and technical foci of so many of us has taken a toll on what we think is relevant to a good life – and a good society. This slicing-up of the psyche into non-inter-relational domains makes it very hard at times to see beyond our own disciplines, our own spheres of interest. This is not a problem for Management alone, but for philosophy and economics and other disciplines as well. As the American philosopher Richard Rorty held, philosophy departments have become the domains of a highly professional set of intellectuals, whose work continues to recede from relevance to anything that is of interest or importance to the society at large. Once driven by a sense of wonder and even deep spirituality and public commitment, philosophers have become a shadow of their former selves. The same is true of the field of economics. Economics, though now thoroughly fatigued with the charge that it is filled with wanna-be natural scientists, still behave, more often than not, like wanna-be natural scientists. In so doing, they limit the number and types of variables that they think important in doing economic analysis and in giving the rest of us what economists are supposed to give us – clarity if not predictions about macro- and micro-economic matters. As I have already discussed, there are economists who argue that the failures of the economics profession have to do with taking too few variables into consideration, and with specifically holding to a notion of human beings as rational in a very narrow sense of the word. To a large degree, economists take neither political economy seriously, nor affective dimensions of culture, but assume instead that human beings can be boiled down to a sort of static calculating, utilitarian rationality, that human beings are best understood as acquisitive utility maximizers whose satisfaction can only come from the marketplace. This model of economics education is centered on quantitative skills and the construction of quantitative models that, as some have argued, have little connection to the real world, as this extended quote suggests:

> All but a few of these [economics] programs in the United States focus on a narrowly-conceived foundations of economic theory, statistics, and mathematics. For example, consider aspects of two such programs always ranked among "the very best," Stanford and M.I.T. Here is Stanford's description of the desirable academic background for prospective graduate students in economics:
>
> > Most of our recent successful applications have had scores above the ninety-fifth percentile on the quantitative GRE, and received excellent grades in economics and math courses. The department requires competence in the calculus of several variables, linear algebra, and probability and statistics as they are used in modern economics. Applicants are not required to have been undergraduate economics majors, but some substantial preparation in economics is desirable (Stanford University web site).

According to the M.I.T. web site, the 'core requirements' for its PhD in economics include the following courses:

Two courses in microeconomic theory

Two courses in macroeconomic theory

Two courses in mathematics for economists

Two courses in econometrics (statistical economics)

One course in economic history

Most striking about these two programs is not what they include but what they leave out. Here's a list of subjects that one does *not* have to study as a graduate student to get a 'doctor of philosophy' in economics at Stanford or MIT, and why the omission of those subjects is potentially crippling to students of economics:

Philosophy of science and methodology, to explore the appropriate basis for and limits to scientific practice;

Ethics, to consider what kinds of economic relations and outcomes are just in a good society;

History beyond a single course, to help economists understand the evolution of the economy over time;

Psychology, to examine the actual nature of economic behavior, as opposed to assuming that all people are rational, calculating, and utterly self-interested;

Political Science, to study the intersection between political power and the economy;

Sociology and anthropology, to understand group dynamics and the myriad forms of organization human society manifests;

Ecology and other sciences, to grasp the influence of natural factors and technology on the economy; and so on.[12]

There is no doubt but that counterarguments can be made here. One such counterargument is that there is really no time in the normal graduate curriculum to consider all of these subjects. Another counterargument is that all of the subjects listed may be assumed to have been covered during the undergraduate years. Good points. But here are three rejoinders. First, it is simply not true that there is no time in the graduate business school curriculum to consider such subjects *and* their applicability to business. Any good text in business ethics will hit upon all of them, and any good instructor will weave in supplementary materials to make points about each, and their relation to the commercial sphere. The impatience of the student to complete a program is not a sufficient reason to remove from the curriculum, in the interests of catering to such impatience, an important component of business and management education. Second, the undergraduate years are years of intellectual maturation. The big questions of life, of community, and of politics are only beginning to be explored. It is at the graduate level that students can come around to thinking more deeply about the world, and of how they will interact with and shape it. Third, it is irresponsible to educate people concerning the stewardship of vast resources – resources that belong to *others* – contained within institutions that have the power, literally, to transform the lives of thousands or, conversely, cause great harm to them, without teaching them to reflect on their stewardship responsibilities to the society that grants them that opportunity and privilege. Ethics education may sound 'merely theoretical' (and I admit, it can be taught that way), but it must be at the core of the management curriculum, not relegated to the periphery, to a 'mini-course' or module that allows students to tick some box and that treats the subject as merely perfunctory or a dispensable nicety.

Just look at the costs of bad behaviour. Can anyone any longer say with a straight face that ethics education should be marginalized in business and management curricula?

4 THE OTHER WALL STREET: A LOOK AT OUR ANIMAL SPIRITS

Toward the end of the civil war, Abraham Lincoln warned: 'We may congratulate ourselves that this cruel war is nearing its end. It has cost a vast amount of treasure and blood ... It has indeed been a trying hour for the Republic; but I see in the near future a crisis approaching that unnerves me and causes me to tremble for the safety of my country. As a result of the war, corporations have been enthroned and an era of corruption in high places will follow, and the money power of the country will endeavor to prolong its reign by working upon the prejudices of the people until all wealth is aggregated in a few hands and the Republic is destroyed. I feel at this moment more anxiety for the safety of my country than ever before, even in the midst of war. God grant that my suspicions may prove groundless.'

Jeff Gates
Democracy at Risk, Rescuing Main Street from Wall Street[1]

Addressing comprehensively the more general cultural and philosophical roots of the problems that have led to the scandals and disruptions of recent years seems like a very large undertaking, and many who have attempted to address the scandals and disruptions do not appear to have employed the holistic philosophical, psychological, political and sociological analyses that are required – especially when it comes to taking more seriously the primal animal spirits that are causally implicated. Beyond this, addressing the more general cultural and philosophical roots of the problem may actually require one to critique a *system* in which one is significantly and profoundly *invested*. Additionally, there may be the sense that 'grand narrative' forms of critique are passé, and that we have arrived at a condition in which, generally speaking, capitalism is the clear winner, having vanquished all challengers.

After the collapse of experiments around the globe with various iterations of Marxism, few wish to step into the role of general culture critic and risk sounding shrill, dour (and anachronistic) about what appears to be the only game left to play – the game of global capitalism. Indeed, we are all enmeshed in the system of global capitalism, in one way or another. Thus, Jonathan Charkam writes, in his 1995 study of corporate governance and, of course, long before the financial crisis of 2007/8, that

> Everyone is to some extent imprisoned by their history, social, political, and economic. The way we think and the assumptions we bring to bear are ... the consequences of a long historical development which touches us throughout our lives without our understanding it. Only when we strike our shins on some iron protrusion of another system does the pain make us realize why we were so blind to it and why our imagination did not even contemplate the possibility of its existence.[2]

We resort to quick administrative or legal fixes. The impulse for quick fixes, the impulse to sweep unsightly remnants under the rug, to apply bandages to wounds that need more acute medical attention, are common. Our homeostatic impulses want a return to the appearance and most of the substance of normality, as we construe it. Getting rid of the worst of the problem that has beset us, even if we have not gotten rid of all of the collateral features and remnants and residues of the problem, seems sufficient. 'Why make the perfect the enemy of the good?' we ask. We cross our fingers and proceed, hoping that the lessons of the past have been learned and will stay learned. We have no hankering for what Josiah Royce called 'the lost cause'. We want to *see* our efforts come to some fruition in the reasonably immediate future – the future in which managers, politicians, most policy analysts, and lawyers live and move and have their being. However, Royce argued that

> Loyalty to lost causes is ... not only a possible thing, but one of the most potent influences of human history. In such cases the cause comes to be idealized through its very failure to win temporary and visible success ... All the more, in consequence, does this cause demand that its followers should plan and work for a far-off future, for whole ages and aeons of time; should prepare the way for their Lord, the cause, and make his paths straight ... All this larger and broader devotion of those loyal to a lost cause is colored and illuminated by [their] strong [emotional commitment to that cause].[3]

Royce's use of such mind-boggling temporal spans as 'ages' and 'aeons' is, of course, somewhat hyperbolic – and from a trader's or broker's point of view, may seem, simply, eccentric. But from the point of view of one who cares deeply about his or her children's future, about his or her country's health and success, Royce's point is far from eccentric. To the contrary, it rides the firm backs of our better instincts and our higher resolves.

The sorts of changes that are needed may actually take longer than many are willing to accept. Yet, the options before us are not binary. We must be careful not to succumb to the fallacy of the excluded middle – internal (systemic) melioration on one end of the continuum of options (the sorts of things called for in the spate of books referenced earlier), or sweeping structural change on the other end (*a la* Marx). It is possible to make greater strides than can be accomplished through procedural fixes alone, and at the same time accomplish some of the 'far off' goals that one would hope could come about via sweeping structural change. One approach would be to focus less on structures and more on *people*. We can seek to reform the citizenry itself. After all, the social institutions, including markets, are essentially an expression of the will of the citizenry – a fact that is both burdensome when contemplated, but neglected at our peril. And if the citizenry is too large a set of human beings to contemplate for such a project, we can start with a subset – i.e., our business leaders and those being trained to enter their ranks. For these persons operate (in part) from the same primal animal spirits that (in part) motivate everyone else in civil society. This necessitates a sustained project of soulcraft.

Executives, Managers and Corporate Soulcraft

The idea of soulcraft lends itself to our discussion of financial markets reform, and reform of corporate conduct in general. There are two thinkers from whom I borrow the idea of soulcraft (or 'soul-making') – the American intellectual and political pundit George F. Will, whom I have already referenced several times, and the philosopher Kwame Anthony Appiah (although the voices of Edmund Burke, Lionel Trilling, Walt Whitman, Ralph Waldo Emerson, Amitai Etzioni, Matthew Arnold and even Cicero are relevant to me, as well). It hardly matters for my purposes that these thinkers are on opposite ends of the political spectrum much of the time, Will being a political conservative (American-styled), and Appiah being a political liberal (American-styled).

Will's idea of soulcraft in his book *Statecraft as Soulcraft* attends a general belief that government has a role to play in shaping citizens and the citizenry, a belief that does not construe government to be some creature that operates as something separate and apart from the citizenry. The basic idea of soulcraft in respect of government has to do with the general Aristotelian notion that what matters to healthy social order is not merely that citizens can behave according to a list of rules impressed upon them by others, but rather that they have the capacity, as well, to govern themselves because they have been *molded* (socialized, acculturated, initiated) to possess certain habits of mind that conduce to the advancement of the interests of the polity. In that regard, government's role is not merely coercion in its most blunt and sometimes objectionable forms. It has a role to play via public pronouncements, proclamations, and education, in cultivating self-regulative capacities in the citizenry. Dodd-Frank was a sweeping piece of legislative coercion. But, as we have seen time and again, coercion is not enough.

Appiah, in his book *The Ethics of Identity*, uses very similar language when he speaks of 'liberal soul making'. In that book, Appiah writes:

> 'A liberal democratic polity does not rest on diversity, but on shared political commitments weighty enough to override competing values', Stephen Macedo writes, and he stresses that the 'abstract ideals of liberal justice lay claims of mutual respect on

every group in society, whereas the claims of particularity advanced by pluralists create no necessary claim for tolerance or respect' ... What he calls transformative liberalism suggests that one legitimate function of a liberal state is, and has been, to attenuate the strong, *Blut-und-Boden* identitarian commitments it encounters: to process the surly sources of alternative authority – whether Catholicism or English nativism – and leave something diluted by broader liberal commitments ... Historically speaking, this is precisely what the American republic has done, which is what some find so alarming. And yet it is not enough to find a balancing of interests between We the People and We the Peoples; we must also consider the interests of Me the Person, while acknowledging the enmeshment of them all ... [So, if] intolerance of other identities is built into an identity, or if learning the views of others except as shameful error is one of their norms, *we [Western liberals] will be seeking, in public education, to reshape those identities so as to exclude this feature. This is liberal soul making ... Actually existing liberalism, of almost any description, is more than a procedural value: it places a substantive weight on creating a social world in which we each can have a good chance at a life of our own.*[4]

If, Appiah argues, the citizenry of a liberal state is to be molded by collections of forces *in any event* (it is simply inevitable that they will be), what's wrong with it being molded, actively and deliberately, pursuant to the general political and philosophical commitments that make its civilization what it is – commitments to which they have at least in general outline, explicitly or tacitly, assented? This strikes me as eminently reasonable, although it might be problematic for those committed to a version of robust libertarianism which abjures any idea that the political community as such, in the form of government, has a role to play in actively creating even *liberal* souls. Such an objection strikes me, as it appears to strike Appiah, as an objection to reality itself, as well as, depending upon the degree to which the objectors wish to take their objections, a performative contradiction when voiced as more than a passive criticism (for the robust and vocal critics' decisions to enter the fray on this point is in effect an activity that has its own impact on soul-making). For the purposes of financial services cultural reform, the sort of soul-making I have in mind here may be understood if we replace *'Blut-und-Boden'* with *'Geld-und-Reichtum'* – an attempt to reshape identities so as to exclude an inordinate desire for either, or both. *Blut-und-Boden* and *Geld-und-Reichtum* fixations are both species of unhealthy, community-corrosive idolatries.

Soul making is an activity that is concerned with the maintenance of *a particular type* of civilization, and it is effected by cultivating particular types of citizens. Certain worrisome behaviours in the commercial sphere, although purportedly based upon the very economic theories and philosophical views that make that sphere as robust as it is in societies with more or less free markets, actually serve to undermine it and run contrary to the principles and beliefs that are at the heart of the civilizations and societies of which those markets are a part. Thus, Handy asks, in the previously referenced *Harvard Business Review* article, 'Could capitalists actually bring down capitalism?'[5] One of the worst offenders is

Wall Street, the culture of which is a breeding ground for anti-civilizational and anti-social forces (indeed, 'anti-social forces' is not mere hyperbole here), forces (notwithstanding its positive contributions to society, of which there are many) that, because of the growing interdependence of societies and markets, can do great damage to economic and political stability, and can cause great harm to important institutions – and disrupt the lives of billions (yes, *billions*) of people.

The cycles of scandal and high-profile commercial crimes that have been with us for so long are in large part due to an unwillingness to call out the anti-social and anti-civilizational behaviours of business leaders for what they are. Instead, what tends to happen is that there is a rush to 'normality', spurred on by both explicit and oblique complicity among citizens, business leaders, and policy makers. The rush to have things return to 'normal' removes the time needed for reflection on the part of all of those referenced, and so the process of edification and soul making never take hold. The result is a pre-mature *rapprochement* between civil society and the perpetrators that does not permit the underlying issues to be properly addressed – and many of those underlying issues are attitudinal, characterological, and cultural; *they are not merely structural*. In such a rush to normality lawmakers and regulators obtain their pounds of flesh and institute some new rules (Glass-Steagall, Sarbanes-Oxley, and Dodd-Frank, for example), and the scandals fade from the headlines and from memory. The lawmakers and regulators are then faced with new issues with which to grapple, and attention and funding are redirected to the new matters that are extant. The new rules become 'compliance' issues, and lose their political and moral meaning. The compliance issues then become 'headaches' and 'cost burdens'. Industry lobbyists and industry lawyers go to work to remove the 'headaches' and 'cost burdens', employing colourful language about the 'choking of business by burdensome government regulation' (one need only look at the blistering attack on the Volcker Rule, in the United States, if one has doubts about this).[6] The next scandal or high profile commercial crime happens, and the cycle repeats, with looks of puzzlement about how such a thing could happen. (For a useful summary of the history of financial scandals, see *Separating Fools from their Money: A History of American Financial Scandals*, by Scott B. MacDonald and Jane E. Hughes.)[7]

One shoots the bullets one has. The reason that this cycle repeats has to do with the fact that corporate executives – especially those employed by large institutions – and policymakers are not trained (generally) to effect attitudinal, characterological and cultural reconditioning; they are focused on systemic matters. They know how to use the law as a bludgeon and how to implement policies and procedures but, in general, nothing in their training gives them any feeling of competence when it comes to shaping human behaviour and cultures from the inside out. How, after all, do you mandate good attitudes and good character? How do you manufacture healthy cultures? Before I sketch out my answers to these questions it is important that we consider, briefly, the role of the executive manager in today's world. That is, we will consider what the role of the executive manager ought to be in today's post-financial-crisis world which is, history sadly tells us, a world already approaching the next crisis.

The Agency Problem (Again)

In the aftermath of each of the corporate scandals of the past two decades or so, talking heads, pundits and just ordinary people sitting around their kitchen tables asked how such things can happen, and just what kinds of people do the sorts of things that have been revealed in newspapers and TV news broadcasts. Earlier, I quoted Jim Cramer, who asked how people that do the extremely greedy and destructive things that are done can live with themselves. Well, apparently they can live with themselves just fine. One of the ironic and surreal facts about the Enron scandal, for example, is that the company's board of directors had approved a new corporate code of conduct document just prior to the firm's collapse.[8] It was an aesthetically pleasant document, even wrapped in a plastic cover that gave it a sort of gravity, as though the company's principal executives really cared about what was in it. It contained all of the normal declarations concerning the company's commitment to shareholders, employees and the community, sort of like a man or woman who has just exchanged wedding vows makes all sorts of declarations of love and fealty, but has already arranged a string of one night stands to commence as soon as the honeymoon is over. The moral, of course, is that corporate codes of conduct mean almost nothing if the culture of the firm (and/or of the industry) undermines and belies what is in them. As MacDonald and Hughes tell us, concerning this culture, in respect of some of the more recent financial scandals:

> The appetite for partying among these men was only exceeded by their appetite for success. In examining the track record of those at the core of major financial scandals, a broad profile emerges of energetic, creative, ruthless, and highly aggressive, even hubristic, individuals. *The very nature of high finance helps foster a business culture of aggressiveness.* This is frustrating for those on the other side – the reformers and regulators – leading one financial journalist to comment in 2004: "Some even argue that attempts at reform are futile in a business where aggressively courting risk can pay out such rich rewards".[9]

They go on to address the probability that regulation is the answer to scandal and crises caused by serious moral lapses:

> Despite all the efforts to regulate the nooks and crannies of the financial world, innovation and greed run counter to control. This means that the existing framework (bolstered in the United States by Sarbanes-Oxley and other measures) ultimately fails to fully take into account the danger posed by financial scandal in a major insti-

tution. Technology, innovation, and globalization have augmented the danger of contagion. Indeed, it can be argued that efforts to create a more homogenous financial system could actually increase systemic fragility.[10]

Many if not most executives in large, public companies step into roles that are fraught with dangers (to themselves, to the firm, and to the public at large) with which they are ill-prepared to deal. Whether they come up through the ranks or are minted in the best business schools, they are not fully aware of these dangers since their preparation for their roles is focused on the nuts and bolts issues and concerns that are directly relevant to job performance. They devote little time to the 'theory' or 'philosophy' of executive management. Devoting little time to theoretical considerations (that is, considerations that have to do with a full conceptual grasp of their stations in society) is something that is fine for a line worker in an automobile assembly plant, or a bookkeeper in a medical office; however, it is not something that executives and other managers in large public companies or large private companies can do without.

George Will again: 'Americans are overreachers; overreaching is the most admirable and most American of the many American excesses. But in the first half of the nineteenth century, many Americans felt they were reaching for the wrong star. Before and since, there have been episodes of anxiety that something – some sphere of life, perhaps the citizenry itself – was getting out of control, and taking on a pace and style of life, and a dimension of character, that was unworthy of citizens of a city on a hill'.[11] Notice how Will speaks of the malady as something that is not quite *understood*, something that it is hard to put one's finger on. That is because, to the ordinary eye, things seemed to be going on as they always had been. Like a virus, the agent that was causing the malady was not something that could be seen by the naked eye because it was connected to attitudes, to character, to perspective, to ways of seeing that were not guided by the proper recollection of 'first principles'. It was precisely a set of attitudes and perspectives, and a collection of bad characters, that were among the root causes of the more or less recent scandals. When we ask how it is that an Enron or a Tyco or a Countrywide Financial can happen, we seem, as well, to be at a loss to understand. But the answer is not mystical. The men (and it is usually men) who cause these scandals are so teleopathic, so driven by the tyranny of goals, that larger, exigent concerns drop from view. They are the individuals who exhibit the pathological set of characteristics referenced by MacDonald and Hughes.

The worst, most hubristic executives and other managers use the corporate mission and culture as cover to pursue what are really personal financial and ego interests, not the interests of the firm and its diffuse stakeholders. This is what Alan Greenspan, former chairman of the Federal Reserve, did not realize when he assumed that corporate executives would act 'rationally', i.e. navigating around or limiting risks that would or could sink their firms. 'Those of us who have looked to the self-interest of lending institutions to protect shareholders' equity, myself included, are in a state of shocked disbelief', Greenspan, in 2008, told the House Committee on Oversight and Government Reform, as the details and consequences of the sub-prime mortgage and credit crises were becoming apparent. When Mr. Greenspan was asked if his ideology (Greenspan is a market libertarian and at the time a devotee of Ayn Rand's Objectivism, an egocentric, extremely libertarian, and voluntarist ethical and political philosophy) pushed him to make decisions that he wished he had not made, Mr. Greenspan responded, as has been widely reported and discussed: 'Yes, I've found a flaw. I don't know how significant or permanent it is. But I've been very distressed by that fact'.[12]

The flaw was that *as long as there is* a significant divergence between the interests of executives and other managers and the interests of the enterprise itself (the old agency problem, but now on steroids), the risks that executives will tend to mitigate are the risks to their *own* short-term financial gain, something that banking regulators in the EU have recently moved to address by limiting the amount and mode of bonus payments, instituting, among other things, clawback provisions.[13] Often, the size of that gain may correlate directly to significant increases in risks to the firm. Too many executives see the acquisition of corporate authority and the remuneration that comes with it as their primary foci. Because of some general shifts in the public culture, this often means, as well, amassing that power and remuneration *as quickly as possible*. The sooner options vest, the better; the sooner other compensation-padding goals are reached, the better. Thus, senior executives are too often incentivized to pursue, aggressively, a series of *short-term enhancements* to the business bottom line and the stock price – enhancements that may be fraught with long-term danger to the firm and its stakeholders. Many executives will deny this, but their actions and lifestyles too often betray them.

This sounds like an indictment of all executives and other managers in large public and private companies, but it is not intended to be that. It does appear, unfortunately, to describe too many executives and other managers, however. At some point, mitigating risks to the executive, which seems to revolve around wealth accumulation, and the risks to the enterprise, which should revolve around its ability to continue to produce its goods or services in the long-run, diverge. That might be explained away as, simply, human nature. But executives are not entitled to the 'human nature' defense, insofar as they are deemed to be fiduciary agents and, I and others argue, quasi-public servants, which is the position in which the rarified heights of the c-suite places them. The law views executives and other managers of corporations as fiduciaries with the obligation to act in the best interests of their corporate employers. Generally, a person (agent) is a fiduciary as regards another person (principal) if the agent has the authority to exercise discretion or power, if the agent can unilaterally exercise that power or discretion to affect the principal's legal or practical interests, and if the principal is particularly vulnerable to or at the mercy of the agent holding the discretionary power. So the 'I-might-do-the-same-thing-if-I-were-in-their-shoes' argument is available neither legally nor ethically, given the status that executives have with respect to the interests of their firms. Because of the far-flung responsibilities that executives have to corporate shareholders and other stakeholders in the context of the public company (whose shareholders can, and often do, span the globe), and because of the staggering level of assets that is placed in their care, civil society has compelling and pragmatic interests to oversee and police their activities, and should also have compelling and pragmatic interests in the kinds of persons they are, i.e. whether they, the executives, are aware of the special status they have in society. While there are executives and other managers who understand this, there are, as well, too many who only understand that they have an obligation to comply with the law, failing to grasp the quasi-public roles in which they find themselves.

This leaves too many executives pressing, constantly, against the limits of acceptable conduct, which, in the minds of many of them, is in fact a *duty: Why do more than what the law requires, especially if doing so has a substantial economic/monetary cost?* It has been argued by Milton Friedman and others that executives have no real obligation to conduct themselves with reference to considerations beyond the basic rules of the road of commercial conduct. As Friedman put it, in a much-referenced *New York Times* article ripping the idea of corporate 'social responsibility':

> In a free-enterprise, private-property system, a corporate executive is an employee of the owners of the business. He has direct responsibility to his employers. That responsibility is to conduct the business in accordance with their desires, which generally will be to make as much money as possible while conforming to the basic rules of the society, both those embodied in law and those embodied in ethical custom ... What does it mean to say that the corporate executive has a 'social responsibility' in his capacity as businessman? If this statement is not pure rhetoric, it must mean that he is to act in some way that is not in the interest of his employers. For example, that he is to refrain from increasing the price of the product in order to contribute to the social objective of preventing inflation, even though a price increase would be in the best interests of the corporation. Or that he is to make expenditures on reducing pollution beyond the amount that is in the best interests of the corporation or that is required by law in order to contribute to the social objective of improving the environment. Or that, at the expense of corporate profits, he is to hire 'hardcore' unemployed instead of better qualified available workmen to contribute to the social objective of reducing poverty. In each of these cases, the corporate executive would be spending someone else's money for a general social interest. Insofar as his actions in accord with his 'social responsibility' reduce returns to stockholders, he is spending their money. Insofar as his actions raise the price to customers, he is spending the customers' money. Insofar as his actions lower the wages of some employees, he is spending their money.[14]

Third-Wave Economic Imagination

Friedman, whom I criticized earlier, was nevertheless right to say that corporate executives are agents with a special obligation to pursue the desires of the firm's principals, i.e. shareholders, which is a reasonable return on their capital investment; but, as has been rehearsed time and time again in the business ethics literature, he was wrong to assume that meeting that obligation is simple or that investors are entitled to immediate returns, rather than returns based upon a well-thought-out management plan that takes time to unfold. Business firms, and especially public firms, are not to be run in the interests of *traders*, but rather in the interests of true investors, although the law is not entirely clear on the distinction between traders and investors in terms of ownership rights. Most business firms are not hedge funds; the stated missions of the latter are to swing for the fences when it comes to seeking total return, at least in many cases. Most businesses, rather, are operating companies with a wide range of objectives and responsibilities, and a far broader base of stakeholders than that of a hedge fund, which is perhaps the purest expression of the classical profit-seeking model of the corporate form. Further, we are not considering corporate social responsibility per se (although it does enter into our analysis), but rather the problems that arise when executives and other managers fail to understand their actual (i.e., non-idealistic) standing in civil society, without regard to other public policy considerations that some in civil society may wish to impose upon corporations for a variety of sometimes idiosyncratic reasons. So, for example, I am not arguing that corporations should involve themselves in public policy matters that extend well beyond their business missions (providing a school system for children in inner-cities or poor rural communities, for example). While those acts of philanthropy may be heart-warming and laudable, they obviously run well beyond the commercial mission and, in that sense, Friedman is correct – executives spending any substantial amount of corporate assets for such purposes would be stealing other people's money.

No one who has considered bad corporate conduct thinks that executives and other managers need to conduct themselves in a supererogatory manner (in a manner far above ethical norms). What is clearly needed are executives and other managers who understand the distinction between the supererogatory and what I will call fully-cognizant corporate conduct which is based upon a social imaginary in which stewardship is a central guiding principle and upon the idea of social and economic *ecology* in which social institutions, including commercial institution, are seen as interlocking systems, as part of an ecosystem that permits the members of society to flourish. Fully-cognizant corporate conduct is effected on the basis of constant *recollection* that the corporation/firm is a part of civil society and has the power to harm as well as to deliver benefits.

The executives and other managers who operate with full cognizance come to feel the weight of that seemingly banal fact, produced by civic mindfulness and civic reflection. They possess a third-wave economic imagination by which they understand that:

1. The firm is embedded in society and is a creature of it (i.e., is part of an ecosystem of commercial and noncommercial actors and institutions);

2. 'Economics' is not limited to a grasp of merely macro-economic data – facts and figures about productivity, unemployment and the like; and

3. A proper commercial social imaginary is affectively and intellectually sensitive to the fact that the firm is a *key agent of social welfare* that is linked with other key agents of social welfare, such as governments and nongovernmental organizations.

All of this is to be kept in mind as the plastic bottles, cans of hair spray, rolls of tissue, or flasks of oil career down the rollers of manufacturing plants, or as shares of equity are sold by and corporate analysis is issued from Wall Street's broker-dealers and banks. And all of this *can* be kept in mind where the executive manager is *properly initiated into his or her role*. I call this third-wave economic imagination as compared to what I will call first-wave economic imagination, which persisted in the early days of the industrial revolution and in which firms were assumed to be run expressly and solely for the enrichment of the owners of capital, with little or no regard for employees or the community at large, and second-wave economic imagination, which was ushered in after the *Lochner* era and which evolved in response to a number of high profile and socially impact-ful events (among them, the Triangle Shirtwaist Factory fire of 1911) and in response to the development of more sophisticated and holistic management theories (such as those developed by Mary P. Follett and Peter Drucker, among others) that arose along with a wave of social reforms that began or came to maturity in the Progressive Era. There was a burgeoning recognition that while firms produce useful and valuable goods and services they can also do substan-tial harm and those harms can rebound on the firms themselves. The typology – first-wave, second-wave, and third-wave – is rough, admittedly, but I use it as a heuristic to plot out a growing awareness of and appreciation for *just what a business firm is* as a unit of civil society, and how it and the rest of civil society (and the natural environment) play off of one another. The trajectory has been away from conceptualization of the firm as insular and self-referential, toward the ecological conceptualization sketched above.

If you think that many executives already possess the third-wave economic imagination and take decisions that may be characterized as fully cognizant, you are right. But while many executives are or at least endeavor to be fully-cognizant, there are things that undermine them and force back-sliding to occur. Take the recent crisis that led to the insolvency or financial crisis of US and European banks. Bank executives operated without due consideration of what would happen if their banks failed. A review of the failures of several large US banks, and the near-failure of others, led to policy proposals that called for the banks to adopt 'living wills', i.e. prescribed and preapproved remedies that would lead to their proper unwinding if they found themselves in a catastrophic situation so that taxpayer money would not have to be used to bail them out and in order to avoid a cascade of negative events through the financial system. Dodd-Frank specifically called for living wills in the case of large financial institutions.[15] Such legislation and proposals have, in this case, mandated what third-wave economic imagination would or could implement without legislation – that is, *thinking* about the full repercussions of the firm's activities and existence, and what it would mean if those activities and existence ceased. The creation of a living will requires executives to think through the interests of all stakeholders, including those who may seem far-flung (such as the taxpayers).

It is better to initiate corporate executives into the habits of thinking and planning that lead to third-wave economic imagination, which leads to fully-cognizant corporate conduct. The third-wave economic imagination should be seen as quotidian, i.e. not something that is only required when considering catastrophic possibilities. It can also be used to head-off the problem of free-riding, by creating robust private sector solutions to looming or extant public costs and externalities, without government having to act. It is axiomatic that commercial enterprises have an obligation to act in their own interests, but it is a superficial (yet widely held) notion of 'self-interest' that leads to corporate scandals of one variety or another. We have recourse to many examples of corporate scandal, of course, and I have already touched upon several. Most if not all of these scandals were caused by or substantially enabled by an inadequate notion of 'self-interest'. Had the executives implicated in these cases operated from the perspective of one who possesses third-wave economic imagination, which would have prepared them to deliberate over variables that were relevant to the longer-term interests of all tenable corporate stakeholders, they would have made much better decisions.

Behind such holistic thinking must be something more: a strong sense that there are interests larger than the immediate interests of the firm – and its executives. Without it being explicitly articulated, what stands behind third-wave economic imagination is *the civic sense*, which is a strong sense that, while it is not always expressed in work-a-day life, there is something that is more foundational than immediate exchanges of goods and services for payment, and that something is the commonweal. This should not sound grand. But to too many ears it does sound grand. That is the problem, exactly. To the contrary, what we need, and what third-wave economic imagination calls for, is the capacity to

truly *think*. How do you make *thinking* part of the fiber of managerial deliberation? You tell stories and deploy rhetoric aimed at edification, and you do so via
various channels and social organs: educational and governmental institutions;
media; movies and novels; even corporate communications. To craft commercial
souls so that they act in ways that are in line with the core values of the commonweal, these organs will be needed, although there is no particular algorithm that
can be proffered to make it so.

Soulcraft is precisely the objective of the now well known 'MBA Oath',
crafted by management graduate students themselves. Here is the Oath (I have
underlined certain words for reasons that I will get to momentarily):

> As a business leader I recognize my role in society.
> My purpose is to lead people and manage resources to <u>create</u> value that no
>   single individual can create alone.
> My decisions affect the <u>well-being</u> of individuals inside and outside my enterprise,
>   today and <u>tomorrow</u>.
> Therefore, I <u>promise</u> that:
> I will manage my enterprise with <u>loyalty</u> and <u>care</u>, and will not advance my
>   personal interests at the expense of my enterprise or society.
> I will understand and <u>uphold</u>, in letter and <u>spirit</u>, the laws and contracts governing
>   my conduct and that of my enterprise.
> I will refrain from <u>corruption</u>, <u>unfair</u> competition, or business practices <u>harmful</u>
>   to society.
> I will <u>protect</u> the <u>human rights</u> and <u>dignity</u> of all people affected by my enterprise,
>   and I will oppose <u>discrimination</u> and <u>exploitation</u>.
> I will protect the right of <u>future generations</u> to advance their standard of <u>living</u>
>   and <u>enjoy</u> a <u>healthy</u> planet.
> I will report the performance and <u>risks</u> of my enterprise accurately and honestly.
> I will invest in developing myself and <u>others</u>, helping the management profes-
>   sion continue to <u>advance</u> and create sustainable and inclusive <u>prosperity</u>.
> In exercising my professional duties according to these principles, I recognize
>   that my behavior must set an example of <u>integrity</u>, eliciting <u>trust</u> and <u>esteem</u>
>   from those I <u>serve</u>. I will remain accountable to my peers and to society for
>   my actions and for upholding these standards.
> This oath I make freely, and upon my <u>honor</u>.[16]

The MBA Oath, however, has been criticized because of its unilateral nature
– the fact that it amounts to no more than a pledge to oneself (although sign-
ers of the oath are now identified by name on the web). It has also been argued
that the MBA Oath is akin to the sign-off one is asked to make upon receiving a
company's code of conduct. This may be, but deliberating and even debating the
significance and utility of the MBA Oath is, in itself, an activity of commercial
soulcraft. The Oath itself is intended to publically state a commitment to be fully-
cognizant managers determined to engage in fully-cognizant corporate conduct,
and to spread the values of fully-cognizant corporate conduct across their firms.

It arises from an awareness of what is often missing or inadequately addressed in management education, and an awareness of the rapacity and puerile teleopathy bolted into the identities of executives and other managers and, to harken back to Appiah, it is an attempt 'to reshape ... [those] identities so as to exclude [these features]'. Many of the pledges contained in the MBA Oath speak to general moral and even political commitments, which is precisely the way executives and other managers ought to be thinking about their activities. 'I will protect the right of future generations to advance their standard of living and enjoy a healthy planet' is a statement that serves as a signal (and a warning) to any firm hiring someone who makes it. Should the firm's actions begin to run counter to the pledge, the pledger will oppose the firm's interests as a matter of moral commitment. Any firm that hires such a manager is, in effect, making a public declaration about its own values and ethics, which in some measure is the larger purpose of the Oath.

Of 'Ethics'

I'd like to drop a marker here about the use of the word 'ethics'. The word 'ethics' – as in 'We need more business ethics courses in our universities' – packs little punch these days, and is mocked or given short shrift in business circles – dismissed as trite by many managers, executives and directors who have their eye fixed on the nuts and bolts of running their businesses. Many in Harvard's MBA program who considered signing the MBA Oath doubted that the Oath would be effective, largely for the reasons referenced by MacDonald and Hughes, mentioned previously i.e. because 'aggressively courting risk can pay out ... rich rewards'.[17] But aggressively courting risk is not the same thing as *recklessly* courting risk, or recklessly placing one's firm on a collision course with the core values of one's civilization. Aggressiveness and recklessness are not the same thing, just as greed and aspiration are not the same thing.

In order to change conduct we may have to adopt language that serves our purposes better. We won't get much change in the behaviour of executives and managers (or those who report to them) if the word 'ethics' (admittedly, a word that I have used continually) is most prominent as we consider ways to navigate companies away from scandal and enforcement actions by regulators, and toward fully-cognizant corporate conduct and toward third-wave economic imagination. This is because the word 'ethics' is, today, largely bloodless. Also, unless one digs deeply into the body of literature that concerns 'ethics', one tends to construe 'ethics' in a more or less *negative* way. That is, for many, 'ethics' is about *constraints* rather than *affirmative actions and goals*. People respond best when their emotions are engaged, which is why they find narratives, whether concerning real or fictional events, so compelling. They tend to respond to *animal spirits* such as those that attend loyalty, honour and solidarity. The positive animal spirits associated with a feeling that one is in good standing in one's society are the vectors from which a new type of thinking concerning corporate conduct will emerge.

The American philosopher Richard Rorty was right when he said at the 2005 Annual Meeting of the Society for Business Ethics that:

> At the beginning of the twentieth century, businessmen like Henry Ford imagined ways in which the US might become a relatively classless society. Some of those dreams actually came true, at least for that brief shining moment in US history that historians now describe as the Great Leveling. Ford, like FDR and Walter Reuther, glimpsed possibilities for industrial capitalism that had been beyond Marx's and Lenin's imagination. I hope that now, at the beginning of the twenty-first century, at least a few executives of the great multinational corporations are thinking about the need to create a global economy that will, far down the road, make possible global social justice. These men and women are the people with the best sense of the directions in which economic forces are presently driving the nations, of where the real levers of power are to be found, and of the possibilities that remain open for both governments and business enterprises. If none of them are dreaming up idealistic, utopian scenarios for the formation of a morally decent global society, it is unlikely that such a society will ever come into existence. Perhaps the business ethics community will provide an environment in which such dreams are encouraged.[18]

What I am referring to here as animal spirits is what Will was referring to when he sketched soulcraft as a disposition to consider 'whether certain [actions] accord with worthy ends for the polity', and what Royce was referring to when he invoked 'emotion'. Any concern about worthy ends for the polity should be construed as caught up in a concern for solidarity – the idea of a *we* that has goals that extend beyond narrowly construed economic ones. But there are forces that work against the gelling of solidarity, and these float upon fallacies concerning profit, rationality, incentives, growth, and efficiency, which I critique below.

As for what word might supplant 'ethics' in terms of the plans and actions undertaken in the commercial sphere, in the commercial ecology of the larger social ecosystem, perhaps, given the importance of the concerns that we have given our commercial culture, we might set aside the usual preference for linguistic parsimony and go with two words instead of one. The two words that might better frame our deliberations – because they trigger our imaginations and emotions (our positive animal spirits), are 'trust' and 'stewardship'. Trust is what has repeatedly been broken and has gone missing in the scandals that continually beset society, as political scientist Francis Fukuyama has argued at some length.[19] 'Stewardship' speaks more directly to the care that might animate Fully-Cognizant Corporate Conduct. In tandem, they may help frame a new social imaginary, not only of leaders in business but also in all of society's important institutions. You may note, as well, that the words of the The MBA Oath triggers emotional, not merely intellectual, responses: 'honor', 'serve', 'dignity', 'promise' and 'spirit' are words that rally the *emotions*, activate collections of positive metaphors, and kindle narratives of valiant and even heroic behaviour with which we have been familiar since childhood. Good leadership is really about 'trust' and 'stewardship' and a stable and profitable organization will be a place in which the words of the Oath come to life.

Attacking (Some of) the Fallacies

One of the ways to address the primal animal spirits at work in our commercial lives is to have a clearer *understanding* of what commerce is all about, or should be about. Meeting the primal animal spirits that drive our existential fears with the positive animal spirits that form us into a political community can have its uses, but what is also of use is *understanding* – understanding the nature and purposes of commerce and of the social structures in which it takes place and which, alternatively, support it. To that end, pointing out and demolishing the fallacies that stubbornly drive the thoughts and actions of many market participants is important.

Fallacy 1: The Raison D'être of Business is Profit

The first fallacy is that the purpose of business is the maximization of profits. This is one of the most pernicious of the fallacies, and one that I have already touched upon in the preceding pages. A commercial transaction is an exchange – money for goods or services, or, less common, a barter of goods for goods, services for services. The exchange has to do with a need or a want of some kind. The business enterprise exists to satisfy a need or a want. A successful business enterprise will generate repeat patrons, those who 'customarily' return to the business to satisfy a particular need or want. The stability of the business, as well as the growth of the business, will usually depend upon the repetitious character of patrons, i.e. customers. Profit follows. No business ethicist believes that business can ignore profits. But there is a danger in conceptualizing business as only about profits, as my pyramid diagrams attempt to illustrate. For one thing, when profit is placed above all other considerations, moral hazard is created. We have seen such moral hazard at work in the SAC insider trading and Wall Street research scandals, as well as in many, many others.

Profit (that is, money left over after all expenses are paid, generally speaking) is the result of satisfying the customer or client. There are at least two ways to undermine profitability. Bad management is one way. The other, and perhaps the most corrosive way, is to consistently disappoint (*dis-appoint*) those whom you are trying to make customers. Putting profits ahead of all other considerations, then, is suicide in slow motion – and sometimes in fast motion. An organization with poor customer/client satisfaction and bad management is an organization that is doomed. An organization with great customer/client satisfaction and bad management has everything it needs to survive by simply replacing its bad managers (since the customers are still loyal). An organization with great customer/client satisfaction and great management is virtually unstoppable, all else being equal. Of course, this is a bit simplistic, since bad managers can undermine customer satisfaction by making poor decisions about quality and customer support. But as a general rule, I think the point is clear. Great managers don't focus on profits to the exclusion of all else, they focus on great products and great services. They focus on providing customers with great value, and they make them ambassadors for the business, people who spread the word about the great experience they have had with the business. Further, great managers understand the environment in which the business operates, and are sensitive to respect all stakeholders to the degree required.

The auto industry in the United States, for example, ceased to make great cars that gave consumers good value, and in the late 1970s and 1980s it paid the price, just as has happened more recently, when Japanese car makers rolled out a spate of efficient, high quality automobiles. Have a look at the classic book about the auto industry of that period, *The Reckoning*, by the late and celebrated journalist David Halberstam, for a full accounting of the auto industry's travails. The difference between Japanese and American manufacturing and quality was stark, and Japanese auto makers had no intention to stand still and cede the market share they had gained. They were making quality automobiles using quality manufacturing processes that focused on, well, quality:

> In the early eighties, American executives, because of joint production deals, were often visiting Japanese factories, and they were finding out how good the Japanese were, especially at the basics. One executive who had made that trip and reached that conclusion a decade earlier was Hal Sperlich, then of Ford. Touring a Japanese auto factory in the early seventies, he had noticed that there were no repair bays alongside the line, areas into which defective cars in the process of assembly were pulled for fixing. "Where do you repair your cars?" Sperlich asked the engineer with him. "We don't have to repair our cars," the engineer answered. "Well, then," Sperlich asked, "where are your inspectors?" "The workers are the inspectors," his guide answered. Sperlich left that factory somewhat shaken: In America, he thought, we have repair bins the size of football fields.[20]

Profit is but the way a business keeps score, a way of measuring whether or not the business is being managed properly, from a number of different perspectives – whether it is getting and keeping *customers*. If you replace the idea that 'business is *about* profit' with the idea that 'profit is only a way that a business *keeps score*' you will be closer to a perspective that allows the business to have both sustained profitability and longevity. There are many forces that work against such a point of view, however. One of them is Wall Street, which punishes businesses and their managers for not bringing in consistent short-term profits – for 'missing the numbers'.

Businesses need profits, but their *raison d'être* cannot *be* profits. When businesses focus on their own needs, *when they are self-regarding rather than other-regarding*, they invariably fall into trouble.

Fallacy 2: 'The Public' and 'The Private' Refer to Separate Social Realms

Look no further than the recent government bailouts of various banks, as well as at the interconnections between governments and foreign markets around the world, and you will see that the separation of social reality into a realm that is public and a realm that is private creates and perpetuates a dangerous fiction. Government and public institutions perform certain necessary functions; and the private (for example, families and commercial enterprises (businesses)) perform certain other necessary functions. When one sees the division of 'the private' and 'the public' in terms of division of labour based upon unequal strengths and economic efficiencies, once can see the division as functional rather than as ontological or ideological. Seeing the split as functional is best, because it admits that there is mutuality and intercourse (and should be!) between the various institutions that order and minister to society. Sadly, there are too many people, on both wings of the political spectrum, who hold that there is an inviolable separation, a dark black line, between the public and the private, somehow ordained by the gods. But this perspective is seriously factitious, at the service of ideological commitments that pit government and public institutions against commercial and private ones, as though their interests are mutually exclusive. If one views the roles played by government and the roles played by business as *functionally* different, on the other hand, each performing the *functions* best or better suited to it, one will have a better grasp of the reality. The public and the private are always in *partnership*.

The myth of the public-private split is a myth that has its political foundations: many liberals and leftists tend to emphasize public and communal endeavors and values that *override* private interests, and conservative libertarians tend to see civil society as driven by private interests the values of which are foundational to the social order. Leftists are suspicious of private interests, and conservative libertarians are suspicious of government and communal endeavors other than those necessary to protect private concerns.

It can be argued that we do well to supplant such views with the general Liberal view (and here I mean Liberal with a capital 'L' – Liberal in the sense that Thomas Jefferson, John Adams, Ronald Reagan and Bill Clinton were all Liberals), and understand that there are reasons why certain tasks are assigned to different players. Government makes very poor decisions about prices and what goods should be produced, and how many. Private enterprises make very poor decisions about land use and environmental protection and other things of value that are not the subject of sale in the marketplace, often leading to what is called the tragedy of the commons and other social maladies.

Fallacy 3: Only Stratospheric Remuneration Incentivizes

Many studies have shown that high levels of executive compensation are not well correlated to the growth or success of a business, and have also pointed out that the notion that compensation is set pursuant to truly arms-length negotiations is delusional due to 'management capture' and other factors.[21] Charles M. Elson and Craig K. Ferrere offered a searing critique of the types of peer benchmarking that has not only inflated CEO compensation but has inflated compensation packages across the corporate suite, at the expense of shareholders. They view untenably high levels of compensation as the extraction of rents from shareholders and boards:

> We argue that: (I) theories of optimal market-based contracting are misguided in that they are predicated upon the chimerical notion of vigorous and competitive markets for transferable executive talent; (II) that even boards comprised of only the most faithful fiduciaries of shareholder interests will fail to reach an agreeable resolution to the compensation conundrum because of the unfounded reliance on the structurally malignant and unnecessary process of peer benchmarking; and (III) that the solution lies in avoiding the mechanistic and arbitrary application of peer group data in arriving at executive compensation levels. Instead, independent and shareholder-conscious compensation committees must develop internally created standards of pay based on the individual nature of the organization concerned, its particular competitive environment and its internal dynamics.[22]

The more pernicious assumption underlying astronomical levels of executive pay (in particular) have to do with a model of economic thinking that is itself in retreat. This is the model of human beings as *Homo Economicus,* and that holds that our *primary* values are economic values, and that which motivates first and foremost are our economic interests. But this is patently false at all levels of society, not only in the corporate suites, although there is no doubt that economic interests often take priority. But there is a difference between taking priority at times and assuming a position in our hierarchy of values that is *totalizing.* People value and are motivated by a wide range of things: the desire to innovate; the desire to create something new; the desire to solve an intractable problem; the desire to be perceived as a good professional or good leader; the desire to be in a position to assist others; the desire to create; or even act just for the fun of the game, whatever it may be. A CEO of a Fortune 100 company may make $10 million or $20 million per year (or more), but to suggest that that CEO would not perform at a high level were his or her compensation $5 million a year reduces him or her to a mere calculator, with no interest in anything other than personal wealth.

Associated with the assumption that CEOs are only incentivized by exorbitant levels of compensation (in the largest firms, 300 to 400 times the level of the average worker's) are two other problematic assumptions. First is the assumption that the for-profit company's CEO is commensurately more valuable than a similarly qualified and driven hospital administrator or university president. Second, there is an assumption that the CEO should enjoy a piece of the new wealth that he or she has helped to generate for shareholders. Both assumptions are questionable – from both a risk/reward perspective and an agency theory perspective.

Fallacy 4: Rationality May be Divorced from Cultural Values and Communal Goals

The market is assumed to operate through participants making rational calculations about the baskets of goods and services that will provide 'the greatest utility'. The assumption that markets operate in this mechanistic way, must operate without the meddling of 'extraneous' values or axiological considerations, has been sufficient to silence many critics who have argued that markets and businesses can more directly affect problematic social conditions (homelessness, poverty, juvenile crime, etc.). Because of the prevailing dogma, there was substantial pushback against the notion that such factors as sustainability and social return on investment (or 'SRI') were other than forms of market 'interference'. But sustainability, SRI, and even the impact of business activities on particular communities are becoming accepted as important considerations in corporate governance and management – as part of what I have been calling Third-Wave Economic Imagination, which removes factitious barriers between human activities, which barriers are based upon ideological and/or misguided assumptions about 'the public' and 'the private'. We are expanding our notions of what can be done to improve lives and communities, even nations, through intelligent partnerships between businesses and other elements of civil society. Given that, old models of 'profit maximization' are slowly going by the boards, and are being replaced with more holistic views concerning the nature and use of the for-profit enterprise.

It is anticipated that 'impact investing' – investment (and business activity) focused on both the commercial mission and the potential to solve social problems – will likely grow substantially in just a few short years.[23] Many see impact investing as anything but chimerical, and have built their business models around its positive prospects.[24]

Fallacy 5: Economic Growth Assures that a Society Will Do Better

There is no doubt that economic growth is very important to the health of a society. But many studies have shown that economic growth does not guaranty that the least well-off will participate in the larger pools of wealth that are created by such growth. Economic growth is a necessary but insufficient condition for improved standards of living, especially among the least well-off. Economic growth in societies with high rates of inequality divert the increased wealth toward those already at or near the top. The problems with such unequal wealth distribution is highlighted in many books and in documentaries about the current problem of inequality in United States, most notably, perhaps, Thomas Piketty's *magnum opus, Capital in the Twenty-First Century*, and the Robert Reich documentary, 'Inequality for All' (2011). America has seen periods of strong economic growth, but the real wages of average Americans have remained stagnant for decades:

> The bad news: [Wages are] down from the end of 2008, broadly flat over the past decade, and on an inflation-adjusted basis, wages peaked in 1973, fully 40 years ago. Apart from brief lapses, like in the late 1990s, wages have been falling for a generation.[25]

Fallacy 6: 'Business Ethics' is an Oxymoron

No endeavour, institution, or undertaking can turn out well without care for others as human beings and respect for the property of others. None can be wholly inward looking, focused only on its own needs rather than on the needs of others. No endeavour, institution, or undertaking can turn out well without trust. *None.* Beyond this, nothing need be said about this particular fallacy. Yet it remains, and likely will remain for some time, stubbornly persistent.

5 REFORM OR *METANOIA*? – BEYOND DODD-FRANK

We have met the enemy, and they are us.

Walt Kelly

Let's carry on our analysis of The Other Wall Street.

The psychologist James Hillman has written that human beings, whether they are aware of it or not, have 'a terrible love of war'. There is something in us that is attracted to the manic state, the sense of urgency that war creates. We romanticize war in books and films. The theme of war repeats in our artistic output, from kitsch to the magisterial, even as we understand (or think we understand) the butchery that war is. Another psychologist (and philosopher), William James, who is known as the father of American psychology, wrote a fascinating essay titled 'The Moral Equivalent of War' (1910). In that essay, James wrote, concerning the draw to and fascination with warfare:

> The *Philosophie des Krieges* [Philosophy of War], by S. R. Steinmetz is good example. War, according to this author, is an ordeal instituted by God, who weighs the nations in its balance. It is the essential form of the State, and the only function in which peoples can employ all their powers at once and convergently. No victory is possible save as the resultant of a totality of virtues, no defeat for which some vice or weakness is not responsible. Fidelity, cohesiveness, tenacity, heroism, conscience, education, inventiveness, economy, wealth, physical health and vigor – there isn't a moral or intellectual point of superiority that doesn't tell, when God holds his assizes and hurls the peoples upon one another. *Die Weltgeschichte ist das Weltgericht* [The world's history is the judgment upon the world]; and Dr. Steinmetz does not believe that in the long run chance and luck play any part in apportioning the issues.
>
> The virtues that prevail, it must be noted, are virtues anyhow, superiorities that count in peaceful as well as in military competition; but the strain is on them, being infinitely intenser in the latter case, makes war infinitely more searching as a trial. No ordeal is comparable to its winnowings. Its dread hammer is the welder of men into cohesive states, and nowhere but in such states can human nature adequately develop its capacity. The only alternative is "degeneration."[1]

War is thought to be part of human destiny, 'the essential form of the State'. War quickens. It brings on feelings of ecstasy (the feeling that one is standing outside of oneself). It creates bonds of community and friendship that are deeply felt and often life-long. 'Fidelity, cohesiveness, tenacity' are part and parcel of warfare. For a brief moment, on September 11, 2001, and for several months thereafter, we experienced this heightened state of alertness and 'togetherness', and we were ready to set aside our normal disagreements over policy and politics. In the United States, Americans bathed in a sense of commonality and felt urgently the need for a shared venture to destroy an existential threat. The treasure and emotional resources were quite literally *marshalled* by political and other leaders, and something felt right about this, at least for many.

In the preceding pages I urged that the only way to properly address serious issues in commercial ethics is to bring to the surface the existential realities of people's lives, rather than to instantiate a checklist of dos and don'ts to be followed if one is to be a decent citizen, or rehearse the insights of normative ethicists. In both war and commerce the existential looms, most pronouncedly as existential *threat*. I continue to hold that the model we should hold out in our commercial lives, and especially in our duties as employees, executives, and entrepreneurs, is the model of *service*, The Ministerial Model. That is, as you will recall, I urged that we need to reframe our understanding of our commercial selves so that we first and foremost see ourselves as beings engaged in *service*, rather than in acquisition and conquest. But, of course, the flip side of service will always be the need to acquire, to appropriate what we, as individuals and as persons (the terms do not have the same meaning), need for our survival and for flourishing. Our fragility, our dependence, is recalled by a constant series of triggers encountered all throughout our lives, starting with the gnawing in our stomachs, but extending to the gnawing hunger for recognition, adulation, respect, and even (for many) immortality.

The existential threat, our neediness, fragility, and dependence, are fully engaged in commerce. What many philosophers who disdain business and commerce refuse to or fail to appreciate is that business and commerce are at the heart of what it means to be human, not peripheral to it. It is, in many ways, much simpler to understand the marketplace as a vale of seekers, hunters, sowers (recall the reference to the 'harvesting of companies' from the business of private equity – an expression that caused US presidential candidate Mitt Romney (2007) not a little trouble) rather than as a vale of ministers seeking to service the needs of others. For isn't it our individual neediness that brings us to market in the first place? Isn't it our awareness of what we need and what we want that drives us into commerce, at least most of the time? Isn't the hope that drives us the hope that one day we will be secure and sated, so that we can withdraw from commercial life, and no longer need to appear as supplicant, enduring the often monotonous rhythms of workaday existence, the indignities of callous, tyrannical or sometimes reprobate bosses, the sometimes inanity or abrasiveness of colleagues, the gritty monotony of the commute, the agonism of the pursuit? Isn't it the hope that we will be able to retire at a young-enough age, with all of our earthly needs provided for and our wits intact, to go and live the life we prefer to live, secure in the understanding that the maladies of poverty and disrepute are far from us?

What is sought is a sated autonomy, but we want to achieve it by 'winning' the 'game', 'winning' the 'war'. One gets one's repose through 'manly' and aggressive engagement in the 'battlefields' of commerce – 'battlefields' because everyone else seeks the same things, for the most part, and the money and status and access sought – to power and opportunity – are limited, scarce. To get what one wants and what one needs one must compete. Competition is not always docile; sometimes it is bruising; often it is unfair. Again, it is *agonistic*. To 'play the game' you have to learn to outmaneuver your competitors (adversaries), outsmart them, and 'vanquish' them when necessary. No one is going to hand you what you want; you must *take* it. And in commerce there are various ways that we position ourselves to take it, depending upon the 'point of access', whether the point of access is via a farm, a factory, or an executive suite. Maslow would seem to have been right – the human body and the human psyche are usefully described as, and within, a hierarchy of needs. If you don't get what you need – whether somatically or psychologically – you perish, or are at least wounded, may turn on yourself and pronounce yourself a 'loser'. We human beings prefer to surround ourselves with both people who are 'winners' and people who can help us to 'win'. There is little room for 'losers'. This is why the poor are so often forgotten, why those with mental illnesses are so often relegated to social 'dungeons', and why those who are the recipients of public assistance are stigmatized. Our primal animal spirits have a large role to play in all of this.

Isn't this how many (though certainly not all) people approach the world of commerce, albeit with an endearing Elmer Gantry smile and glad-handing – social niceties that mask the real 'game' that is afoot – 'the kill', the acquisition? In fact, it even gets romanticized in a way. Herbert Spencer was quick to construe aspects of Charles Darwin's *On the Origin of Species* as providing an explication for 'the survival of the fittest' (Spencer's term; it was not coined by Darwin) and to suggest that human society is a struggle for survival against others, others who are sometimes more powerful, more cunning, more swift. Spencer joined others in creating various notions of 'Social Darwinism', which expressed itself in the age of the robber barons in America (many of whom saw Darwin's theory, as well as Spencer's own social and political theories, as justification for ruthless business practices). Since the agonistic is written into nature, since we cannot help but strive against forces that threaten our existence, since nature is red in tooth and claw, should we not shift our attentions and concerns away from those who are weak and learn from (and celebrate) those who are strong? These discredited ideas have been turned-back in modern, civilized societies, but they are still pervasive enough and they bubble just below the surface of the constraints and particulars of civility. It is, alas, a rather primal mindset, reinforced from our youths, and tied to our amygdalae. And it is as real in the worlds of philanthropy and academia as it is in the commodities trading pits, although, perhaps, not always expressed to the same degree or in the same ways. That community, compromise, and mutualism have marked the evolutionary ascent of humanity is not an idea that captures the imagination in quite the same way as the fears that attend our neediness and the imperatives of agonistic contest.

The frame of agonism works its way into other fora. We have 'Chainsaw' Al Dunlap and Raj Rajaratnum and Jeff Skilling as focal points of those who pursued 'the edge' in business (as discussed earlier), but 'edginess' is not limited to corporate suites and hedge fund managers. We find it throughout the culture. In our entertainment, we are enthralled by the 'bad ass' hero, who quickly dispatches all who oppose him, even if he is on the wrong side of the moral fence. We admire Superman, but we admire, as well, Don Corleone, and in our popular music we indulge in 'gangsta rap', which has kept several generations of young and not-so-young people bopping and flowing in primal affirmation, albeit sometimes muted and latent affirmation, to the sounds of performers such as Ill Bill:

> Hey yo, I smoke dust and shoot cops, sold guns to Tupac
> Smoked blunts with Biggie Smalls and sold drugs on newlots [New Lots Ave., Brooklyn]
> I was too young, couldnt get up in clubs back in the old days
> We used rob and terrorize kids in front of homebase
> If Funkmaster Flex was inside, rockin the whole place
> We was outside, smacking kids and snatchin gold chains
> Baggin mad pigeons [young women], catchin mad digits, bad bitches
> And when they husbands came around we had to blast bisquits [handguns]
> A bunch of bad Brooklyn kids that always had pistols
> Broken dreams and broken homes, we always had issues
> And mad problems worshippin gangstas and bankrobbers
> Watchin star [friends] fade startin fights and rap conscience (?)
> Until we realized how to get the real money
> Steal money, kidnap money, kill money
> Its funny how the money make the whole world love you
> Jealous cats hate you, dime pigeons
> Little ghetto children run up on you, wanna touch you
> Got the IRS lookin at you, wanna fuck you
> Sniffin so much blow, you don't know if you can trust you
> Ecstasy react to what the cocaine and the dust do
> Go against the Ill Bill, and Non Phixion [a rap group] will crush you, bust you
> Leave you with a tube and ya throat to suck through
> We truck jewels, we dust brothers fuck mothers
> You thugs love us, the gunslingers and drughustlers
> Where my gangstas at?[2]

'You thugs love us', goes the lyric. The 'You' is, of course, *us* – all of us, at least to some degree – or that is at least what the rapper hopes or assumes. In these lyrics one will find Maslow, the existential need for recognition, the celebration of the move from social powerlessness to a place of social power – a power that we all crave, to one degree or another. The truth of gangsta rap, regardless of whether it is to one's taste, is that it is the understandable (shall we say, natural?) *cri de couer* of the once outcast, the once powerless, who seems to boil the truth of human existence down to its most elemental, primal forms – the struggle to survive and thrive. Gangsta rap is social Darwinism cloaked in a gritty and captivating urban aesthetic, just as Wall Street is, all too often, social Darwinism cloaked in Hugo Boss, Ferrari, Patek Phillipe, and Hamptons retreats. These urban neologisms express the sentiments of many on Wall Street, to varying degrees. Gansta rap may as well be the background music in many Wall Street trading rooms– even the more or less quiet ones.

Gangsta rap is the red light district of music (or at least one of them) and,as I have said,Wall Street is the red light district of commerce. What draws people to listen to Ill Bill or to watch Don Corleone is their *audacity*, the pure festival of *seizure*. For in a world in which what you want or need will not yield, one must take by force. If you fail to take you will be taken, and so the world is divided into two sets of people, the takers and the taken. If you are not a taker, then you will be a 'muppet', or in gangsta rap jargon, a 'sucka'. 'It's funny how the money make the whole world love you', the lyric goes. And just as we are fascinated by such audacity, drawn to it, romanticize it (as we still romanticize tales of piracy on the high seas), we celebrate audacity concentrated in a single 'place' where we can see it lived out, played out, on a daily basis. In commerce, that place is Wall Street. The bell rings to open trading, just as it rings to commence pugilism, and both close with a bell. This is the *tradition* – what is handed down to us. Agonism is what fills the time in between. What does Jordan Belfort say? – 'Let me tell you something. There's no nobility in poverty. I've been a poor man, and I've been a rich man. And I choose rich every fucking time'. And:

> My name is Jordan Belfort ... I'm a former member of the middle class raised by two accountants in a tiny apartment in Bayside Queens. The year I turned 26 as the head of my own brokerage firm I made 49 million dollars, which really pissed me off because it was three shy of a million a week.[3]

You don't counteract primal animal spirits such as these by rehearsing the 'Categorical Imperative', or with talk about *phronesis*, or with discussions of *arete*. This is the problem with business ethics education, in my view – it does not engage our primal animal spirits head on, as the lion tamer must address the lion's inveterate animal spirits head on, or be eaten. I have been before students rehearsing Kant and Mill and Aristotle, and I could see the 'lion' in the eyes of some of them, could detect it in their body language and in the tone of their voices –

perhaps future Jordan Belforts, who had already concluded that all of this talk about Kant, Mill and Aristotle (or even real cases that highlighted the principles discussed) were but interesting thought experiments with no real application, save for those who opt to be the taken rather than the takers.

How to tame the 'lion', bring it under control? It was not too long after those first few classes that I realized that it was necessary to reach into the students' *souls* if I wanted to get my message across; to guide them, slowly, out of their more animalistic assumptions about business and commerce, and introduce them to another nature, equally powerful, that could take their positive animal spirits (powerful spirits of loyalty, care, community and even patriotism) and direct them toward the needs of the commonweal. I had to let the students know that I have primal animal spirits, too. I see the 'lion' in their eyes because there is also a 'lion' in my own. But there are also other spirits, the spirits of community, of brotherhood and sisterhood, of *we*. There are also the positive animal spirits that are fed when others respect you, cheer for your success, stand ready to aid you when you are in need, and will comfort you when you are sick, and (you are certain) will converge at the hour of your death to deliver orations regarding a life well-lived. These thoughts stir us, too, and can stir us even more than the spirits of seizure and commercial warfare.

We Have the Wall Street We Want

My students come from both the United States and from far flung places where the story of the inner 'lion' is reinforced again and again – by parents, teachers, peers, movies, video games. Sometimes, they arrive from countries that are impoverished, and so they are hungry, eager to finally 'make it' and end the cycles of poverty that have so plagued their families, their people. The taste for 'the kill' is introduced early in life, well before they show up to my classroom. It is incubated in their wrinkled stomachs, and if not theirs then in the wrinkled stomachs of those who surrounded them in their cities, towns, and villages. In this there is more than a small clue to the problem of Wall Street's pathologies. And in the United States and the rest of the developed world, Wall Street is the quintessential place for fast riches, riches that can end – quickly – generations of deprivation, as well as keep the cycles of stunning wealth turning with an ongoing sense of entitlement.

Wall Street will never be completely reformed until the citizenry reforms itself. Reform the Wall Street we have by means of coercive regulation alone and another will spring up, unless we change, as a civilization, how we understand work, markets, money, leisure, success, and commerce. For it is the citizenry that, unconsciously, *wants* Wall Street to exist. They want it as a place where they can roll the dice and win their freedom from financial mediocrity or poverty. They want it because they want a place to which their kids can go to 'make a killing' even if they cannot. They want Wall Street because Wall Street is controlled warfare, and so offers a form of martial romance. I have students who tell me, despite all they learn in my classes, that they still admire Gordon Gekko (as part of their studies they have to watch the film *Wall Street*, and many others). The audacity of the character entrances. Gordon Gekko takes, he extracts, he is both immoral and amoral because the world of morality is for 'suckers' and 'losers' – he is therefore more alive than others, having liberated himself from the constraints that block the path to the life and capabilities that only wealth, it is assumed, can provide. He is the *Übermensch* for whom conventional morality is 'slave morality'. It does not matter that he is also a species of sociopath. To these students he is simply a realist, living in a world in which *extraction* is the name of the game. We may recall Gordon Gekko's famous 'greed is good' speech:

> The point is, ladies and gentlemen, that greed – for lack of a better word – is good. Greed is right. Greed works. Greed clarifies, cuts through, and captures the essence of the evolutionary spirit. Greed, in all of its forms – greed for life, for money, for love, for knowledge – has marked the upward surge of mankind. And greed – you mark my words – will not only save Teldar Paper, but that other malfunctioning corporation called the USA.[4]

Gekko's conclusions sound compelling, but they are half-baked, untutored, ill-informed, and plagued by a category error that conflates a nation-state and a corporation. Had he (and the real 'Gekkos' who emulate him) had the intellectual resources to draw upon he would have found the 'better word' that could have allowed him to remain in the game of intelligent investing and trading (functions needed in any economy, we should not forget) without setting himself on a path to self-destruction and deeper sociopathology. The better word that Gekko might have selected in his famous, or infamous, 'Teldar Paper' speech, is 'Aspiration'. *Aspiration* is right. *Aspiration* works. *Aspiration* clarifies, cuts though, captures the spirit of growth and improvement. *Aspiration*, in most of its forms – for life, for money, for love, for knowledge – has marked the upward surge of humankind. For *Aspiration* is the steadfast longing for a higher goal. *Aspiration* is good, *ceteris paribas*. Greed, by definition, is a vice.

Thomas Hobbes told us in his *Leviathan* that the only way to provide security from a life that is 'nasty, brutish, and short' (that is, a life of savagery) is to cede certain of our rights to a sovereign, who alone would have the power to protect our property and our persons. That Hobbes may have granted too much authority to such a sovereign (an understandable error, given the bloodshed that Hobbes had seen in his own country and knew of from history books) does not discount the fact that it is the social compact that provides the conditions for peace, security and welfare, however imperfect that compact may be at times. The Belfort and Gekko mindsets, formed in part through experiencing or witnessing deprivation, are rooted in the awareness of the same sorts of existential threats that led Hobbes to write *Leviathan*. But the real Belfort and fictional Gekko had no faith in the compact, so their law became the law of the jungle, and their business conduct became commercial savagery, however 'civilized' the savagery appeared to be. To make their lives lush and florid (and hopefully long) they would render the lives of others, if necessary, nasty, brutish (and if necessary) short. Beneath their two thousand dollar suits, luxury automobiles and art collection beats the heart of the commercial savage.

We have the power to mitigate the existential threats that stir and provoke the 'lion' within each of us. This is done by replacing market values with communal ones, the virtues of the market with civic virtue, the fear of falling into abject poverty with a social safety net that makes such a fall nearly impossible and that is spread pursuant to the assumption that we are first and foremost members of common political community, bound by a collection of promises, promises that we pledge to defend with our lives. It is all too easy, as market libertarians and some conservatives do, to suggest that there is a downside to the welfare state – that it can infantilize those who rely upon it too much. I fully agree that it can, and I have seen this sort of infantilization myself. But the fear of falling into poverty generates behaviours that are sociopathic, creates the Gekkos and the Belforts that result in the ruin of businesses, communities, and lives, and that erode trust and produce cynicism in the young, which distrust and cynicism get passed on to the next generation. So the worry of infantilization and dependence has a match in the worry that an ethos of egocentric commercial savagery will continue to cause scandal and market disruption, and continue to erode the bonds of trust, which, in turn leads to scandal and raids upon the public treasure. It is not, or should not be, hard to see that in societies with weak safety nets, great inequality, and few paths to upward mobility, corruption is rampant, as each member of the society takes his survival and security into his or her own hands. The ethos of rugged individualism, which for sure has a claim to some admiration, is not an ethos that has a significant place in developed economies with developed markets that rest upon democratic principles.

This apparent leap to a discussion of the welfare state is really no leap at all. It rests upon simple observations and the documentation of scores of development economists. The anomic behaviours – and the behaviours of Belfort (a real person) and Gordon Gekko (a fictional one) are nothing if not anomic – that we see in societies with high levels of poverty and inequality are sowed in the soil of existential threat. Reduce that threat, and you reduce the anomic behaviours and, equally important, you reduce the *excuses* for, and tolerance of, commercial savagery. Human beings will always tend to 'go anomic' if we feel insecure, and we will justify such anomic behaviours by pointing to what we take to be a world that has no real interest in who we are, what we hope for, the things we love or, indeed, whether we live or die. There is a direct relationship between our scandals and our social insecurity, even where the scandals are the result of the actions of financial elites.

The welfare state was not only constructed out of compassion for others, it was constructed in view of the knowledge of what deprivation and fear can do to a political community, to civic virtue, to a desire to carry out the duties of citizenship. What goes missing, however, in our recollections of the rise of the welfare state is that such deprivation and fear form people with certain characters, and those characters, once the deprivation and fear are abated, have been shaped so that avoidance of the previous conditions is the highest priority. Yet, I already hear the objections by those who would suggest that linking the scandals of Wall Street to the need for a robust welfare state is untenable or problematic. Some may hold, for example, that a little fear is good for the soul. That it is the desire to get ahead in the world (our aspirations) that motivates us, that it is the pot of gold at the end of the commercial rainbow that motivates us to build successful businesses and careers, that we live for the coming reward, to reap where we have sown.

All of this is true. A little fear is indeed a good thing, as is the pursuit of the things and style of life to which we aspire, assuming it is not indecent. And we should certainly reap what we sow, a principle famously championed by the writer of 'Ecclesiastes'. But in a society where it is possible to find oneself in dire straits through no fault of one's own, commercial savagery will remain a latent and live option for many. We can decry such commercial savagery all we wish, but such won't change the fact. When one can go bankrupt and homeless in a matter of months after the loss of a job or after suffering a financially catastrophic event, one thinks of ways to live above the vale of personal disaster, to establish a personal bulwark against the 'slings and arrows' of 'outrageous fortune', to rise above the need to 'grunt and sweat under a weary life', to borrow a few locutions from *Hamlet*. A society in which the citizenry takes seriously the bonds of the political compact, in which each citizen is seen as an equal fellow with a special moral demand upon our own time and resources (and this mutually), in which all the members are seen as members of a fraternal and sororal order (as political 'brothers' and 'sisters') – that society will replicate itself such that the highest value is placed not upon the needs of the market but rather upon the maintenance of the fraternal and sororal bonds that markets are established to serve, and will make as pervasive the duty of mutual care and relief as it makes pervasive the duty of industriousness, innovation, and personal responsibility.

Wall Street's transgressions are rooted in the bygone ethos of a world well lost, a world of robber barons and of social institutions that failed to take proper care of those who funded them, or upon whose backs they were built. One need only read the realities of such a world (in, for example, the writings of Jonathan Swift, Charles Dickens, Jacob Riis, and Upton Sinclair) to understand why we have endeavored to leave that ethos behind. Yet, too many on Wall Street valorize this ethos, the ethos of a world well lost. Obviously, the conditions that obtained in the works of the writers referenced have been mitigated to a great degree (though with the kicking and screaming of moneyed interests every step of the way), yet the ethos abides, and like a virus that hides dormant for a time in the body's occult organs, it lives on in the occult places of the commercial world – in the culture and values of Wall Street, among other places. We are not now concerned with the working conditions of the Chicago meatpacking industry that Upton Sinclair shined a light upon and exposed, but rather with something that is in many ways far worse – the self-dealing manipulation of the fortunes of billions of people, and the creation of systemic risks that can bring down the economies of nations and smother the prospects and aspirations of countless millions. Look back at the crisis of 2007/8 and it will be difficult to conclude that what I say here is hyperbole. While Dodd-Frank and other checks have been set in place, the thinking has barely changed. The virus has been better contained, but not killed. Only a *metanoia* can do that.

I have been pretty hard on Wall Street in this book, but I want to make it clear that many honest and decent people are employed there, and these include investment bankers, hedge fund principals, traders, brokers, analysts, accountants, risk officers, compliance officers, marketers, portfolio managers, and sales people. These people want reform as much as Wall Street's harshest critics do. I hope that what I have written here will lead not only to more discussion among Wall Street's critics, but will also serve to facilitate discussion among those who earn their living there – a living that has allowed them to take care of themselves, raise families, and contribute to their communities and to those in need. Indeed, some of the most generous people I know work on Wall Street. My hope for all of them is that they will be freed of the 'patina of shit' – to reference *Michael Clayton* one last time – that coats the financial services industry. Perhaps they will use some of the recommendations that follow in the next chapter to start new conversations about what must be done.

6 WALL STREETS, 2025

Part of the problem was that only in an environment of crisis can the self-regulators galvanize themselves to actions that they couldn't otherwise take. We had Congress pressing us against any of these [difficult reform] initiatives. We had Congress constantly bearing down on the Commission: 'Don't take steps which would hurt the firms, don't take steps which would change the way business is being done' ... When Congress sees these scandals taking place ... [it becomes] the latter-day Elmer Gantry, protecting investors that [it] had abused so badly before.

Arthur Levitt[1]

Changes in Wall Street culture will, as I have argued, be the result of a combination of an industry and public *metanoia* (the public *metanoia* having to do with The Other Wall Street) and concrete reforms in the way financial services firms conduct business, which in turn will depend on the leaders of these firms cultivating a Third-Wave Economic Imagination. In ten years' time, Wall Street can be well on its way to a different sense of itself and enjoy a very different public perception, although to expect wholesale change in ten years is probably to entertain delusion. Nevertheless, one cannot merely hope for change, one must draw a roadmap to it. So what I would like to do now is lay out some proposals that can move us toward cultural reform, can serve as a partial roadmap.

The proposals that are included in this chapter were drafted in October of 2011, at the height of the so-called Occupy movement (centered in Zuccotti Park in lower Manhattan, New York City, and subsequently spreading to other cities (and countries) from there), and submitted to those in the movement (by various means, including handing them out on the streets of New York City). There were and are 50 proposals, introduced by an essay that was both critical and supportive of the movement (titled '50 Proposals for Reform and Reclamation: In Solidarity with the Wall Street Protesters and the 99 Percenters'). Herein, some of the proposals are fleshed-out substantially, with others left more or less in their original form. The proposals are grouped, loosely, by theme. Some have to do with large, even sweeping, changes, such as Proposal 1, which calls for the overturn of the *Citizens United* decision, handed down by the US Supreme Court in 2010 (which removed limits on the amount of money corporations may spend in political campaigns, and which I believe is more than tangentially relevant to Wall Street cultural reform, given the banks' and broker-dealers' oft-demonstrated lobbying power), while others have to do with changes that are more or less 'inside baseball' and that only Wall Street operatives would grasp on first blush. *The issues or problems addressed by each proposal should be taken as representative of similar issues connected to it (issues of trust, fairness, accountability, etc.).*

I have little doubt but that some of the proposals are controversial, to one degree or another. The proposal regarding the overturn of *Citizens United* will be criticized by libertarians (for political and other reasons), but so will certain 'inside baseball' proposals, such as concerning the banning of soft dollars and calling for a financial transactions tax. Certain of the proposals were, very consciously, written into torrents of existing opposition, but that is because I am not at all convinced, at least so far, by the counterarguments. I hope what follows contributes to the conversation and debates.

50 Proposals for Reform and Reclamation

Public Policy Proposals

Proposal 1

The Supreme Court's decision in Citizens United v. Federal Election Commission ('Citizens United') *warrants an amendment to the United States constitution, so that the decision will be, effectively, overturned.*[2]

As *The New York Times* editorial board put it just after the court ruled,

> With a single, disastrous 5-to-4 ruling, the Supreme Court has thrust politics back to the robber-baron era of the 19th century. Disingenuously waving the flag of the First Amendment, the court's conservative majority has paved the way for corporations to use their vast treasuries to overwhelm elections and intimidate elected officials into doing their bidding.[3]

Here is an excerpt from the oral arguments in the case, beginning with Justice Jean Paul Stevens, who wrote a blistering dissenting opinion:

> *Justice Stevens*: One of the amicus briefs objects to – responds to Justice Kennedy's problem by saying that the problem is we have got to contribute to both parties, and a lot of [corporations] do, don't they?
>
> *[Solicitor] General Kagan*: A lot of them do, which is a suggestion about how corporations engage the political process and how corporations are different from individuals in this respect. You know, an individual can be the wealthiest person in the world but few of us – maybe some – but few of us are only our economic interests. We have beliefs,

we have convictions; we have likes and dislikes. Corporations engage the political process in an entirely different way and this is what makes them so much more damaging.

Chief Justice Roberts: Well, I suppose some do, but let's say if you have ten individuals and they each contribute $1,000 to a corporation, and they say, "we want this corporation to convey a particular message," why can't they do that, when if they did that as partnership, it would be all right?

General Kagan: Well, it sounds to me as though the corporation that you were describing is a corporation of the kind we have in this case, where one can assume that the members all sign on to the corporation's ideological mission, where the corporation in fact has an ideological mission.[4]

Citizens United was wrongly decided. It was a decision that harkens back to the 'business shall rule' climate of the *Lochner* era in the United States at the beginning of the twentieth century, the era of First-Wave Economic Imagination during which a narrow view was taken concerning the rights of businesses to operate without the 'police powers' of government brought to bear on their decisions and operations in the interests of larger public policy objectives.[5] But it is, unfortunately, the law of the land in the United States. The citizenry, composed of real and not artificial persons, must make it clear that it does not wish to go in the direction that the Court has taken it. Whether or not the notion that 'corporations' should maintain and enjoy some of the *indicia* and regard of natural persons need not be at issue, since such indicia and regard have served very useful social purposes (on this point I generally *disagree* with leftist critics of corporations who abjure corporations' status as artificial persons, and I view such criticisms as shallow and unduly sentimentalist).

This does not mean, however, that the power of for-profit corporations should be permitted to be arrayed against real citizens as is now permitted. The argument of transitive rights (that for-profit corporations are merely expressing the will of the stakeholders who control them, one of Justice Scalia's arguments) rings hollow in the face of enormous corporate power. For one thing, it is hard to know just what the interests of those stakeholders are, and it is an assumption that the corporation's financial interests take precedence over the other, and perhaps many, interests of those stakeholders, even though those stakeholders would see the corporation perform well.

While I understand the substance of the arguments on both sides of the decision in *Citizens United*, the net result is further perversion of the democracy – a hidden triangulation of powerful wealthy interests against the needs and aspirations of average citizens, who are real and not merely artificial persons. The effects of purely theoretical and academic arguments do not uncommonly have undesirable effects when they become written into public policy, unless, that is, they are appropriately seasoned by experience. Justice John Paul Stevens, with an eye to such worldly experience (the centuries of worldly experience with corporate abuses and betrayal of the public) had this to say in a passionate, almost derisive, dissent from the majority (one may take special note of his characterization of the majority's approach):

> The Court's blinkered and aphoristic approach to the First Amendment may well promote corporate power at the cost of the individual and collective self-expression the Amendment was meant to serve. It will undoubtedly cripple the ability of ordinary citizens, Congress, and the States to adopt even limited measures to protect against corporate domination of the electoral process. Americans may be forgiven if they do not feel the Court has advanced the cause of self-government today ...
>
> When corporations use general treasury funds to praise or attack a particular candidate for office, it is the shareholders, as the residual claimants, who are effectively footing the bill. Those shareholders who disagree with the corporation's electoral message may find their financial investments being used to undermine their political convictions.[6]

It is precisely this 'footing of the bill' by shareholders that was at issue almost a century ago in the famous debate between Adolph Berle, Jr. and E.M. Dodd, Jr., discussed below. Ironically, it is also the concern often expressed by market libertarians, such as the late Milton Friedman. It is the concern, not only about the dissipation of shareholder assets by managements (the old agency problem), but the interference of corporations in public policy formation that goes well beyond the interests of the business.

Shareholders (many of whom are citizens) are the ultimate owners of (though not the only stakeholders in) corporate assets, though they often forget that fact. They have the power, if properly organized, to compel the corporations that they own to limit the level of shareholder money that can be expended on political campaigns, in lobbying and in other forms of issue advocacy. This could entail using the proxy rules promulgated by the SEC, which permit shareholders to call for a vote on matters affecting shareholders and shareholder rights (see Appendix II). In addition, state legislatures can pass legislation that would make it easier to compel corporations (and other forms of organized entity), domiciled in their states, to allow a shareholder vote on the expenditure of corporate assets in political elections/campaigns. These measures would be needed because managers resist shareholder 'meddling' in corporate decision making. It is important to note that federal and state initiatives would be required to make this work since, in the United States, corporations are (for the most part) creatures of the various states. That will be discussed in my next proposal, below.

Beyond these measures, concerned voters could force state legislatures to pass laws that would act as a drag on the expenditure of corporate assets on political campaigns. These could include detailed, mandatory reporting explicating the reason for and nature of contributions. Corporations should be forced to demonstrate that their contributions to political campaigns (or issue advocacy) have more than a tenuous connection to actual business interests. At the federal level, corporations could be required to disclose detailed contribution reports in federal filings and post the information, conspicuously, on their corporate web-sites.

There are, clearly, other things that need to be done now, at the grass roots level. It is no exaggeration to say that there is much at stake. Not only does *Citizens United* mean a clear and present danger to democracy (not just the actual democracy comprised of laws, practices and institutions, but the very *idea* of democracy, as properly construed in modern political philosophy), it makes the thoughtful, historically-minded observer recall the roles that corporations played in the Germany of 1933 to 1945, and what President Eisenhower warned about, i.e. a military-industrial complex that has grown so powerful that the citizenry has lost control of it. Only now, it is not the military-industrial complex that we must fear, but a newer and more robust corporate-political complex that far exceeds anything that we have yet seen.

When it comes to *Citizens United* and Wall Street, one need only review the drag placed on the adoption of the Volcker Rule (a rule that was adopted under Dodd-Frank to ban most proprietary trading by banks) to understand the problem of unlimited amounts of money being spent to sway elected officials. (Though proposed in 2009, because of the relentless efforts of bank lobbyists, final rules to allow the Volcker Rule's implementation were not adopted in 2014.) Corporate lobbyists representing the biggest banks in the country descended on Capitol Hill by the scores, being paid tens of millions of dollars to block the Volcker Rule's inclusion in the Dodd Frank reform law, and then, once that failed, to water it down substantially. It can be debated whether banks' ability to engage in proprietary trading, in general, was a major cause of the financial crisis of 2007/8. But it is *clear* that proprietary trading had a *substantial* role to play, since it was banks' *principal* (rather than agency) exposures to troubled proprietary investments that caused some of the largest among them, perhaps most notably Citigroup, to find themselves in serious trouble.

The fact is that the 2008 final crisis forced policymakers to revisit the very purposes of banks in the financial system (a process of *recollection*, which is, of course, not the first time this has had to happen). First, banks are indispensable – as *banks*, not as hedge funds which take substantial risks with investors' money and are designed for just this purpose. Banks exist to safe-keep money in the form of deposits, and to provide credit to keep businesses and consumers flush with needed (or reasonably desirable amounts of) liquidity. But it was a full-court press of lobbying efforts (including campaign contributions to both parties) on the part of the banking industry that changed the traditional business model of banks. The Financial Crisis Inquiry Report tells us:

> [T]he financial industry itself played a key role in weakening regulatory constraints
> on institutions, markets, and products. It did not surprise the Commission that an
> industry of such wealth and power would exert pressure on policy makers and regu-

lators. From 1999 to 2008, the financial sector expended $2.7 billion in reported federal lobbying expenses; individuals and political action committees in the sector made more than $1 billion in campaign contributions. What troubled us was the extent to which the nation was deprived of the necessary strength and independence of the oversight necessary to safeguard financial stability ... [The banks and other financial firms] took on enormous exposures in acquiring and supporting subprime lenders and creating, packaging, repackaging, and selling trillions of dollars in mortgage-related securities, including synthetic financial products. Like Icarus, they never feared flying ever closer to the sun. Many of these institutions grew aggressively through poorly executed acquisition and integration strategies that made effective management more challenging. The CEO of Citigroup told the Commission that a $40 billion position in highly rated mortgage securities would "not in any way have excited my attention," and the co-head of Citigroup's investment bank said he spent a "small fraction of" his time on those securities.[7]

It is no wonder that, with the enormous amount of 'free speech' (read, money) directed at policymakers by the industry, banks and other financial institutions were given an increasingly free hand to transform their traditional business models in ways that would yield greater profits, greater freedom of movement, and greater risk. No one in a capitalist society begrudges institutions increased profits by taking on greater risk in a reasonable manner. The willingness to assume rational risks is the hallmark of entrepreneurship and innovation, as well as personal growth. Without risk there is stagnation. But banks are given their public charters for a reason – to be *banks*. When lobbyists, and those whose bidding they do, slowly chip away at the fundamental logics upon which the economy and the financial markets rest, 'free speech' (in the form of money) has gone too far. When the Volcker Rule finally emerged from its long gauntlet through the paths of its enemies, here is what one newspaper wrote:

> When the long-awaited Volcker Rule finally emerged last week, the outside world took out its magnifying glass. The advance buzz had said it would be 'tougher than expected'. But soon enough, critics were poring over the text, spotting weaknesses, comparing notes, and even, in a few cases, calling it things like 'Washington's latest bonanza for lawyers and lobbyists'.[8]

As is often the case with corporate lobbying, the banks have been somewhat disingenuous in their opposition to the Volcker Rule, throwing up a dust storm of dubious arguments that were sure to bedazzle the US Congress (many members being untutored in the arcane language of finance) and, most certainly, the average citizen. One of the things that the banks argued is that it is hard to tell the difference between a 'proprietary trade' and a trade done for, say, you or me, as a bank customer, otherwise known as an 'agency trade'. This is an interesting but cheeky argument. The accounting departments of banks have always been able to determine when revenue is coming from trades for other people (agency trades because the banks are acting as agent for someone else) and trades done for 'the house' (proprietary trades). At a minimum, they have had to do this for tax and management reporting purposes. The banks, and their cohorts in the securities industry, wanted the regulators and Congress to believe that the difference between a proprietary trade and an agency trade is so fuzzy that, well, gosh, who can *tell* the difference? This is, of course, nonsense, although around the margins some confusion will exist. If the banks got away with this cheeky argument it would have been business as usual in a very, very big way. It would have been as though the trauma of the financial crisis never happened, as far as domestic banking was concerned. But it did happen, and it almost destroyed the financial system, and did actually ravage the savings and retirement accounts of hundreds of millions of people around the globe. It was not all the fault of banks' proprietary trading and risky investments, but much of it was.

The Supreme Court decided *Citizens United* on the grounds of the constitutional right to free speech, which has indeed been extended historically to entities such as labor unions and other forms of corporate association. A major problem with *Citizens United* has to do with the drawing of the right kinds of distinctions and focusing on the real issue, which is not that all institutions pose the same sorts of threats to democratic decision-making, but that extremely wealthy interests can 'speak' so loudly in the protection of narrow corporate interests over and against, say, the interests of a town or hamlet or even a demographic (say, children or the elderly) that a way must be found to, as they say in the law, 'balance the equities'. It rests upon a principal of just proportion and fairness which may be enough to trump free speech rights in certain cases. That is to say, 'balancing the equities' may be enough to permit corporate speech (its content, as well as a certain level of substantial scope), while not allowing domination of other important voices. In a democracy actual edification is a value. Where edification is aborted because of the dominance of the voice of special, narrow pecuniary interests, especially ones whose goal is to distort the truth (there is a very significant history of lies and distortions coming from business interests which are quite easy to present as evidence with a simple internet search), then harm is done to the democratic processes of governance, and to democratic culture which consists in a mind-set of truth telling and trust and the open flow of information (all things that capitalism and free markets purportedly require for them to work as they should). This is equally true if the spending (the 'speaking') is done by labour unions or even charities. But of course, labour unions and charities do not have endless pots of cash to spend on political speech, and their focus is directly on the aid of human beings as such – workers, the environment, the elderly, scientific research, etc., and not narrow business interests. Those who argue that businesses also have as their goal an increased quality of life for human beings as such are confusing, at best, outcomes with goals – an error frequently made in defense of extreme *laissez-faire* capitalism, as I have argued earlier. The 'voices' of Institutions whose *raison d'etre* is improved quality of life for actual human beings should be given a special standing in a democracy for at least two reasons.

First, business is rife with narrowly self-interested people, and the business's own interests are more or less narrow, though with residual social benefits, even when businesses rightly see their mission as the creation of customers rather than maximizing profits. Second, businesses cause negative externalities of a sort that is rarely akin to those created by not-for-profit interests, and their capacity to generate these negative externalities is not infrequently connected to their power to pressure and coopt (or corrupt) policymakers.

This second reason is linked to the first. Businesses, though extremely critical to society, minister to society *only derivatively and indirectly*. Not-for-profits in general, as institutions, minister to the needs of society directly, and often maintain themselves with difficulty in doing so. The relative purity of the social missions of not-for-profits (including labour unions, which, let us not forget, exist to create bargaining parity with the managerial class that speaks on behalf of the interests of capital), their being involved more primarily in the public service, should give their voices priority, at least often, over the voices of powerful for-profit corporate interests, however valuable in a derivative way to society. The court was correct when it concluded that 'political speech is indispensable to decision-making in a democracy, and this is no less true because the speech comes from a corporation'. But it erred, as expressed in Justice Scalia's concurring remarks as elsewhere, when it makes no room for a distinction between types of corporate entity:

> The dissent says [writes Justice Scalia] that when the Framers 'constitutionalized the right to free speech in the First Amendment, it was the free speech of individual Americans that they had in mind' ... That is no doubt true. All the provisions of the Bill of Rights set forth the rights of individual men and women – not, for example, of trees or polar bears. But the individual person's right to speak includes the right to speak *in association with other individual persons*.[9]

With this, it is hard to quarrel, and I do not quarrel with it. But the observation is banal and only facially compelling. Scalia and the others in the majority seem oblivious to the following, which is why their conclusions read like the ruminations of ivory tower legal symposiasts who are out of touch with the natures of commercial and politics:

First, while in the United States the right to free speech is *nearly* absolute and unlimited, it is in fact *not* absolute and unlimited, a fact made plain to the public imagination by Justice Oliver Wendell Holmes, Jr. in *Schenck v. United States* (one does not have a right to falsely shout *Fire!* in a crowded theatre), as well as in *Chaplinsky v. New Hampshire* (which concerned 'fighting words'). Public peace and safety considerations can, at times, trump free speech rights;

Second, speech and money are *not* equivalent – no more equivalent than money and the right of assembly or the right to worship as one pleases are equivalent. Money is (or can be), rather, a tool for the *amplification* and distribution of speech. It is the amplification that is at issue, since it can drown out the voices of others. This distinction is lost on those who blithely equate money and speech;

Third, large for-profit enterprises have, for many decades, used their vast resources to hone the art of public manipulation, and are masters of irrational persuasion, subliminal messaging and deception – something that advertising laws have addressed squarely for decades. We don't let corporations get away with making untruthful claims in advertising, so we already regulate their speech, and have been for many years;

Fourth, those in opposition to *Citizens United,* for the most part, are not claiming that businesses do not have the right to publish their views and convictions through general means of communication. Therefore, the argument that limiting the expenditure of money by corporations to influence elections is a form of censorship is in fact specious. The public interest is best served by making sure that others who do not possess the resources for unlimited amplification of their speech are given a fair opportunity to be heard, and heard before it is too late – before a vote is cast by a legislator, for example; and

Fifth, the social harms done by unlimited amounts of money spent by pecuniary and narrow corporate interests are stacked high. While there are many examples of this, one need only think of the example of the tobacco industry, which was, through the expenditure of enormous amounts of money, able to squash scientific research and honest narratives that were in competition with its narrative that the health risks of tobacco are 'inconclusive', and so able to delay for generations, and only after countless millions of deaths, the truth about that claim (it was a lie, and the industry knew it was a lie). What the court marginalized is the *fact* that free speech can also include distortions and outright lies, and unlimited amounts of money gives wings to those distortions and lies. Sophisticated 'spin' is the wheelhouse of corporate marketing, communications, PR, and investor relations departments, as has been made very clear by many scholars and whistleblowers over the years, such as Wendell Potter. In Wendell Potter's book *Deadly Spin,* we are treated to a detailed accounting of how certain corporate interests manipulate the public – using vast amounts of money – to shape the narrative that will get them what they want in the marketplace. In this regard, unlimited funds provided by corporate interests, such as through Super-PACs, allow them to amplify their narratives indirectly, rather than through media ad buys and other more direct means. It is naive to think that this is some tangential point, for the money is spent to *put the corporate narrative into the mouth of the candidate* – to, in effect, turn the candidate (who may be an incumbent) into a *corporate agent.* This is at the heart of the issue, and there is nothing terribly new about the concern. But *Citizens United* extends the potential of corruption and cooption exponentially. When a public servant owes her office (that is, her income, *future* income, influence, power, and prestige) to narrow corporate interests rather than the people who elected her to serve their various interests, one cannot but conclude that such person is a public servant *in name only*, and is rather, more accurately, *a quasi-covert private agent* of narrow interests, who is permitted to speak and act as she pleases *only* when such speech and action do not impede the goals of her private masters.

Justice Stevens argued two other compelling points in his dissent:

> The financial resources, legal structure, and instrumental orientation of corporations raise legitimate concerns about their role in the electoral process. Our lawmakers have a compelling constitutional basis, if not also a democratic duty, to take measures designed to guard against the potentially deleterious effects of corporate spending in local and national races...
>
> The free speech guarantee thus does not render every other public interest an illegitimate basis for qualifying a speaker's autonomy; society could scarcely function if it did. It is fair to say that our First Amendment doctrine has "frowned on" certain identity-based distinctions ... particularly those that may reflect invidious discrimination or preferential treatment of a politically powerful group. But it is simply incorrect to suggest that we have prohibited all legislative distinctions based on identity or content. Not even close.
>
> *The election context is distinctive in many ways*, and the Court, of course, is right that the First Amendment closely guards political speech. But in this context, too, the authority of legislatures to enact viewpoint-neutral regulations based on content and identity *is well settled*. We have, for example, allowed state-run broadcasters to exclude independent candidates from televised debates. *Arkansas Ed. Television Comm'n v. Forbes*, 523 U. S. 666 (1998) ... We have upheld statutes that prohibit the distribution or display of campaign materials near a polling place. *Burson v. Freeman*, 504 U. S. 191 (1992) ... Although we have not reviewed them directly, we have never cast doubt on laws that place special restrictions on campaign spending by foreign nationals. See, *e.g.,* 2 U. S. C. §441e(a)(1). And we have consistently approved laws that bar Government employees, but not others, from contributing to or participating in political activities ... These statutes burden the political expression of one class of speakers, namely, civil servants. Yet we have sustained them on the basis of longstanding practice and Congress' reasoned judgment that certain regulations which leave "untouched full participation ... in political decisions at the ballot box," *Civil Service Comm'n v. Letter Carriers*, 413 U. S. 548, 556 (1973) ... help ensure that public officials are "sufficiently free from improper influences," *id.,* at 564, and that "confidence in the system of representative Government is not ... eroded to a disastrous extent," *id.,* at 565.
>
> The same logic applies to this case with additional force because it is the identity of corporations, rather than individuals, that the Legislature has taken into account. As we have unanimously observed, legislatures are entitled to decide "that the special characteristics of the corporate structure require particularly careful regulation" in an electoral context ... Not only has the distinctive potential of corporations to corrupt the electoral process *long been recognized*, but within the area of campaign

finance, corporate spending is also "furthest from the core of political expression, since corporations' First Amendment speech and association interests are derived largely from those of their members and of the public in receiving information" ... Campaign finance distinctions based on corporate identity tend to be less worrisome, in other words, because the "speakers" are not natural persons, much less members of our political community, and the governmental interests are of the highest order. Furthermore, when corporations, as a class, are distinguished from noncorporations, as a class, there is a lesser risk that regulatory distinctions will reflect invidious discrimination or political favouritism.

If taken seriously, our colleagues' assumption that the identity of a speaker has *no* relevance to the Government's ability to regulate political speech would lead to some remarkable conclusions. Such an assumption would have accorded the propaganda broadcasts to our troops by "Tokyo Rose" during World War II the same protection as speech by Allied commanders. More pertinently, it would appear to afford the same protection to multinational corporations controlled by foreigners as to individual Americans: To do otherwise, after all, could "'enhance the relative voice'" of some (*i.e.*, humans) over others (*i.e.*, nonhumans) ... Under the majority's view, I suppose it may be a First Amendment problem that corporations are not permitted to vote, given that voting is, among other things, a form of speech.

In short, the Court dramatically overstates its critique of identity-based distinctions, without ever explaining why corporate identity demands the same treatment as individual identity. Only the most wooden approach to the First Amendment could justify the unprecedented line it seeks to draw.[10]

Proposal 2

States should adopt statutes that allow for alternative charters and other mechanisms that give shareholders greater voice, including such greater voice as would allow managements to use substantial corporate resources to run companies in a way that reflects shareholders' disparate reasons for investing in the company and that permit longer term conclusions concerning what encompasses a company's 'best interests' and the 'best interests' of equity owners and creditors. Among other things, this will remove or lessen concerns that some shareholders will bring law suits alleging violations of fiduciary duty by boards and managements. The SEC should do all it can to lend support to these state-level changes.

Going back as far as the debate, playing out in the pages of the Harvard Law Review in 1932, between Adolph Berle, Jr. and E.M. Dodd, Jr., concerning the control of corporate assets in an age in which shareholder ownership and shareholder control had diverged, there has been a concern about allowing managers and executives (agents) to use corporate assets in any way but in pursuits of the narrow business interests of the shareholders who own the corporation. Berle won that debate. Dodd argued that corporations are social institutions with responsibilities to a wide range of what were effectively stakeholders. But Berle argued that such a position would effectively place corporate assets in the hands of managers and executives to employ to satisfy these various stakeholders, effectively removing control from shareholders and dissipating their assets in ways they had not been contemplated by them when they invested their capital. In such a situation, executives and managers could run amok. Proper control of corporate assets, for the good of the corporation, its shareholders (who are substantially removed from day to day operations and engagement with management, and so need extra mechanisms of protection) is best effected where the managers and executives, as agents, are restricted as to how corporate assets may be expended. Doing otherwise would and should, on Berle's account, be actionable, even in the form of derivative claims against management on behalf of the corporation and its shareholders.

The agency concerns raised by Berle are apt, and are still discussed today:

> We define agency relationship as a contract under which one or more persons (the principals) engage another person (the agent) to perform some service on their behalf which involves delegating some decision-making authority to the agent. If both parties to the relationship seek to further their own ends, there is good reason to believe that the agent will not always act in the best interests of the principal. The *principal* can limit divergences from his interests by establishing appropriate incentives for the *agent* and by incurring monitoring costs designed to limit the aberrant activities of the agent ... *However, it is generally impossible for the principal ... to ensure that the agent will make optimal decisions from the principal's viewpoint.*
>
> Since the relationship between the stockholders and the managers of a corporation fits precisely the definition of a pure agency relationship, it should come as no surprise to discover that the issues associated with the separation of ownership and control in the modern diffused-ownership corporation are intimately associated with the general problem of agency. The problem of inducing an "agent" to behave as if he were maximizing the welfare of the "principal" is quite general. *It exists in all organizations at every level of management in firms, in universities, in mutual companies, in cooperatives, in governmental authorities and bureaus (and) in unions.*[11]

While Berle's position still remains sound, at least in the minds of most who have given serious thought to the subject, the assumptions about what constitutes shareholders' interests have evolved, and it is no longer assumed that corporate assets need be expended under a notion of interests that is extremely narrow. Today, corporate expenditures on community activities, scholarships, and even charities can all be construed as within the sphere of corporate interests, disquotationally construed. Archer Daniels Midland Company ('ADM'), the agricultural company, has declared specific commitments to the communities and societies in which it operates (and the Archer Daniels example is but one of many). Here, demonstrating Third-Wave Economic Imagination, is what the company published concerning its broader interests:

> For more than a century, Archer Daniels Midland Company has connected the harvest to the home, transforming crops into products that serve vital needs for food and energy.

Today, we are a global leader in the production of food ingredients, animal feeds, and renewable fuels and chemicals, with 30,000 colleagues worldwide. Although our company has grown over the last century, the foundation of our business remains unchanged: our commitment to agriculture, our stakeholders, our colleagues and our communities.

Through our *ADM Cares* program, we're working to sustain and strengthen this commitment by directing funding to initiatives and organizations around the world that drive meaningful social, economic and environmental progress ...

ADM Cares is a corporate social investment program comprising three distinct focus areas: Strong Roots, Strong Bonds, Strong Communities.[12]

These initiatives are, however, at the discretion of the Board of Directors and corporate executives, who are usually human beings (so far, although in certain places, such as the United Kingdom, so-called 'corporate directors' have been plentiful, though reforms have forced companies to have at least one 'natural person' (or human being) on the company board).[13] This commitment to a wider class of stakeholders could be strengthened if the foundation of such commitment were included in the corporate charter. Archer Daniels Midland Company's certificate of incorporation states its corporate purposes using the typical minimalist language of corporations incorporated in the state of Delaware (the go-to state for the majority of US incorporations): 'The purpose of the Corporation is to engage in any lawful act or activity for which corporations may be organized under the General Corporation Law of Delaware'. That's it – the same language used by a closely held, private beauty shop, car wash, or magazine stand, established in corporate form. While there may be sound legal reasoning behind this, there seems to be an incongruity.

Suppose that the certificate of incorporation were amended, by vote of a majority of shareholders, to include the larger purposes and goals of this important and dynamic corporation, which better reflects the corporation's social and economic impact. For example, *The purpose of the Corporation is to provide agricultural and related products and services, broadly construed, to pursue other lawful business as determined by its shareholders and/or its board of directors from time to time, and to use a portion of its profits to support the interests of stakeholders in a manner congruous with its corporate purpose.* While this language may need to be amended in view of legal concerns, the point is that such language recognizes the distinction between an organization such as Archer Daniels Midland Company and an incorporated and privately held beauty shop, while at the same time gives the board and executives and other managers the explicit authority to expend assets outside of the narrow and parsimonious language that implies that an important economic agent such as Archer Daniels Midland is in the business to do anything, so long as it is lawful.

Why would such a rewrite of the corporate charters of public companies actually matter?

The shareholder democracy movement has been in full swing for some years now, and it relates to what has just been said. The idea that shareholders should have greater say as to what is done with the businesses they own – an idea that goes well beyond typical notions of shareholder activism, which often aims at the realization of value in the short-term – is one that has gained traction. It is more important now than in decades past, since shareholders are becoming increasingly distant from the corporations they own (much more than was the working assumption in the debate between Berle and Dodd, which took place long before high-frequency trading), as their ownership is more often than not indirect (via pension funds, mutual funds, and other derivatives). Luis A. Aguilar, an SEC Commissioner, pointed this out in a 2009 speech he delivered to the New America Alliance Latino Economic Forum:

> One of the most significant changes in our financial markets since the 1930s and '40s has been the decrease in the relative percentage of securities owned directly by retail investors and the substantial increase in direct holdings by institutions. Estimates indicate that in the 1950s, individuals directly owned more than 90% of public companies, and today that number is closer to 30%.
>
> These trends in retail ownership and market participation raise very important questions for shareholder participation in the capital markets and financial regulation. Accordingly, I believe the SEC staff should undertake a study of the growth of institutional ownership and the consequences for shareholders and the capital markets.
>
> The study should look into the causes and consequences of this trend, and what the SEC's response should be. Should our rules take into account whether they may create incentives for retail investors to invest through institutions rather than directly? Is that good or bad? Do we need to change the manner and content of our required disclosures? These are difficult questions that delve into many of the Commission's regulatory responsibilities. How we proceed will have profound effects on retail and institutional investors, mutual funds, advisers, operating companies, and others.[14]

Beyond this, it is my belief that general US for-profit corporations should consider charter revisions for the purposes stated above, or consider conversion, which might entail corporate redomicile to another state, to the form of 'public benefit corporation' which would make the corporation's commitments to an array of stakeholders, the communities in which it operates, and even to the environment, explicit and so clear. There are now many states with public benefit corporation statutes, including Delaware. Reorganization from the typical for-profit corporation form to the public benefit corporation form can send a serious message to managements, employees, customers and clients, and to the public about the desire of the business to be a responsible and useful economic actor, demonstrating its commitment to Third Wave Economic Imagination. Such would go beyond merely publishing social responsibility reports and distributing codes of conduct to employees. It would root the very existence of the enterprise in an ethos of stakeholder awareness and responsibility.

Proposal 3

*Regulators who violate the public trust through collusion with the firms they regu-
late (otherwise known as 'regulatory capture') should be subject to severe sanctions,
up to and including imprisonment.*[15]

While regulators obviously influence the businesses that they regulate (in any
industry), the regulated also influence regulators. To some degree this is simply human nature at work. Constant associations between regulators and those
regulated can give rise to relationships in which regulators see themselves as
industry partners, rather than watchdogs in the service of the public interest. Further, the notion of 'the public interest' is off the mark if it contains an
assumption that the regulated are no part of it. So an extension of sympathy to
the regulated by regulators is understandable, especially where there is no apparent effort to thwart regulation. While there is public pressure to maintain an
inimical posture toward regulated businesses, this is seldom beneficial. It causes
unnecessary tensions that lead regulated businesses to see government as an
enemy, and so they circle the wagons, which usually means diminished flows of
or highly guarded communication, and higher legal and compliance costs for no
other reason than to prepare for the next fight.

That being said, regulators must be made aware that the public interest
involves more than the desires of the industries that they oversee, however beneficial those industries are to society, and it certainly involves more than the interests
of regulators to obtain lucrative jobs should they decide to leave government. The
desire to be lenient on regulated businesses in view of a future step through the
revolving door that leads from government service to a high-level appointment as
a manager or executive in the industry once regulated can lead to actions that in
fact violate the public trust, even if no explicit *quid pro quo* is its basis. Regulators
who leave a trail of e-mails, text messages, or other communications indicating
that they are being lenient on members of the industry they are regulating should
be susceptible to serious sanction where a *quid pro quo* is implied in the context
of the communications. There are ways for regulators to be fair to the regulated
without any form of *quid pro quo* in the works, and indeed regulators should be
fair, even when there is mounting political or bureaucratic pressure not to be
(such as was the case in the financial services industry after the 2007/8 crisis,
where regulators took out hammer and tongs on even technical violations).

Anti-revolving-door rules must be strengthened to avoid regulatory capture
to the fullest extent practicable, which could mean longer periods during which
regulators are precluded from going to work in the industries they once over-
saw. There is no room here to provide more than a sketch of steps that would
strengthen policies to avoid regulatory capture, but they should include: time
constraints upon certain high level regulators that preclude them from going to

work in the regulated industry for some period of time after leaving government or self-regulatory organization service, and/or constraints upon working for specific companies or specific sub-sets of companies (rather than debarment from the industry as a whole), and/or rules that would require that former regulators recuse themselves from any form of lobbying – broadly construed – on behalf of their new employers within the industry, including assisting in any way in regulatory examinations on inquiries, other than through legal counsel representing the affected company or companies.

Proposal 4

Companies in industries that supply vital health and welfare services (pharmaceuticals, medical devices, defense, medical insurance, etc.) and who use Wall Street to raise capital should be barred from the use of Wall Street's capital raising mechanisms and firms for a period of at least two years if they violate the public trust through any form of material misrepresentation.

Executives of such companies who lie to the public, as was done, for example, in the tobacco industry's 'seven dwarfs' testimony before Congress, should be barred from serving as an officer or director of a public company, or serve in any equivalent capacities for a public company. But beyond that, the companies they serve should be barred from the use of any regulated broker-dealer or bank in capital raising. This could be a default position, with exceptions made for extenuating circumstances. However, with the threat of this hanging of the heads of companies in these industries, much more robust efforts will be made to assure that managers and executives are conducting themselves with the highest degree of integrity.

Serious financial sanctions that come down hard on a firm because of the shenanigans of one or two managers or executives within the firm are not unheard of. A few years ago, the Securities and Exchange Commission adopted rules that would preclude investment advisers from doing any kind of business with any state or municipality under certain circumstances. The rule has three horns: (1) the rule prohibits an investment adviser from providing advisory services for compensation – either directly or through a pooled investment vehicle – for two years, if the adviser or certain of its executives or employees make a political contribution to an elected official who is in a position to influence the selection of the adviser; (2) the rule prohibits an advisory firm and certain executives and employees from soliciting or coordinating campaign contributions from others – a practice referred to as 'bundling' – for an elected official who is in a position to influence the selection of the adviser; and (3) the Rule prohibits solicitation and coordination of payments to political parties in the state or locality where the adviser is seeking business. The rule also prohibits an investment adviser from paying a third party, such as a solicitor or placement agent, to solicit a government client on behalf of the investment adviser, unless that third party is an SEC-registered investment adviser or broker-dealer subject to similar pay to play restrictions. Though these restrictions are not directly related to the debarment discussed in this section, they do speak to the tainting of an entire organization regarding the pursuit of certain business, because of the actions of one or a few. The inability of an investment adviser such as Fidelity or Vanguard to conduct business with, say, the state of New York or California for as long as two years could mean tens of millions of dollars in lost revenue, and opportunity costs that are literally incalculable.

Radical libertarians may argue that such sanctions applied to the important industries referenced above will ultimately harm society as a whole, and unjustly interfere with those businesses. I take that to be short-term thinking, typical of the radical libertarian mind. The point is to create a climate and an ethos wherein stronger internal policing takes place, in order to avoid the costs of external policing. Similar libertarian arguments have been made about sanctions imposed on the banking industry after the crisis – 'It will only hurt innocent shareholders'. What is forgotten in the libertarian analysis is that the economic definition of a 'shareholder' is 'holder of the residual risk' of the enterprise. Shareholders actually sign-on, when investing in a company, to absorb the company's risks in exchange for the potential of dividends and/or capital gains. So the argument that punitive measures, such as those proposed, 'harms innocent shareholders' is spurious. If shareholders – such as myself – do not want to be harmed by the shenanigans of the companies that they own, it is incumbent upon them (us) to make our voices heard, and demand that management and governance are both first-rate and carried on in the interests of all stakeholders. Such, of course, applies to shareholders of all corporations, not just those in particular industries.

One of the interesting things about much of the call for more integrity and responsibility on the part of directors and managers is that the role of shareholders in creating more integrity and responsibility has not been emphasized. Shareholders that get burned in corporate scandals should not behave as though they are hapless victims. Some of their suffering is the result of too much trust in their agents. The myth of the hapless, innocent shareholder is one that we should dispel as soon as possible, for an enormous amount of power resides with shareholders. What shareholders lack, however, are the mechanisms to wield that power more effectively. Shareholders need greater and more diverse means to influence managements and boards, and to do so more directly – for the notions of responsibility and power without capacity and the means to exercise it, respectively, are hollow. In a comment letter to the SEC that I wrote concerning proxy reform proposals, I made this plain.[16]

Proposal 5

Legislation should be passed that limits the power of lobbyists of/for profit interests, severely restricting the manner and mode of their engagements with elected officials. Lobbying communications, in substantial detail, must be made a part of the public record promptly.

In 2009, former head of the Commodity Futures Trading Commission, Brooksley Born, in her acceptance of that years John F. Kennedy *Profiles in Courage Award* said this:

> When I spoke out a decade ago about the dangers posed by the rapidly growing and unregulated over-the-counter derivatives market, I did not do so in expectation of award or praise. On the contrary, I was aware that powerful interests in the financial community were opposed to any examination of that market. Yet I spoke out because I felt a duty to let the public, the Congress and the other financial regulators know that that market endangered our financial stability and to make every effort I could to address that problem.[17]

The pressure that Brooksley Born was referring to was, in large part, the pressure of lobbyists, who put pressure on Congress, who in turn put pressure on regulators, which led to something called the Commodity Futures Modernization Act of 2000 (hereinafter called the '2000 Act'). The 2000 Act exempted OTC derivatives, such as Credit Default Swaps ('CDS'), from regulation by the Commodity Futures Trading Commission (the 'CFTC'), even though these derivatives had many of the characteristics of the financial futures contracts that were already regulated by the CFTC. CDS would not be regulated by the CFTC *as a matter of law*. What is noteworthy, as well, is the implication that some OTC derivatives maintained the indicia of gambling (bets) of the sort referred to by the United States Supreme Court in *Gatewood v. North Carolina*. In *Gatewood*, the court defined a 'bucket shop' as '[a]n establishment, nominally for the transaction of a stock exchange business, or business of similar character, but really for the registration of bets, or wagers ... on the rise or fall of the prices of stocks, grain, oil, etc., there being no transfer or delivery of the stock or commodities nominally dealt in'. While it is true that many OTC derivatives have useful purposes, others, such as naked CDSs, where the buyer of protection is doing no more than placing a bet with no risk exposure to the referent security, is nothing more than gambling. The wording of the 2000 Act suggests knowledge of this fact, and thus the provisions to protect OTC derivatives, including naked CDS contracts, from regulation. But why? How did this happen?[18]

It happened because, *at best*, ideology trumped stewardship, as government insiders, including such powerful figures as Lawrence Summers, Robert Rubin, Alan Greenspan, Senator Phil Gramm, and Arthur Levitt (then Chairman of the Securities and Exchange Commission, engaged in a turf war with the CFTC) joined hands with powerful interests within the financial services industry to beat back any suggestion that OTC derivatives, as just described, should be regulated – by any agency, including the CFTC. The then head of the CFTC, Brooksley Born, attempted to draft regulations that would have captured CDSs and other OTC derivatives in the same regulatory net as other financial derivatives that were regulated by the CFTC, largely because of the systemic risks they might pose. She was concerned that the hidden size and pervasiveness of these instruments could possibly lead to financial disaster down the road. I have elsewhere stated my agreement with some who wrote a dissenting opinion in the Financial Crisis inquiry Report, i.e. derivatives exacerbated but did not cause the recent financial crisis. But that is a side issue in the face of whether policy makers, as high as the White House and Treasury Department, turned a blind eye to bad public policy decisions under the ideological cloak of a commitment to 'free markets'. The answer seems clear – they almost certainly did. The lobbying pressure from banks, hedge funds and broker-dealers was enormous and effectively beat-back Born's attempts to place some constraints on CDS and other OTC derivative instruments. Born's proposed constraints seemed, simply, sane. But with a money party going on in derivatives, nobody wanted the punch bowl taken away – other than a few thoughtful public stewards, like Born.

The story is a sad one. It is a story about how policy makers breached a trust of stewardship to the country, a trust that required that they protect it from the rapacity of certain business interests, from the pitfalls of ideological blindness, and from certain types of 'establishment', such as bucket shops, that spur rampant speculation rather than economic growth. It is noteworthy that under Dodd-Frank CDS are still with us, and in a very big way, notwithstanding the hyperbole of some of the stellar critics of these instruments (Buffet, Soros, *et al.*). This speaks to the inherent utility of these contracts in mitigating risk, and even in generating revenue for firms. But we now have, because of Dodd-Frank, and following on concerns raised by Born, much greater transparency into the contracts themselves as well as into those institutions that use them. In Europe, reporting requirements were recently imposed for certain derivatives transactions. In February 2014, the European Commission adopted regulatory technical standards specifying the derivatives contracts 'that are considered to have a direct, substantial and foreseeable effect within the Union or to prevent the evasion of rules and obligations'.[19] Hedge funds and similar fund vehicles now have to report their exposures to CDS and other derivatives, in some cases quarterly. It becomes clear in hindsight why the attempts by Born to institute similar, sound regulation was so fiercely beaten back. It was Senator Phil Gramm, then head of the Senate Banking Committee, who made sure that the CFTC was blocked by force of law from actually *doing its job* – from regulating instruments that it made all the sense in the world for it, or some other government agency, to regulate. (Phil Gramm's spouse, Wendy Gramm, was once head of the CFTC herself, it might be of some interest to note.)

Changing the way that lobbyists can communicate with government officials does not require that lobbying go by the boards. There is no need for such extremism, as lobbying, per se, is not the issue. The issue is the sort of access that lobbyists have to legislators and their staffs, and, let us not forget, to the executive branch. Since what lobbyists are communicating to elected officials is their side on a particular issue, there is no reason that this cannot be done through written proffers submitted through special portals, on line, with requests for review and comment within a certain time period – much the way registration statements for securities offerings are filed with the SEC, using the SEC's Edgar system. The moment the lobbyist files his or her proffer, it will become available immediately to the public, and can then be scrutinized by the press and experts, giving an opportunity for quick rebuttal of dubious data or claims. This does not preclude oral communications with legislators, but it is in the public's interest that such communications be effected so that there can be near-real-time reaction, such as what happens on analyst calls involving public companies. This approach to lobbying has the virtue of allowing lobbyists to say all that they wish to say, to make their case, while allowing legislators and the public the benefit of other points of view. Such an approach would actually give legislators – always worried about offending various industries – some cover from industry reprisals, since legislators will be able to simply point to the public and expert rebuttals as the reason for voting against industry interests. This approach would be intellectually honest, transparent, and above reproach. It would keep the lobbyists employed, but it would save a great deal of T&E expenses for all concerned.

Proposal 6

A financial instruments transactions tax should be implemented over five to seven years, rolled-out across one asset class at a time (first equities, then fixed income securities, then derivatives of all types) to determine the effects of each, to adjust the imposed tax, and to preclude deleterious effects on the next asset class. A federal financial transaction tax on all financial transactions would bring in billions of dollars per year in new revenue, directly from the industry that continually produces externalities (or equivalent harms) for the rest of society.

An outcry is often heard from banks, broker-dealers, market libertarians, and exchanges upon the mere mention of a financial transaction tax. The logic is knee-jerk, in part: a financial transaction tax will dissuade investors from participating in securities markets; it will dry-up liquidity; it will cause issuers of securities to go elsewhere, etc. Not all criticism, however, is merely knee-jerk, and some is based upon models and analyses of the experience of countries in which various forms of financial transaction tax (or 'FTTs') have been attempted. Experiences with FTTs have been mixed. But according to a study conducted by the Institute of Development Studies, as reported by *The Guardian* newspaper, a '0.005% tax on foreign exchange trades alone might raise around $26bn a year (£17.6bn) worldwide, with the UK accounting for about $11bn (£7.7bn)'.[20] The report held that 'An FTT is unlikely to reduce market volatility as claimed by some campaigners. Despite theoretical models suggesting otherwise, the evidence shows that higher transaction costs are typically associated with more, rather than less, volatility. As a result the rate of the transaction tax should be a small percentage of existing transaction costs to minimise market distortions'.[21]

The accountancy firm PriceWaterhouseCoopers, in November 2013, released a study of the viability and utility of a FTT in the EU, with specific reference to the EU-11 member states.[22] The study, *Financial Transaction Tax: The Impacts and Arguments – A Literature Review*, was commissioned by a consortium of European institutions. The section of the report addressing the impacts and arguments for and against a FTT was commissioned by over a dozen market participants and advocacy organizations, including the British Bankers Association and the Alternative Investment Management Association. The report begins by noting that the notion of an FTT is not new, something that gets lost in discussions of a FTT on television talk shows and among ideologues:

> Despite the recent attention given to the concept of a tax on financial transactions, it is far from a new idea. Indeed several countries, such as the United Kingdom, have levied stamp duties on certain financial transactions for several centuries. However, the concept of a FTT was only fully articulated in 1936 by the renowned economist John Maynard Keynes. Keynes' rationale for a FTT centered on its potential to bring stability to markets and raise additional revenue for government.
>
> Most recently, Nobel Laureate economist James Tobin's proposal for a specific currency transaction tax (CTT) in the 1970s as a way of managing exchange-rate volatility has been conflated with Keynes' FTT, and the term "Tobin Tax" is used interchangeably to describe either tax.
>
> Although the debate surrounding FTTs is clearly not a new one, substantial impetus has been added to it by the wake of the financial crisis. Financial market stability has become a key priority for governments and regulators, resulting in a resurgence of proposals for the implementation of FTTs or similar taxes due to their suggested volatility-reducing properties and ability to dissuade investors from entering into unproductive trades. Most prominent among these proposals has been the EC's plan to implement a FTT in the EU-11.[23]

In proposing a FTT, I am not suggesting that it should be implemented in an incautious manner, as should be clear in the wording of my proposal. And my proposal is for a US FTT, imposed at the federal level. While I am sympathetic to the need to be cautious – the road to hell, as they say, is paved with good intentions – I think there is enough experience with FTTs in other countries to give adequate guidance as to where the pitfalls may be so that implementation can achieve the desired results. One thing is clear: the financial services industry continues to generate substantial costs (negative externalities) for the rest of civil society, and despite the billions of dollars it has paid in fines and restitution (and shall no doubt pay in the future, as new scandals emerge), civil society remains largely uncompensated. Since, given the history of the banking and brokerage industries, there is scant reason to believe that new scandals are not already in the works, with severe costs to be imposed on the innocent, the costs of such scandals should be absorbed by the industry that creates them – a notion axiomatic in macroeconomics. I say the preceding well aware that the financial crisis that began in 2007 was not solely the fault of financial institutions, but it is quite clear that financial institutions carry much of the blame for what happened.

While this is not the place for a lengthy discussion of the merits of a FTT, a few things must be said. Critics of a FTT often point to the impact of a FTT on GDP. But there is no God's-eye view of the proper level of growth of GDP in any country, nor is there a God's-eye view on the proper level of trading frequency or liquidity that must obtain. Critics of *any tax* like to talk as though there is, and so critics of a FTT are no different. The level of growth of GDP, as the level of trading frequency in any asset class and the level of liquidity that exists in a market *are not context-independent*. They are, in fact, embedded within a nexus of numerous political, economic, and cultural decisions, which themselves rest upon political, economic, and cultural values, some of which remain in constant competition. Whether there is a VAT, a FTT, or an income tax, or whether certain expenses should be permitted to be deducted on tax returns, or netting against taxes paid in other jurisdictions (etc.), are decisions that are not based upon context-independent assessments of what is best for a society or upon financial calculations alone. They are based upon *judgments* by policy makers whose job it is to make those judgments, taking into consideration all the relevant variables. One relevant variable (although it does not seem to be too relevant to many of the critics of a FTT) is the pain and dislocation caused by an industry that from time to time runs off the rails and straight into our living rooms. Further, it is no argument to point to the good that this industry does. The good it does it is chartered to do by civil society. No, the focus must be on the bad that it does in considering whether the costs the industry imposes should be isolated within the industry itself. The purpose of a FTT is to accomplish just this isolation, not after but before the bad news breaks. The costs on market participants (like myself) will be countered by the benefits that come with avoiding the pain of taxpayer bailouts of failed banks and other institutions. FTT could go directly into a fund that will accrue to guarantee that the costs of such bailouts will be paid by the market participants that are closest and most responsible for the problem, not the public more generally. It will also help to guaranty that sufficient resources will be on hand for this purpose, so that no surprise $700 billion bailout legislation is proposed out of the blue in order to save the world from financial Armageddon, as was the case in September 2008 when Treasury Secretary Hank Paulson proposed such a gargantuan bailout in a mere three-page bill drafted by his staff and foisted on Congress in what columnist Maureen Dowd once called, concerning another national emergency, a 'wigged-out state of Apocalyptic readiness'. Let us not forget that 'too big to fail' is alive and well, and the biggest banks have only gotten bigger, thought others perished in the wake of the crisis. So an FTT would not be a punitive tax measure. To the contrary, it would be no more than prudence. The costs would be discounted into trading deliberations, just as ticket charges, commissions, and brokerage house account fees have been. Further, the proposed FTT would be so *de minimis* to a single transaction that they would hardly be noticed. A tax of, say, .0005 on a million dollar trade would be $500. This is absorbable to most market participants, but enough of a deterrent from frequent trading to tamp down needless speculation.

Of course, critics might complain that market liquidity would be tamped down too but, again, I am aware of no God's-eye view of the level of liquidity needed in a market for it to be considered an 'optimum' level. At some point the call for more and more liquidity becomes an argument for 'gaseousness'. Gaseousness of this sort might best be critiqued as *ignus fatuiis*. Neo-classical economic purists want *unlimited* liquidity, not adequate or even super-adequate liquidity. When the desire for a good, because it is a good, leads to the conclusion that no extreme quantity of such a good is absurd – whether the good is penicillin, food or liquidity – one is already alerted to the unreasonableness of the demand. The gun lobby in the United States operates pursuant to a similar demand, and one of the most effective arguments against it is that it brooks no notion that there can be a limit on gun ownership, including the quantity of guns one may own. Such a position is simply absurd on its face.

Proposal 7

Civics education should become part of the core curriculum in high schools and colleges across the nation.

As mentioned in the Introduction, I teach a course at Rutgers University titled 'Citizenship and Corporate Cultures'. The course is a bit of a departure from the conventional business ethics courses that I teach. The course treats of business ethics from the perspective of the interplay between citizens/citizenry and business enterprise. One of the unusual texts I use for the course is Hanauer's and Liu's *Gardens*. In the course, the first book that the student reads is this book. The purpose is to condition the student's mind to take up the rest of the readings from the perspective of a citizen, with powers, rights, and duties – to show that the citizen, as an individual social actor in civil society, is not a waif, or hapless, or a victim but an agent with power to effect change.

Of course, by the time a young person enters university, many of his or her habits of mind are set. This does not mean that those habits of mind can't be reset, but it is more difficult. That is why citizenship studies must again become part of the high school curriculum, perhaps even earlier, although at the junior high school level there may not be sufficient capacity to accede to the seriousness of citizenship, as youth of junior high school age are too far removed from the time in which they will have to actively, and primary, take charge of their own lives, and begin to engage the political world as voters, civic leaders, etc. The advantage of a book like *Gardens*, as well as Hanauer's and Liu's other book, *The True Patriot*, is that they are accessible, and therefore useful across a wide age range. As Hanauer and Liu tell us in the opening pages of *The True Patriot*, which they consider a political pamphlet in the mode of Thomas Paine's *Common Sense*:

> We freely admit that there is not one original idea in this pamphlet. We simply cap-tured the essence of what America's civic leaders and heroes have been saying for over 200 years. It was through our year of research that we realized America doesn't need a new politics, it simply needs to reconnect with its original patriotic traditions.
>
> Those traditions are grounded in civic virtue, in the simple precept of country above self. They rest on a notion of public morality, which is a very different notion of morality than the one that dominates contemporary elections. Ultimately, we seek the revival of a civil religion: a patriotism that every American can be proud of.
>
> Why patriotism as the template for our beliefs? The first reason is visceral: we simply love this country. We want to make it safer for other people to say that – and we want to make it harder too. No one should feel sheepish about professing patriot-ism, but no one should be able to get away with mere professions. Patriotism may begin in reflex but it must lead to reflection – and result in action.[24]

Such notions are not merely for Americans, caught up in a politically nasty period in domestic politics. They resonate with concerned citizens around the world: in France, in Britain, in Japan, in Canada, in Hungary, in Jamaica. The notion of tak-ing the time during our years of formal education to connect with a fundamental truth about our lives, that we are members of political communities that will only be as good as we are good, as moral as we are moral, as charitable as we are charitable.

In many ways, in the business scandals that plague us, we are merely reaping what we have sown. Decades of Thatcherite-Reaganesque rhetoric that sug-gest that 'government is the problem' (when government is really the organ of the people, at least in democracies, carrying out the people's wishes – a *tool*), of hagiographic paeans to the god of the free market, and the belief that char-ity is a private affair and that the welfare state is not our deepest and grandest expression of charity – the desire to care for others who are in need, and who are members of the same political compact and community as we are – have eroded the bonds of *sororitas* and *fraternitas* that are crucial for a people to think of itself as one, joined in a common effort to create and improve the commonweal.

The tools for civics instruction go well beyond the books of two interesting and needed writers, of course. There are many books, videos, and magazines that can be pulled together to construct citizenship curricula. Further, and last on this point, citizenship studies should not be relegated to the section of a course in social studies or history. It should have its own standing, its own course codes, within the curriculum. It is *that* important to preventing the incubation of future generations of scoundrels, knaves, con artists, boiler rooms and merely weak-kneed employees with no courage to stand-up and take action when their bosses or the institutions for which they work are going down the wrong path. Citizenship studies, if done well, can help to do what Aristotle made the subject of his ethical writings – they can instil civic virtue, and shape good characters.

Proposal 8

Political campaigns should be financed from public funds alone, with attendant accountability for expenditures, and formulas that govern limits but that allow for reasonable expenditures. Political offices should not be for sale to Wall Street or any other commercial interest.

Senator John McCain, who had for many years pushed for campaign finance reform, told us:

> Questions of honor are raised as much by appearances as by reality in politics, and because they incite public distrust, they need to be addressed no less directly than we would address evidence of expressly illegal corruption. By the time I became a leading advocate of campaign finance reform, I had come to appreciate that the public's suspicions were not always mistaken. Money does buy access in Washington, and access increases influence that often results in benefiting the few at the expense of the many.[25]

Senator McCain, along with Senator Russ Feingold, sponsored significant campaign finance reform legislation which was passed, against substantial opposition by members of Senator McCain's own party (Senator McCain is a member of the Republican Party). The law's title was the 'Bi-Partisan Campaign Reform Act of 2002' ('BRCA' otherwise referred to as 'McCain-Feingold'). McCain-Feingold was the subject of attack by other members of Congress, and *Citizens United* served to gut important provisions.

While political campaigns are expensive affairs, there is no good reason to assume that, at least in Congressional campaigns, public financing of elections won't work. While rolling back the current system, in which unlimited amounts of money pour into political campaigns, will be difficult, another truth obtains alongside this fact: It must be done if we want to end corruption in the political system. Limiting the amount of money that can be spent on political campaigns does not mean that those candidates will be hamstrung. Initially, the limit on spending can be set quite high, at least as high as is presently the case with unlimited political contributions coming from private donors, such as corporations and Super PACs (see Proposal 1). But over time, the amount of money permissible can be scaled back, as well as indexed to reflect the needs for each district or state. Again, as with other proposals proffered, change will take time, but that is no reason not to start reforms that everyone agrees are needed. Repeal of *Citizens United* is not enough. The amount of money spent on certain campaigns, especially state-wide and national campaigns, has reached 'pornographic' levels – a display of excess that only serves to undermine the noble enterprise that politics is at its best.

Industry-Specific Proposals

Proposal 9

'Eat what you kill' must end.

The idea that aggressive sales pressure should be done away with. As well, the idea that certain Wall Street producers can thrive only by their own efforts is a cancerous part of a rabidly individualistic and hedonistic culture that is in need of real transformation. The very *language* of Wall Street indicates a warped ethos, the corrosion and undermining of critical values of community and service to others. Sales and marketing efforts must be focused on the needs of the customer and client, and not merely the wallets and purses of Wall Street professionals. Salary-based compensation removes some of the incentive to 'rape and pillage' the wallets or balance sheets of customers and clients. Commissions and bonuses should be the desserts, not the main course. In a study of the commission system undertaken some 20 years ago, such trusted sages as Warren Buffett and others concluded that the commission system is flawed and, were the industry being redesigned from scratch, would not be recommended (see Proposal 10).

Firms create brands. Firms maintain systems for operation, physical plant for employees, purchase insurance policies for reasons of potential liability. Yet, it is not the firm that a customer signs on with when one opens an account at many broker-dealers. One is effectively the client of his or her broker, not of the firm, and the broker is often deemed, more or less, an 'intrapreneur'. But 'intrepraneur' is a knock-off of 'entrepreneur', that is, of the term for real risk takers who must concern themselves with all of his or her business's operations, and who risk a great deal of his or her own capital. But for the intrepreneur, the payout ratio is all that matters, at least in many cases. They want only the upside and none of the downside. They go where the payout is highest, and sometimes this can mean as high as eighty or ninety percent of the commissions generated. Such persons are mercenaries, not truly concerned about the firms whose names are on the business cards he or she hands out and which lends them the prestige and support systems to do what they do. In most cases, they couldn't care less about their firm's growth; they are only concerned with the growth of their own wallets. This may seem like too broad an indictment. To my mind, it is largely true.

Proposal 10

Wall Street leaders should end the commission system by 2025, which system provides a constant inducement to 'manage' compensation upward, often at the client's or customer's expense.

This proposal is similar to Proposal 9, but not quite the same. Here I focus on the commission system itself, which is rooted in the dogmas I discussed earlier. The commission system of compensation is based, untenably, on the idea that only variable compensation, with the potential for high financial rewards, is required to motivate people to do their jobs and to do them well. Further, making investments is not like buying new tires or washing machines. While sales people are involved in both, the stakes are much higher when it comes to making investments, which often represent money for important life goals, such as retirement, college educations, medical expenses, and simply to achieve some reasonable measure of financial security.

A review of some of the regulatory actions brought against brokers and traders tells the tale. Television commercials for Wall Street firms even reference the conflicts of interest that exist between investors and firms with which they invest. The combination of commission-based compensation and Wall Street's culture of entitlement are, combined, an invitation to steal, and most people know it.

I am not alone in calling for changes in the commission system. Arthur Levitt, SEC Chairman in the 1990s, was also critical of the system. In testimony before the US House of Representative's Subcommittee on Telecommunications and Finance (September 14, 1994), Levitt indicated his concerns:

> In addition to education, I want to touch on the subject of compensation. The public's trust and confidence in the securities industry are strongly affected by registered representative [i.e., broker] compensation. Investors develop trust and confidence in a registered representative based on their interactions with that individual. When a registered representative recommends a security, the investor should not have to wonder whether the investment is in his or her interest or whether the registered representative is simply trying to make a quick buck. Investors should feel that their registered representatives are looking out for their best interest.[26]

But in a report that was prepared by a special committee, commissioned by Chairman Levitt, to review Wall Street compensation practices (see Proposal 9), this is what the committee concluded:

> If the retail brokerage industry were being created today from the ground up, a majority of the Committee that developed this report would not design a compensation system based only on commissions paid for completed transactions. The most important role of the registered representative is, after all, to provide investment counsel to individual clients, not to generate transaction revenues. The prevailing commission-based compensation system inevitably leads to conflicts of interest among the parties involved. But the current compensation system is too deeply rooted to accommodate radical alteration in the near-term. And by all accounts, it works remarkably well for the vast majority of investors. At the same time, the beginnings of a shift towards other forms of compensation, such as fee-based charges for various investment-related services, is taking shape.[27]

Twenty years later, most firms still lean heavily on the commission system, although there are some exceptions. The one line in the preceding is that the commission systems works 'remarkably well' for most investors. I suppose that depends upon what 'remarkably well' means. The number of cases of unsuitable trades, account churning, and related games run on investors is *astounding* – unheard of in any other industry (and I am excluded instances where firms have been sanctioned for minor or technical violations of various regulations (some of which are the result of regulatory overreach, pedantry on the part of regulatory novices and zealots, and/or revenue-seeking) – the sorts of violations bound to be uncovered in any complex industry). FINRA's October 2014 'Disciplinary and Other FINRA Actions' went on for forty-five pages, and such volume is not atypical. It is tallied in monthly statistics by FINRA and other regulators. One must assume that what was meant by 'remarkably well' was that the system works for those fortunate enough to have never been burned by their brokers (and let me suggest that among this set of investors, most would never know for sure if there were or not). As far as the culture into which the commission system is embedded, and the attitude of brokers regarding firm clients, the committee confirms a long-understood reality on Wall Street, which is that brokers see the clients with which they deal as *theirs*, not the *firm's*, as I have just indicated:

> [R]egistered representatives occupy a unique and often problematic position, and few who have not held that job can fully appreciate its challenges. While most firms consider customers to be clients of the firm, the [registered representative] generally talks about 'my book' and 'my clients.' Likewise, when customers refer to 'my broker' they are often referring not to the brokerage FIRM but to their individual registered representatives. There is an implicit understanding that the RR is there to advance their interests.[28]

While the committee undertook a review of extant compensation practices, point out that some were better than others, the report struck me at the time it was published as no more than capitulating to a compensation system that is rife with obvious conflicts of interest, ironically made clear by the fact that a majority of the committee members – which included Warren Buffett of Berkshire Hathaway and Daniel P. Tulley, then Chairman of Merrill Lynch – would never have adopted a commission system of compensation if they had their druthers. In Levitt's book, *Take on the Street: What Wall Street and Corporate America Don't Want You to Know – What You Can Do to Fight Back* (a rather scrappy and scornful title for a person who spent his career on Wall Street), Levitt actually says that 'Brokers may seem like clever financial experts, but they are first and foremost salespeople'.[29] *That is most certainly true.* Another way to say that is that their financial interests, far too often, come before the financial goals of their clients. How can such a system be permitted to continue?

Much more recently, a study was conducted by The CFA institute: 'Restricting Sales Inducements – Perspectives on the Availability and Quality of Financial Advice for Investors'. The study concluded the following, among other things:

A lack of proper enforcement of existing rules meant to combat mis-selling and inducement abuses is also a problem because a number of regulators lack either the resources or the ability to enforce investor protections already in existence.[30]

Also, more recently, there has been a storm of controversy regarding the question of the application of the fiduciary standard to registered representatives. The problem with the application of such standard to registered representatives is that, as Arthur Levitt quite correctly told us, registered representatives are sales people. How can people primarily focused on selling be fiduciaries trusted to advise investors without a serious conflict of interest? That the question may be asked at all shows just how badly reform is needed, because it is asked in the face of an entrenched culture that will fight tooth and nail to keep things as they are.

Proposal 11

Reduce asset-based management fees for retail mutual funds dramatically by 2025. The proximity to other peoples' money does not infer taking a large portion of it for oneself.

John Bogle of Vanguard has had a lot to say on this subject. He has repeatedly pointed out that given the returns investors have reaped from most mutual funds, in part due to the erosion of their investments by fees and commissions, funds should roll-back fees. Bogle has made this point in several books, dozens of speeches and interviews, and in many articles and white papers. This is an especially crucial issue today, as US 'baby boomers' (those born between 1946 and 1962) are looking to retire and, as well, for the generation coming just after them, which can't be certain that the social safety net will be there for them or that they will even have pensions on which they can rely. Bogle joins New School for Social Research economist Theresa Ghilarducci (author of *When I'm 64: The Plot Against Pensions and the Plan to Save Them*) in predicting a retirement train wreck, with many Americans having a woefully insufficient nest egg upon which to rely, a condition that will force many people to work well into their golden years or, perhaps, succumb to poverty – the thought of which is a damning indictment of the entire society. Bogle and Ghilarducci argue that the money that should be swelling retirement accounts have instead lined the pockets of investment firms.

> John Henizl, investments reporter and columnist, recently wrote the following in *The Globe and Mail* (April 26, 2013), which captures the essence of the problem. In it, he recounts a recent warning by Bogle in the US Public Broadcasting Service's news and current events program, *Frontline*:
>
> *Frontline* interviewed index fund pioneer John Bogle, who compared the performance of two hypothetical equity portfolios – one earning 7 per cent, and the other earning 5 per cent (7 per cent less 2 per cent in fees).
>
> Two per cent may not seem like much in any given year. But over a long time period, the impact is enormous: Assuming a 50-year horizon, the second portfolio would have lost 63 per cent of its potential returns to fees, Mr. Bogle said.

"What happens in the fund business is that the magic of compounding returns is overwhelmed by the tyranny of compounding costs. It's a mathematical fact," he explained ...

Okay, let's assume there are two investors: Investor No. 1 owns a portfolio of stocks worth $100,000, pays no ongoing fees (apart from commissions when he purchased his shares) and earns the market return of 7 per cent annually. Investor No. 2 owns the same stocks in a mutual fund that charges 2 per cent in fees, and he therefore earns a return of 5 per cent ...

If you've done everything right, you should see a "future value" of $2,945,702.51. This is what Investor No. 1 would end up with after 50 years at a growth rate of 7 per cent. To figure out his return, subtract the original $100,000, which gives you $2,845,702.51.

Now do the same [calculation] for Investor No. 2. The only number you need to change is the interest rate, which is now 5 per cent. Hit "calculate," and you'll get a future value of $1,146,739.98, for a return of $1,046,739.98.

You'll notice that Investor No. 2's return is less than half of Investor No. 1's. In fact, consistent with Mr. Bogle's example, Investor No. 2 made about 63 per cent less than Investor No. 1 – and all because of just 2 per cent in fees charged every year.

Here's something else to consider: The longer the time horizon, the bigger the bite that fees take. Taking our example a step further, after 60 years, fees would eat up 69 per cent of returns. After 100 years, 85 per cent. Nobody invests for that long, of course, but you can see the trend here: As the time horizon approaches infinity, the proportion of returns eaten up by fees approaches 100 per cent.

Why does this happen? Because, over extremely long time periods, even small differences in compounding rates have a gigantic impact on returns.

Also note that Investor No. 2's fees increase over time. In the first year, he pays about $2,000 in fees (2 per cent of $100,000). In the second year, because his portfolio has grown to $105,000, he pays about $2,100 in fees. In the third year, $2,205. And so on. This is money that could otherwise be compounding in his favour.

Fees are the silent killers of investment returns. Don't make the mistake of thinking a couple of percentage points don't matter – in the long run, they're huge.[31]

One might argue that the same sort of analysis can be applied to a financial transaction tax. Won't a tax eat into investment returns? Yes, of course. But what Bogle is talking about here are relentless asset-based investment management fees, not transaction costs the accumulation of which can be controlled by the investor. Trade less (buy and hold as a true investor should, all else being equal), and the impact on long-term performance becomes far less impactful. Of course, broker-dealers want investors to trade, not hold low-turnover investment portfolios. The financial transaction tax would take investment dollars away, for sure, but it would also create an incentive to truly invest. They would also buy some security for future market and financial crises, the value of which (to investment portfolios) cannot be calculated in advance.

Proposal 12

Get rid of soft dollars and asset-based selling concessions.

Soft dollars and asset-based selling concessions charged by mutual funds (such as 12b-1 fees), along with contingent sales charge arrangements work against the investment returns of investors, despite the clever arguments used to support them. The arguments in favor of the use of investors' own assets to pay for things that portfolio managers should provide in the ordinary course of business is unfair to people who are trying to save and invest for their own and their families' futures, especially in view of the substantial financial destruction that has impacted investors' portfolios in recent years. This is something that well-informed investor advocates, such as John Bogle, have been saying for years. For just as long the industry has rebuffed them.

The SEC has been leery of soft dollars for decades, which led it, in 2006, to tighten the parameters for their use. Most recently (2014), the European Securities and Markets Authority ('ESMA'), in a 349 page proposal titled 'Markets in Financial Instruments Directive II', called for a general ban on the use of soft dollars, or 'dealing commissions' in the parlance of the proposal.[32] Of course, there is much gnashing of teeth within the industry over the proposal, but there is a reason that regulators, knowing full well how soft dollars are used (and often misused), keep seeing conflicts of interest. 'Soft dollars' refers to the use of client money to buy something (research) that the investment manager will use in the management of the client's portfolio. There is no doubt that third-party research prepared by broker-dealer analysts can be useful to investment managers. So is, for that matter, the education of the manager's professional staff, its computer systems, and other things that go into establishing and running an investment management business. It is curious that research is treated as categorically extraordinary, and so should be obtained with the client's own money. In addition, once a manager has such research, it will certainly use it for its own purposes (which may include the management of proprietary or affiliate investment accounts), as well as for other client accounts. So the additional commissions paid by a client to obtain research are shared broadly.

Consider an example from outside of the industry. Suppose Jones is engaged to paint your house. You assume that Jones has everything he needs to do the job. Of course, the job calls for buying the actual paint, and you know that part of what you, as Jones's customer, are paying includes the cost of paint, in addition to Jones's labour and expertise. But suppose that Jones by-passes the local paint supplier and goes to a special high-end, out-of-town supplier. When the job is complete, you ask Jones for a breakdown of the bill, which he supplies. The itemized bill shows that the paint costs were twenty percent more than you expected them to be. Jones argues, 'Well, that's because I have an arrangement with an out-of-town supplier. When I buy paints there I get a special discount on brushes, pails and such that I will use in my general business, some of which were used on your [Jones's] house'. Jones replies, 'Well that may be, but the paint you are using is the same paint sold at the local paint supply store, and that paint is twenty percent cheaper, and would have covered my house the same. It seems to me that if you need brushes, pails and such to run your business, well that's just the cost of being a house painter, is it not?

Why don't you buy your own trade materials, and let me see your bid on the fee for service, without this hidden component built in?'

Or you can consider a similar example by John Keefe, writing for *PlanSponsor* magazine:

> Here is how soft dollars work. Imagine you earn your living as a contractor, building kitchens, bathrooms, and dormer windows. One day at the lumberyard, the salesman pulls you aside and says, "If you buy more lumber here, I'll give you whatever tools you want for free. Of course, I'll have to charge you 50% more for the wood, but the extra cost will come out of your client's pocket, not yours." Switch your investment manager with the contractor, and its brokerage firms with the lumberyard, and you've got soft dollars: managers using clients' assets to pay inflated commissions, and receiving free services that benefit their businesses. Sometimes the managers disclose it, sometimes not.[33]

It is no surprise that regulators keep revisiting the use of soft dollars. The real surprise is that they have not been outlawed. (Well, it's not really a surprise, once you consider how entrenched the use of soft dollars is and the power of the industry's lobby.[34])

Proposal 13

Get Research Professionals Completely Away from Selling Pressures.

Research of public companies (and into the merits of investment in them) must be conducted completely away from sales pressures of any kind. 'Sell side' analysts should provide reports based upon, and only upon, their professional analyses and best professional judgments. Sales or marketing considerations or pressures (even such considerations as the firm's brand) should not enter into their thinking. Reforms in this area, though they have gone far, have not gone far enough and still allow for tension and a fundamental conflict of interest to remain, permitting coercion on research professionals to take more veiled forms. There is still room for sales pressure to appear in research reports, while allowing analysts to live up to the letter of the new rules that were adopted after New York Attorney General Eliot Spitzer skewered Wall Street broker-dealer over its research practices.

In the early 2000s, Spitzer took aim at Wall Street research (that is, sell side Wall Street research, written by broker-dealers, not investment advisers). At issue, among other things, was the conflict of interest that obtained between research staff and investment banking staff, and the corrupting influence the investment banking department had on research analysts. The investment bankers, needing to paint the best picture of their clients financial strength and prospects for the future, needed to tell the best story they could in an effort to raise capital for their clients in the capital markets. In that effort, warts are minimized or elided, and outright problems with corporate clients were 'spun' to paint the rosiest picture possible. In some ways, this is the job of an investment banker whose job it is to advocate for its clients (within the bounds of truth, of course).

But advocacy should not be the job of the research analyst, whose constituency is far flung – is, in many ways, the public at large, though reports are written to guide the firm's investors on the merits of investing in particular companies (or industries) covered by the analyst. In many ways, research analysts are scholars, and should operate with the same level of objectivity and independence. Investment bankers want to close deals for the firm's banking clients, while the research analyst is supposed to be interested in one thing only: performing good analysis and publishing accurate reports and sincere recommendations. Prior to the attention paid by Spitzer, analysts were essentially coopted by the investment banking side of the firm, and their research reports were contorted in content and prediction. It was noted that few research reports (one to two percent, depending upon what source you consult), actually contained sell recommendations (indicating that a company was not a good investment, at least for the moment). Research reports were paeans of optimism, often unjustified optimism. Prior to the attention given research reports by Spitzer, research analysts would be verbally castigated by their investment banking colleagues for not playing ball – not helping them to close deals and rake in the millions of dollars in fees charged for taking new offerings to market. Analysts that didn't go along found themselves without jobs, or were forced to take jobs on the buy side (the investment management side) of the industry.

Spitzer's pursuit of this conflict of interest led to a settlement (known as 'The Global Settlement') with a number of very large broker-dealers that had very large research departments, forcing them to separate research and investment banking departments, assure that research analyst compensation was in no way tied to the conclusion of investment banking deals, and to pay substantial fines.

The scandal that was sell-side research speaks to the wink and nod culture of Wall Street, as well as many who regulate it. It should have been obvious to any reasonably intelligent person that a research report should be based upon the best analysis and conclusions of the analyst, upon what he or she believes to be the facts. Otherwise what are all of those years of training in financial and company analysis for? To be hacks for investment bankers or retail brokers? Instead, in a quasi-Orwellian way, the word 'research' was perverted to mean, simply, fancy sales literature.

As recently as 2011, the Financial Industry Regulatory Authority ('FINRA') was still issuing 'guidance' and clarifications about the conflict of interest and tensions that still exist between research and investment banking departments – and functions, housed under the same roof. Of course, what was also included in such guidance and clarifications was the role that *public companies themselves* still play in attempting to corrupt the content of research reports, although the attempts are far less overt than they used to be:

It has come to FINRA's attention that certain issuers [companies that are investment banking clients] may be attempting to extract implicit promises of favorable research by suggesting publicly or directly to potential deal participants in advance of an anticipated offering that positive research coverage will be an implicit or explicit condition to selection as an underwriter or selling group member. The suggestions may take the form of hints, insinuations or other subtle references, but are intended to condition the award of investment banking business on the nature of research attendant to the deal. For example, the CEO of an issuer recently stated in an interview that he was dissatisfied with the tone of research coverage of his company by certain firms that previously served as underwriters for the company. As a result, the CEO reportedly intends to require candidates for the company's next offering to demonstrate "a clear understanding of who [the company] is and [the company's] trajectory, and why [the company's stock] is a stock that investors should own." He further is quoted as saying, "If I'm confident they can articulate that well, they will have a chance" at being selected as an offering participant ... FINRA views these and similar advance statements as attempts to create an expectation that a firm chosen to participate in a subsequent offering will maintain favorable research on the issuer's stock, irrespective of the stock price or the company's ongoing performance ...

FINRA understands that such uninvited pronouncements place prospective offering participants [i.e., broker-dealers engaged in investment banking] in a challenging situation should they seek to compete for a role in the offering. Nonetheless, in circumstances where an issuer makes known, expressly or implicitly, that the selection of an offering participant will be predicated on an expectation of positive research coverage, FINRA will closely scrutinize offering participants' research and other deal-related activities for compliance with, among others, NASD Rule 2711 and SEC Regulation Analyst Certification.

Member firms that choose to compete for or participate in offerings under such circumstances must expressly repudiate to the issuer any expectation with respect to the content of research coverage and document such repudiation. In addition, the firms must implement heightened supervision of their solicitation activities, including pitch meetings and other communications with the issuer, to ensure there is no express or implied acknowledgement or accedence to the research expectation. Finally, members [i.e., broker-dealers] must increase oversight of the preparation and content of their research on the subject company – both before and after deal participants are chosen – including any permissible communications between research and investment banking personnel.[35]

The referenced comments by FINRA highlight the near impossibility of cleaning up Wall Street research short of total separation of the research function (which may mean, spinning it off, since it is hard to understand what else 'total separation' could reasonably mean without a complete spin off of research departments). First, that corporate issuers have been making demands of research firms in the 'form of hints, insinuations or other subtle references' has never stopped, even after the Global Settlement, and this should have been known (and I believe was known) to regulators long before 2011. Water finds the cracks when it meets with the impenetrable obstacle, and the cracks with respect to the research rules that came after Spitzer's pressure were less obvious forms of communication of the wishes of investment bankers and corporate issuers. Hints, insinuations and threats send the same message as tirades from investment bankers. The message is 'Damned your professional objectivity; Get in line!' This more insidious form of pressure is hard to detect, and can be even harder to prove, which is what makes it so pernicious. Further, the notion that a broker-dealer must expressly repudiate to the issuer any expectation that research reports will be favorable is laughable if it is assumed to be a cure. This is because it is no more than a declaration into the air, a declaration that, officially, no such expectation should be construed as part of any engagement. But what does that actually mean in the real world? Broker-dealers can write such a repudiation into engagement documents, which covers them should FINRA inquire. But the golf course (and its equivalents) still exists, and that is where the hints and threats take place.

So there is no real cure for the problem under the present arrangement and even under the more robust anti-conflict rules. Research analysts who write for a living can dance their way, in prose, into deniability that any statement or claim was made to support the investment banking side of the business, or to throw a favorable light on an issuer. The clever use of 'on the one hand, on the other hand' devices (verbal devices of equivocation) can go a long way in providing cover and protection from regulatory sanctions. Further, the 'hints' dropped by corporate CEOs and CFOs can always be denied, or else they will claim that an analyst or banker simply 'misunderstood' what was said – 'Oh no, all I meant in saying that I expected better coverage of our company was just that, better research, research that indicated a real understanding of our business'.

And so the game will go, until research and investment banking are no longer under the same roof.

Proposal 14

Brokerage firms must be required to have a formal code of ethics.

Codes of ethics do not solve all of the ethical problems within a firm, but they help to set a tone and create a corporate ethos that can be useful in guiding conduct. Amazingly, broker-dealers are not required by regulators to have codes of ethics, and it wasn't until 2003 that SEC-registered investment advisers (investment managers) were required to have codes of ethics – which is quite remarkable given their status as fiduciaries.

An effective broker-dealer code should begin with a noble mission statement that will make it plain that the mission of the firm is to assist the investing public to make sound investment decisions, to assist in the procurement of capital for private enterprises and governments, to educate the investing public about appropriate investments, and to assure the proper handling of their portfolios from an operational point of view. The mission statement would be followed by a pledge to make investment selections or offer investment recommendations that are believed to be suitable and effective given the financial goals of the customer, and to take special care to oversee the accounts of investors who, though suitably invested in securities, have the least ability to absorb a substantial loss of principle. Further, as the customer's advocate, the registered representative will resist calls by his employing firm to make investment decisions or recommendations that are based upon the firm's interest to sell-out proprietary positions or to take other self-serving actions if such is not congruent with the goals of the customers to which the registered representative is assigned.

See Appendix 1.

Proposal 16

Reduce the Cost of Raising Capital.

The cost of raising capital must be reduced substantially. The fees charged by corporate lawyers and investment banks must be reviewed. The cost of raising capital should not be prohibitively high to small companies, and capital-raising should not be an opportunity to gouge fees from large businesses simply because they have the money to pay them. Fees should be based upon a model of fairness, and a commitment to the capital raising process as good for the society as a whole. New rules that permit direct public offerings through internet portals should be adopted, which would assign the investment banker to the role of, primarily, expert advisor. There are many ways to effect such a change, in my view, without removing protections from either the issuer firm or the public at-large.

Proposal 17

The bar of entry to Wall Street should be raised.

Full entry into the securities business should be harder than taking a few exams in rapid sequence. The securities licensing model should follow that used for Certified Financial Analysts, who only become fully fledged after taking a series of exams over a period of years. Movies such as The Wolf of Wall Street and Boiler Room demonstrate what can happen when the bar to entry is so low that just about anyone can get in.

Proposal 18

Compensation of brokers and bankers should be based upon a matrix of achievements.

Compensation should be based upon overall performance, including customer satisfaction, avoidance of violations of rules and regulations, and other non-financial variables. Some firms employ such a matrix, but all firms should. Where compensation is based merely upon the level of revenue produced, the firm is sending a clear signal concerning its values and culture. Where non-financial variables matter in setting compensation, production personnel will need to be more careful about how customers (and fellow employees and the firm itself) are treated.

Proposal 19

New brokers must be shadowed by compliance and ethics officers for one year.

New entrants to Wall Street should have to meet with compliance and ethics officers for discussions, training and acculturation for one year so that they are not corrupted by Wall Street's problematic culture and pressures to work against the interests of customers and clients. There are various ways in which this can be done without interfering unduly in employees' day to day responsibilities.

Proposal 20

The core brokerage business of a complex of affiliated financial services firms should not sell proprietary mutual funds.

Proprietary mutual funds should be sold only by a stand-alone unaffiliated broker-dealer with no interface with broker-dealer affiliates that are part of its complex of companies. The core brokerage business should sell funds of other fund companies only.

   A preposterous idea? Consider that the core activities of fund management do not usually reside with broker-dealer affiliates but rather with the funds' investment managers (legally, separate entities). Non-affiliated broker-dealers can just as easily distribute the funds' shares as broker-dealer affiliates can. And the system would have reciprocity built in, since broker-dealer affiliates would replace commission dollars lost by selling non-affiliated funds. What would be gone would be the conflicts of interest pressures that attend selling 'house' funds.

Proposal 21

Compensation of executives and managers should depend, in part, upon the level of disciplinary actions initiated against them or their firms.

Compensation committees should draft employment agreements and establish compensation arrangements that make it clear that overall compensation will depend upon, in part, the firm's recent regulatory history and their part in making it what it is.

Proposal 22

New products should be introduced accompanied by a capital impact study appropriate to the particular product. The study should also include an analysis of the level of systemic risk that may result given the use of the new product (the word 'product' should be construed broadly).

Whether or not such products as credit default swaps caused the recent financial crisis is debatable. Nevertheless, recent history suggests that the use of certain products warrants impact studies that take into consideration various impact scenarios for both the firm and the financial system. The idea of the 'impact study' should be appropriated by Wall Street as one of its risk management mechanisms, and it should be revisited every three years.

Proposal 23

Risk management programs within Wall Street firms must construe risk as both quantitative and qualitative.

Risk must be understood as both qualitative and quantitative. The tragic miscalculations and lapses of judgment that led to the financial crisis could not have been predicted by models and algorithms alone. Risk is not merely mathematical. It must be understood holistically. Risk managers must take such factors as human psychology and human relationships into consideration when assessing risks to the firm as well as systemic risks.

Risk expert Thomas Coleman concurs:

> If there is one paramount criticism of the new 'risk management' paradigm, it is that the [financial services] industry has focused too much on measurement, neglecting the old-fashioned business of *managing* risk. Managing risk requires experience and intuition in addition to quantitative measures. The quantitative tools are invaluable aids that help to formalize and standardize a process that otherwise would be driven by hunches and rules of thumb, but they are no substitute for informed judgment. Risk management is as much about apprenticeship and learning by doing as it is about book learning. Risk management is as much about managing people, processes, and projects as it is about quantitative techniques.[36]

Most of the remaining proposals I present without elaboration, since they are more or less clear without it.

Proposal 24

The current annual CEO certification requirement for public companies, required pursuant to Sarbanes-Oxley, should be supplemented with a quarterly certification requirement, which certifies that substantial and exigent risk and compliance targets, programs and reporting requirements are being met.

Proposal 25

To recoup the costs that Wall Street has created for society, fees and assessments paid to federal and state regulatory authorities should be indexed to capital so that larger firms pay substantially more than smaller firms. The fee system on Wall Street is regressive, in many cases. Making it progressive will generate more revenues for federal, state and local governments now involved in redressing Wall Street's irre-sponsibility and lapses of judgment.

Proposal 26

The practice of customer portability should be studied in terms of the law of agency and other considerations. The model that holds that customers 'belong' to individual brokers or bankers (akin to 'franchisees') creates a lack of loyalty, trust and stability on the part of brokers, bankers, customers and firms. The focus becomes money and money only. Brokers should be 'account representatives' hired to service the customers of the firm. The firm should not be seen as, merely, providing a 'roof' for the broker-'intrapreneur' (see Proposal 9) who holds no loyalty to the firm or responsibility for its success. Brokers who voluntarily resign from firms should not be permitted to solicit former clients/customers for at least 60 days and should not be permitted to 'pre-solicit' clients/customers prior to departure.

Proposal 27

Self-offerings should increase. In the internet age, there is no reason why the role of Wall Street should not shift to that of an advisor (see Proposal 16). Large companies should be able to effect public offerings directly through portals at their web-sites, linked directly with corporate transfer agents and other administrative institutions. This will allow corporations to save tens of millions of dollars on investment banking fees – money that can be used for business operations, dividends, hiring, expansion, and R & D.

Proposal 28

For as long as research is published by broker-dealers, the reports should be filed with regulators, via internet portals, with a series of expanded ethical certifications accompanying each filing. Currently, there is no requirement that research reports be filed with industry regulators. Because of abuses that still exist, some of them esoteric, research reports should be filed at the time of publication, accompanied by statements that affirm that the reports were not prepared to, among other things, condition the firm issuing the report for sought after investment banking business from the issuer that is the subject of the report. All research reports should be made available to the public via the Edgar or other SEC portal 120 days after filing.

Proposal 29

Continuing professional education should include substantive business ethics educa-tion, not merely content that addresses industry matters. Business ethics is considerably more than running through a series of vignettes and flipping through a few cases. It requires discussion and reflection. Proper business ethics education opens-up students to areas of learning previously alien to the student. An industry as plagued with wrong-doing as Wall Street needs a more robust model for ethics education. See Appendix 1.

Proposal 30

Senior executives of larger firms (with net asset values of $100 million or more) should be required to respond to risk alerts by the Financial Stability Oversight Council (which shall issue them), and file a written risk self-assessment, within 21 days, of their firms' vulnerability to the indicated risks.

Proposal 31

Wall Street needs to adopt an 'ethics of care' standard. Wall Street should construct a model of ethics that places customer and client care – even in cases where the customer or client is an institution – as the center of the firm's concern. It needs a transitive standard that looks through to the ultimate beneficiaries of investments and investment decisions – individuals and families. The new ethics of care standard should be codified in new industry rules.

Proposal 32

Larger broker-dealers and investment advisers (i.e., with net asset values of $100 million or more) should maintain a Management, Ethics and Risk ('MER') advisory board (or its equivalent), and should be required to provide an annual statement or report to the MER board and respond to feedback promptly. A majority of the board should be qualified management, ethics and risk professionals; independent persons with no affiliation with the firm who will not have had any affiliation with the firm for the prior two years; and may not take employment with the firm for at least one year after resignation or removal from the MER board.

Proposal 33

Registered Representatives (brokers) should, in order to maintain their licenses, receive ongoing education in taxation, estate planning, new securities products and related subjects at an accredited institution, with a minimum of four credits per year, the costs to be subsidized by firms on a discretionary basis.

Proposal 34

Larger Wall Street firms (with net asset values of $100 million or more) should require Chief Ethics Officers and Ethics Officers with the responsibility to prepare a report to the board of directors or substantially similar body, at least semi-annually. The Chief Ethics Officer should report to the board, and not to another officer.

Proposal 35

Lobbyists for broker-dealers, banks, mutual funds and registered investment advisers should have to prepare monthly reports to the designated examining authorities (regulators) of the broker-dealer indicating their activities and the issues they are addressing, with opportunity for inquiry from industry regulators. Individual lobbyists or lobbying agent-employees of lobbying firms must become registered as 'Government Relations Officers' (a new designation) with the firms that engage them. They should be required to become qualified by examination administered by FINRA or the North American Securities Administrators Association ('NASAA') to represent those firms, since they are acting on behalf of firms on matters that will or may affect the management of those firms. They should not be permitted to work from under the cloak of 'unregulated independent contractor' only.

Proposal 36

Fees and charges imposed on customers and clients must meet tests of reasonableness and fairness. Fees and charges that create disproportionate profits must be delimited. The banking, securities and investment management industries should, working with regulators and consumer agencies, create a series of comprehensive guidelines for fees and other charges, similar to certain guidelines and rules already extant in the securities and investment management industries.

Proposal 37

'Bogle Disclosures' should be contained on the inside first page of all mutual fund prospectuses and 'Statements of Additional Information', and in all mutual fund advertisements, similar to the Surgeon General's warning. The 'Bogle Disclosures' would state that 'Studies have shown that investing in lower-cost index funds can lead to returns that outperform actively managed funds such as this one. You should consult an investment adviser for more information regarding index investing. Management fees and administrative costs can have a substantial and negative effect on investment performance over time'. The disclosure should be accompanied by an illustration (see Proposal 11).

Proposal 38

'Fairness Disclosures' should be included in all offering memoranda and prospectuses, regardless of whether the offer is with respect to a private or public offering. The disclosures would address fallacies or serious alternative points of view concerning such matters as executive compensation, corporate governance, investment risk, and investor rights under the federal and state securities laws. They will also narrate the regulatory histories of all persons who serve the issuer as placement agent, underwriter, auditor, or servicing agent.

Proposal 39

Selling pressure to move securities or other investments from proprietary accounts of a firm to customer accounts of a firm should be prohibited or accompanied by appropriate disclosures.

This proposal bears some elaboration, as it is likely one of the most controversial, at least to Wall Street insiders. It is not a proposal that the securities industry will receive with open arms (not that any of the proposals herein are). The proposal seeks to mitigate the inherent conflicts of interest that obtain when a broker-dealer is selling securities out of its own account. There are exceptions, of course, such as when the firm is responding to a *bona fide* client order (I must say *bona fide* because firms are known to engage in shenanigans when it comes to who is an arms-length client or customer and who is really an insider). Unsolicited, client orders could be satisfied from firm proprietary accounts, so long as the price that the client is paying or the sales price he will be receiving is in line with the market.

The proposal really is directed at firms who own positions but have taken the view that the positions are no longer desirable. It is unconscionable for a firm with that mindset to 'fob off' securities to clients under those circumstances. Firms wishing to 'unload' proprietary positions should only be able to do so facing other sophisticated market participants (that is, other broker-dealers or banks), not the class of those persons who are deemed to be 'customers' under Federal securities laws.

Further, even recommending these securities to customers should be proscribed. If proscription is deemed too draconian then customers and clients should, at least, be made aware of the firm's decision to sell the security out of its proprietary accounts.

Proposal 40

Regulators and Self-Regulatory Organizations must increase efforts to retain personnel. Compensation at all levels should be increased so that there is more incentive to forge careers. Senior officials should be precluded from taking positions with industry firms, in any capacity, including as consultants, for six months after leaving their jobs.

Proposal 41

Securities, banking and investment management firms should provide at least 100 hours per year of financial literacy education on a pro bono basis, especially in underserved communities.

Proposal 42

Wall Street must do more to provide opportunities to persons from minority communities and must do more to move women into senior positions.

Proposal 43

Rating agencies should be required to have substantial codes of ethics, ongoing ethics education for ratings professionals, ethics committees and ethics officers, with the authority to respond to significant conflicts and to report to the board of directors (or equivalent body) concerning their findings at least semi-annually.

General Corporate Proposals

Proposal 44

The fallacies of incentive compensation should be exposed, and there should be a new compensation model that shifts senior executive compensation to salary and bonus, with: deductions for missing certain non-monetary organizational targets; claw-back provisions that extend beyond those required by Sarbanes-Oxley and Dodd-Frank; and delays of severance payments for a period of not less than one year from the time of separation.

Proposal 45

In general, companies that have been found to have violated requirements for material and accurate disclosures should lose their ability to raise capital (in the public equity and debt markets) for a period of not less than one year.

Proposal 46

Boards of directors of public companies, including the directors of mutual funds, should hold meetings bi-monthly rather than quarterly.

Proposal 47

Directors of public companies must sit for periodic computer-based training regarding board duties, new issues facing directors, and related matters. The computer-based training could be designed by a committee or council comprised of representatives from the SEC, the Department of Commerce, the Business Roundtable (or similar organization), the American Bar Association, and FASB. The National Association of Corporate Directors ('NACD') has a noteworthy menu of courses to help train and educate public corporate directors. One-shot continuing education is not enough. Directors need to be reminded of key principles of governance in order to do their jobs in a fully cognizant way. Education should not be limited to nuts and bolts matters, such as financial reporting rules or management nomenclature and theory, but also include 'soft considerations', such as handling overbearing CEOs, board bullies, and management of outside counsel and other advisors. Of course, theoretical education should also be a staple. As should be clear by now, problems of recollection are key. Revisiting questions and issues concerning the nature of the corporation, the source of its authority, and the duty to remain cognizant of the corporate footprint in communities and society in general is very important to keep boards functioning at a high intellectual level, to help them review issues and proposals holistically rather than myopically, and to help them set general policy and oversee management.

Academic and Pedagogical Proposals

Proposal 48

Colleges and universities should create more courses to prepare ethics officers for their duties. Instruction and course material would include material on program implementation and theory.

Proposal 49

Colleges and universities should create more courses on citizenship, citizenship theory, and the institutions of 'global citizenship'.

Proposal 50

Academics should redouble their efforts to reach out to local communities to set-up lectures and teach-ins on matters of civic engagement.

CONCLUSION

In an address before the 2005 meeting of the Society of Business Ethics, the American philosopher Richard M. Rorty said:

> At the beginning of the twentieth century, businessmen like Henry Ford imagined ways in which the US might become a relatively classless society. Some of those dreams actually came true, at least for that brief shining moment in US history that historians now describe as the Great Leveling. Ford, like FDR and Walter Reuther, glimpsed possibilities for industrial capitalism that had been beyond Marx's and Lenin's imagination. I hope that now, at the beginning of the twenty-first century, at least a few executives of the great multinational corporations are thinking about the need to create a global economy that will, far down the road, make possible global social justice. These men and women are the people with the best sense of the directions in which economic forces are presently driving the nations, of where the real levers of power are to be found, and of the possibilities that remain open for both governments and business enterprises. If none of them are dreaming up idealistic, utopian scenarios for the formation of a morally decent global society, it is unlikely that such a society will ever come into existence. Perhaps the business ethics community will provide an environment in which such dreams are encouraged.[1]

I am part of 'the business ethics community', as well as of others. I have faith that one day, perhaps not as far into the future as Rorty suggests, our descendants will look back at the scandals and knavery of the twentieth and early twenty-first centuries in disbelief and disgust. At that time, selfish economic ideologies and dogmas, such as those that are coiled at the heart of radical *laissez-faire* libertarianism, will be relics of the past, read about in schoolbooks (or their equivalent) like kids in the developed world today read about shipwrights, pedal looms, chimney sweeps and debtors' prisons. For them, the idea that markets should be more or less free will live on because free markets hold the key to the creation of the basic conditions for human flourishing on a large scale. But by then, if we remain committed to reform and reclamation, this idea will be *yoked* to a more radical sense of obligation to other human beings, and so conditioned by a much more robust moral sense, a moral sense that is derided today by certain ideologues and market fundamentalists, many of whom compose the power elite or thrive by serving its interests. Among other things, our descendants will wonder why we saddled ourselves with mortgage debt we couldn't easily afford, felt the need to leverage our investment portfolios, and otherwise felt compelled to live beyond our means – and spend *their* money on trinkets and baubles, while the world burned. They may brand this period 'The Profligate Years'. Who could blame them?

Growing inequality at home is linked to great pockets of poverty in societies around the world. The hopelessness and disaffection that we think so distal are in fact, as we now know, not so far away after all. Rich countries cannot continue to ignore or exploit lesser-developed countries (politically or economically) without paying a series of horrible prices. The words of Frederick Douglass spring to mind: 'Power concedes nothing without a demand. It never did, and it never will'.[2] The haves will be confronted by the have-nots (and the have-much-lesses) sooner or later, and the demand will be made. So far, what we have done with exquisite granularity is *study* the contours of the yawing gaps between rich and poor, and of the foundering of the great middle class that is needed to keep the economy stable and thriving. The demand has not yet come, but unless we reclaim and reform our markets and market institutions, and institute an ethics of care and stewardship, the demand will come. I suspect it will not be pretty.

It need not come to this. The self-centred attitudes we have incubated, attitudes rooted in our primal animal spirits, in our existential needs and fears, can be supplanted by an attitude of mutual support and an ethics of care, brought into being through deliberate processes of soulcraft – through rehabituation at all levels of civil society, including our commercial institutions. This does not mean that what we have learned about building strong and resilient economies, fostering innovation and nurturing entrepreneurship need go by the boards. The challenge, rather, is to tie the knowledge we have gained in all of these areas to market-based as well as non-market-based initiatives designed to raise out of poverty those who are locked in it, or who stand on the brink of impoverishment.

As I have argued, Wall Street, in its present form, is not only a set of overlapping industries; it is also a trope for self-centred and profligate acquisition. But it is also a powerful engine for the generation of wealth that can be put to the service of many more than it now is. The question concerns how that wealth generation can inure to the benefit of billions more people, whether in Appalachia or the Niger Delta, whether in rural Ohio or the bustling streets of Mumbai. To some extent, the question is already being answered. Good things are beginning to happen. People are beginning to think differently. In recent years, socially responsible investing has gained acceptance and legitimacy. Corporations have adopted corporate responsibility plans and programs (some cynical, some sincere, and many a mixture of both). More dialogues between NGOs and business leaders are underway. There are more corporate-community partnerships and initiatives. The United Nations Global Compact is being taken seriously by many large businesses. The World Trade Organization is now listening to the apt criticisms of those who point out that the benefits of free trade do not always trickle down to those who need those benefits the most (because of corruption and other factors). 'Impact investing' is gaining traction and real attention from serious investors and businesses who are able to see that they can, without dissipating assets, get a good return on their money while at the same time changing lives and communities for the better. Microfinance has taken root in the imaginations of serious policy professionals and business leaders, and it is now seen as viable, thanks to the dogged efforts of Muhammad Yunus of Grameen Bank, and others. In his book, *The Fortune at the Bottom of the Pyramid*, C. K. Prahalad has given voice to the global poor, showing how they ought not to be viewed as mere supplicants or a 'constituency' or a problem, but rather can become, and in many instances already are, partners with enlightened business and non-business leaders. At the same time, Prahalad has provided business leaders with new visions for the growth of their own enterprises, by showing that the poor (those at the bottom of the wealth pyramid) are not really so poor as most in the rich West think – for they possess abundant assets that can be turned into 'capital' under the right conditions and with the right partnering. Prahalad follows Hernando De Soto's logic in his book, *The Mystery of Capital*, which argues, quite compellingly, that 'capital' arises from certain *conditions*, including legal conditions, which give it its substance and its power to change people's lives for the better.

We do not need a Marxist turn in our thinking in order to mitigate or eradicate social miseries. Indeed, that is the last thing for which the present hour calls, though given the rapacity and irresponsibility of the business community in recent years some turn to Marx and Marxians for alternative economic and social analyses, and understandably so. Along the lines of Rorty's observations, above, we now have before us not only possibilities for solutions that are 'beyond Marx's and Lenin's imagination', we have before us possibilities that are well beyond the imaginations of Henry Ford, Franklin Delano Roosevelt and Walter Reuther. The various movements and initiatives just referenced show what can be done *within* capitalism. What we must do now is transform a hackneyed set of perspectives about Wall Street's purpose (that it is, first and foremost, a place to 'get rich quick') into a new set of perspectives that will allow us to hold on to the best of capitalism while at the same time use its considerable power to transform many more lives for the better than it already, undeniably, has. The problem with modern capitalism isn't that it does not work; the problem with modern capitalism is that it is not *permitted* to work to transform many more lives than it does and has. It does not matter whether we call this transformation 'expanding social justice' or simply 'giving more people a break'. It is outcomes that matter.

As I said at the beginning of this book, we must reject cynicism and fatalism as well as dark views concerning human nature, all of which turns up not only among the average citizen, and not only among those who believe that 'business ethics' is an oxymoron, but it turns up also among those who are very enlightened and sophisticated observers of the history of Wall Street. As I have argued, *The Other Wall Street* operates such that too many people not only *accept* scandal and knavery and the conditions for them, but they romanticize them to one degree or another, as many still romanticize the Gold Rush prospector and the early pioneers in their wagon trains, pushing westward across the continent. The romanticizing, of course, conceals or elides an assortment of hard (if not downright ugly) truths. For example, MacDonald and Hughes (whom I have quoted earlier) give us this conclusion to their well-researched and well-written book, *Separating Fools from Their Money*:

> Whenever there is a whiff of scandal in the air, we think of apples. Are the scandals the result of a few bad apples or is the entire orchard afflicted with blight? The historical record suggests that there are a few bad apples, but they keep coming back. *Then again, without the bad apples, American financial history would be that much more boring, the ups and downs that much less giddy, and the drama that much more insipid. And without some degree of creative destruction, there would be no major advances.*
>
> Financial scandals are part of the landscape of American history. Although this is not a source of pride, *it reflects the Darwinian aspect of business, the pressure to maximize profits and to fulfill individual greed.* Short of completely overhauling the U.S. socioeconomic system, it is difficult to see how this could change, despite the growing inequalities evident in the country. This leaves the words of Mark Twain to be most apt: "If you pick up a starving dog and make him prosperous, he will not bite you. This is the principal difference between a dog and a man." Looking at the likes of Jay Gould, Daniel Drew, and Kenneth Lay, Twain's words have a historical echo that just will not go away.[3]

Thus ends their book. It is an unfortunate and surprising ending, for it is precisely the 'insipid' that society should expect as regards the cultures and behaviours of its ministerial institutions and corporate cultures – that is, if one construes 'insipid' to entail 'scandal-free'. There is no good reason that Wall Street culture cannot be as 'insipid' as corn farming, halibut fishing, or automobile manufacturing. If it is entertainment and titillation that we seek, there are other and less destructive forms than the spectacle of once-respected firms collapsing into the dust of history because of the behaviour of a few selfish rogues in their c-suites, bringing down with them employees, vendors, other stakeholders and the general level of trust in society's institutions. As for the allowance made for greed, I have already addressed the all-too-often conflation of 'greed' and 'aspiration'. To recap: greed is *always* a vice. It is a vice by *definition*. As for the suggestion that the people who defraud and cause scandal are central to the 'creative destruction' that Joseph Schumpeter indicated was a mainstay of capitalism, that too seems off the mark, for Schumpeter's notion of 'creative destruction' had nothing to do with fraud and scandal of the likes we have seen in recent years or, for that matter, over the span of the financial history of the country that MacDonald and Hughes survey. Schumpeter was describing or observing not the results of knavery and fraud, but rather the manner and mode of innovation and commercial progress in free markets. As for the reference to Darwin, MacDonald and Hughes seem to invoke a variant of social Darwinism that was discredited long ago, not long after the robber barons appropriated Darwinian concepts to justify their ruthlessness. Business competition has absolutely nothing to do with Darwin's naturalism, although the myth that it does (apparently) persists. It is as though MacDonald and Hughes believe that scandals, and those who create them, are a kind of 'yeast' that is required for the bread of economic progress and commercial innovation to rise, while at the same time they seem to lament them. And as for the idea that businesses exist to 'maximize profits', that too is a bad idea that refuses to die, as a long line of management theorists has made clear.

We can no longer capitulate. We can no longer accept a 'boys will be boys' mindset, and accede to Wall Street its adolescent corporate cultures. There is nothing romantic about greed or scandal. There is nothing chic or honorable about zero-sum notions of competition in which the 'edge' is to be pursued at all costs. And we can no longer accept the *status quo* mindset that thinks otherwise. It is time for 'the boys' to grow up. We may not realize it yet, distracted as we are by new gadgets and fleeting fashions, but we are at the crossroads. We have to choose which road will be taken. Should we choose to do nothing, and preserve the *status quo*, the forces unleashed by unprecedented inequality and growing disgust with corporate leaders – and especially those on Wall Street (you will recall that the movement was called 'Occupy Wall Street' rather than 'Occupy Big-Ag' or 'Occupy Aviation') – will usher us down a road that may very well be marked by social unrest and coordinated violence. We can act deliberately instead and take the road of soulcraft. Those are our options. This book was written because I believe in soulcraft. Soulcraft is undertaken by small steps – through cultural politics; through enlightened political and corporate leadership; through education; and through deliberation by and among citizens, across civil society.

As George Will writes in *Statecraft as Soulcraft*, our acquiescence to market values and market demands, and our love affair with consumption, may be the sign of our childishness:

> The question is not does capitalism ... work? Of course it does. So did the Pony Express. The question is what do you mean by "work"? There is more to judging economic arrangements than judging how far, smoothly and fast they expand the Gross National Product. De Tocqueville spoke of "a theory of manufactures more powerful than customs and laws," and such capitalism has proved to be. It is difficult for statesmen, or anyone else, to measure what De Tocqueville called "the slow and quiet action of society upon itself," because the action is so slow and quiet. But that action must be watched.
>
> Societies, like individuals, can be, to a considerable extent, defined by their admirations. A society which orients politics to acquisition is apt to be a society in which admiration accrues to the most successful acquirers ... Democracy and capitalism are compatible only as long as the habits of political and economic self-restraint (deferral

of gratification; industriousness; thrift) reinforce one another. The question of what happens when the ethics of commercial civilization – the relentless manufacturing of appetites, and the incitement to gratify them on credit – undermines self-restraint in political and economic behaviour. The essence of childishness is an inability to imagine an incompatibility between one's appetites and the world. Growing up involves, above all, a conscious effort to conform one's appetites to a crowded world. By so thoroughly taking our political, hence our moral, bearings from the low but strong and steady passions, are we in danger of lingering in perpetual childishness? A society that seeks a steady expansion of desires and a simultaneous satisfaction of them may be, at least in the short run, a great place for advertising account executives and manufacturers of small appliances. But over time, it must be unstable domestically and vulnerable internationally.[4]

We are now inundated by the 'steady expansion of desires' – to a degree unimagined by Galbraith (who gave us fair warning about manufactured desire in *The Affluent Society*) and Thorstein Veblen (who gave us the phrase 'conspicuous consumption' in *The Theory of the Leisure Class*). Their notions of excess were relatively earthbound – we have now entered, because of the internet, such a commercialized existence that it can fairly be categorized as stratospheric. The focus on consumption and the ideology of consumerism – as well as the institutions that gain from both – are complicit in the erosion of the propositions that gave rise to our political community. The resulting social and political disintegration must, therefore, be addressed from various vectors, preferably commensurately.

Let's get to work. If we do not, the next wave of scandal, or the next severe economic shock, may take away the peaceful and reasoned options that, for now, are available. If we do not, Frederick Douglass's words, quoted above, will be prophesy and not merely a negotiation heuristic.

APPENDIX 1: THE ROLE OF COMPLIANCE AND ETHICS IN RISK MANAGEMENT

by Carlo V. di Florio
Director, SEC Office of Compliance Inspections and Examinations[1]
NSCP National Meeting
October 17, 2011

Thank you for inviting me to speak at this event. The work you all do is incredibly important, and we appreciate and respect your critical contributions to investor protection and market integrity. Today I would like to address two related topics that are growing in importance: the heightened role of ethics in an effective regulatory compliance program, and the role of both ethics and compliance in enterprise risk management. The views that I express here today are of course my own and do not necessarily reflect the views of the [Securities and Exchange Commission] or of my colleagues on the staff of the Commission.

In the course of discussing these two topics, I would like to explore with you the following propositions:

1. Ethics is fundamental to the securities laws, and I believe ethical culture objectives should be central to an effective regulatory compliance program.

2. Leading standards have recognized the centrality of ethics and have explicitly integrated ethics into the elements of effective compliance and enterprise risk management. Organizations are making meaningful changes to embrace this trend and implement leading practices to make their regulatory compliance and risk management programs more effective.

Ethics and the Federal Securities Laws

The debate about how law and ethics relate to each other traces all the way back to Plato and Aristotle. I am not the Director of the Office of Legal Philosophy, so I won't try to contribute to the received wisdom of the ages on this enormous topic,[2] except to say that for my purposes today, the question really boils down to staying true to both the spirit and the letter of the law.

Framed this way, ethics is a topic of enormous significance to anyone whose job it is to seek to promote compliance with the federal securities laws. At their core, the federal securities laws were intended by Congress to be an exercise in applied ethics. As the Supreme Court stated almost five decades ago,

> [a] fundamental purpose, common to [the federal securities] ... statutes, was to sub-stitute a philosophy of full disclosure for the philosophy of caveat emptor and thus to achieve a high standard of business ethics in the securities industry ... "It requires but little appreciation ... of what happened in this country during the 1920's and 1930's to realize how essential it is that the highest ethical standards prevail" in every facet of the securities industry.[3]

Of course, what has happened through the financial crisis I believe is yet another reminder of the fundamental need for stronger ethics, risk management and reg-ulatory compliance practices to prevail. Congress has responded once again, as it did after the Great Depression, with landmark legislation to raise the standards of business ethics in the banking and securities industries.

The manner in which the federal securities laws are illuminated by ethical principles was well illustrated by the Study on Investment Advisers and Bro-ker-Dealers that the Commission staff submitted to Congress earlier this year pursuant to Section 913 of the Dodd-Frank Act ('913 Study').[4] As described in the 913 study, in some circumstances the relationship is explicit, such as the requirement that each investment adviser that is registered with the Commis-sion or required to be registered with the Commission must also adopt a written code of ethics. These ethical codes must at a minimum address, among other things, a minimum standard of conduct for all supervised persons reflective of the adviser's and its supervised persons' fiduciary obligations.[5]

In other circumstances, an entire body of rules is based implicitly on ethical precepts. This is the case with the rules adopted and enforced by FINRA and other self-regulatory organizations, which 'are grounded in concepts of ethics, professionalism, fair dealing, and just and equitable principles of trade', giving the SROs authority to reach conduct that may not rise to the level of fraud.[6] This has empowered FINRA and other SROs to, for example, not require proof of *scienter* to establish a suitability obligation,[7] to develop rules and guidance on fair prices, commissions and mark-ups that takes into account that what may be 'fair' (or reasonable) in one transaction could be 'unfair' (or unreasonable) in another,[8] and to require broker-dealers to engage in fair and balanced communi-cations with the public, disclose conflicts of interest, and to undertake a number of other duties.[9] In addition to approving rules grounded on these ethical pre-cepts, the Commission has also sustained various FINRA disciplinary actions utilizing FINRA's authority to enforce 'just and equitable principles of trade', even where the underlying activity did not involve securities, such as actions involving insurance , tax shelters, signature forgery, credit card fraud, fraudulent expense account reimbursement, etc.[10]

Other ethical precepts are derived from the antifraud provisions of the federal securities laws. The 'shingle' theory, for example, holds that by virtue of engaging in the brokerage business a broker-dealer implicitly represents to those with whom it transacts business that it will deal fairly with them. When a broker-dealer takes actions that are not fair to its customer, these must be disclosed to avoid making the implied representation of fairness not misleading. A number of duties and conduct regulations have been articulated by the Commission or by courts based on the shingle theory.[11]

Another source by which ethical concepts are transposed onto the federal securities laws is the concept of fiduciary duty. The Supreme Court has construed Section 206(1) and (2) of the Investment Advisers Act as establishing a federal fiduciary standard governing the conduct of advisers.[12] This imposes on investment advisers 'the affirmative duty of "utmost good faith, and full and fair disclosure of all material facts", as well as an affirmative obligation to "employ reasonable care to avoid misleading"' clients and prospective clients. As the 913 Study stated,

> Fundamental to the federal fiduciary standard are the duties of loyalty and care. The duty of loyalty requires an adviser to serve the best interests of its clients, which includes an obligation not to subordinate the clients' interests to its own. An adviser's duty of care requires it to 'make a reasonable investigation to determine that it is not basing its recommendations on materially inaccurate or incomplete information'.[13]

While broker-dealers are generally not subject to a fiduciary duty under the federal securities laws, courts have imposed such a duty under certain circumstances, such as where a broker-dealer exercises discretion or control over customer assets, or has a relationship of trust and confidence with its customer.[14] The 913 Study, of course, explores the principle of a uniform fiduciary standard.

Concepts such as fair dealing, good faith and suitability are dynamic and continue to arise in new contexts. For example, the Business Conduct Standards for Securities-Based Swap Dealers ('SBSDs') and Major Security-Based Swap Participants ('MSBSPs'), required by Title VII of the Dodd-Frank Act and put out for comment last summer, include proposed elements such as

> a requirement that communications with counterparties are made in a fair and balanced manner based on principles of fair dealing and good faith;

> an obligation to disclosure to a counterparty material information about the security-based swap, such as material risks, characteristics, incentives and conflicts of interest; and

> a determination by SBSDs that any recommendations that they make regarding security-based swaps are suitable for their counterparties.

Of course the Business Conduct Standards have not been finalized, but the requirements of Title VII requiring promulgation of these rules, as well as the content of the rules as proposed, illustrate that ethical concepts continue to be a touchstone for both Congress and the Commission in developing and interpreting the federal securities laws.

The Relationship Between Ethics and Enterprise Management.

Ethics is not important merely because the federal securities laws are grounded on ethical principles. Good ethics is also good business. Treating customers fairly and honestly helps build a firm's reputation and brand, while attracting the best employees and business partners. Conversely, creating the impression that ethical behaviour is not important to a firm is incredibly damaging to its reputation and business prospects. This, of course, holds true equally for individuals, and there are plenty of enforcement cases that tell the story of highly talented and successful individuals who were punished because they violated their ethical and compliance responsibilities.

Another way of saying this is that a corporate culture that reinforces ethical behaviour is a key component of effectively managing risk across the enterprise. As the Committee of Sponsoring Organizations of the Treadway Commission ('COSO') put it, in articulating its well-established standards of Internal Control and Enterprise Risk Management:

> An entity's strategy and objectives and the way they are implemented are based on preferences, value judgments, and management styles. Management's integrity and commitment to ethical values influence these preferences and judgments, which are translated into standards of behavior. Because an entity's good reputation is so valuable, the standards of behavior must go beyond mere compliance with the law. Managers of well-run enterprises increasingly have accepted the view that ethics pays and ethical behavior is good business.[15]

In the wake of the financial crisis, enterprise risk management is a rapidly evolving discipline that places ethical values at the heart of good governance, enterprise risk management and compliance. For example, organizations such as COSO, the Ethics Resource Center (ERC), the Open Compliance and Ethics Guidelines (OCEG) and the Ethics & Compliance Officer Association (ECOA) have developed detailed guidance, from the board room to business units and key risk, control and compliance departments, on implementation of effective enterprise risk management systems. Industry and sector specific guidance has flowed from these general standards. As COS notes, integrity and ethical values are the pillars of an effective compliance culture.

The effectiveness of enterprise risk management cannot rise above the integrity and ethical values of the people who create, administer, and monitor entity activities. Integrity and ethical values are essential elements of an entity's internal environment, affecting the design, administration, and monitoring of other enterprise risk management components.[16]

Nowhere should this be more true than in financial services firms today, which depend for their existence on public trust and confidence to a unique degree. Expectations are rising around the world for a stronger culture of ethical behavior at financial services firms of all types and sizes. As the Basle Committee on Banking Supervision recently stated:

> A demonstrated corporate culture that supports and provides appropriate norms and incentives for professional and responsible behaviour is an essential foundation of good governance. In this regard, the board should take the lead in establishing the "tone at the top" and in setting professional standards and corporate values that promote integrity for itself, senior management and other employees.[17]

As the standards for ethical behavior continue to evolve, your firms' key stakeholders – shareholders, clients and employees will increasingly expect you to meet or exceed those standards.

In my first speech here at the SEC I outlined ten elements I believe make an effective compliance and ethics program. These elements reflect the compliance, ethics and risk management standards and guidance noted above. They also reflect the US Federal Sentencing Guidelines (FSG), which were revised in 2004 to explicitly integrate ethics into the elements of an effective compliance and ethics program that would be considered as mitigating factors in determining criminal sentences for corporations. These elements include:

Governance: This includes the board of directors and senior management setting a tone at the top and providing compliance and ethics programs with the necessary resources, independence, standing, and authority to be effective. NEP staff have begun meeting with directors, CEOs, and senior management teams to better understand risk and assess the tone at the top that is shaping the culture of compliance, ethics and risk management.

Culture and values: This includes leadership promoting integrity and ethical values in decision-making across the organization and requiring accountability.

Incentives and rewards: This includes incorporating integrity and ethical values into performance management systems and compensation so the right behaviors are encouraged and rewarded, while inappropriate behaviors are firmly addressed.

Risk management: This includes ensuring effective processes to identify, assess, mitigate and manage compliance and ethics risk across the organization.

Policies and procedures: This includes establishing, maintaining and updating policies and procedures that are tailored to your business, your risks, your regulatory requirements and the conflicts of interest in your business model.

Communication and training: This includes training that is tailored to your specific business, risk and regulatory requirements, and which is roles-based so that each critical partner in the compliance process understands their roles and responsibilities.

Monitoring and reporting: This includes monitoring, testing and surveillance functions that assess the health of the system and report critical issues to management and the board.

Escalation, investigation and discipline: This includes ensuring there are processes where employees can raise concerns confidentially and anonymously, without fear of retaliation, and that matters are effectively investigated and resolved with fair and consistent discipline.

Issues management: This includes ensuring that root cause analysis is done with respect to issues that are identified so effective remediation can occur in a timely manner.

An on-going improvement process: This includes ensuring the organization is proactively keeping pace with developments and leading practices as part of a commitment to a culture of ongoing improvement.

In addition to the effective practices above, the NEP has also seen firms that have focused on enhancing regulatory compliance programs through effective integration of ethics principles and practices. These include renaming the function and titles to incorporate ethics explicitly; elevating the dialogue with senior management and the board; implementing core values and business principles to guide ethical decision-making; integrating ethics into key leadership communications; and introducing surveys and other mechanisms to monitor the health of the culture and identify emerging risks and issues.

The Relationship of Compliance and Ethics with Enterprise Risk Management

We can expand the discussion above beyond compliance and ethics to address enterprise risk management and risk governance more broadly. These same program elements, and ethics considerations, are equally critical, but the scope of risks expands beyond regulatory risk to also include market, credit and operational risk, among others. The roles and responsibilities also expand to include risk management, finance, internal audit and other key risk and control functions. Whether we're talking about compliance and ethics or we're talking about ERM, it is important to clarify fundamental roles and responsibilities across the organization.

1. The business is the first line of defense responsible for taking, managing and supervising risk effectively and in accordance with the risk appetite and tolerances set by the board and senior management of the whole organization.

2. Key support functions, such as compliance and ethics or risk management, are the second line of defense. They need to have adequate resources, independence, standing and authority to implement effective programs and objectively monitor and escalate risk issues.

3. Internal Audit is the third line of defense and is responsible for providing independent verification and assurance that controls are in place and operating effectively.

4. Senior management is responsible for reinforcing the tone at the top, driving a culture of compliance and ethics and ensuring effective implementation of enterprise risk management in key business processes, including strategic planning, capital allocation, performance management and compensation incentives.

5. The board of directors (if one exists in the organization) is responsible for setting the tone at the top, overseeing management and ensuring risk management, regulatory, compliance and ethics obligations are met.

While compliance and ethics officers play a key role in supporting effective ERM, risk managers in areas such as investment risk, market risk, credit risk, operational risk, funding risk and liquidity risk also play an important role. As noted above, the board, senior management, other risk and control functions, the business units and internal audit also play a critical role in ERM. As ERM matures as a discipline, it is critical that these key functions work together in an integrated coordinated manner that supports more effective ERM. Understanding and managing the inter-relationship between various risks is a central tenet of effective ERM. One needs only reflect on the financial crisis to understand how the aggregation and inter-relationship of risks across various risk categories and market participants created the perfect storm. ERM provides a more systemic risk analysis framework to proactively identify, assess and manage risk in today's market environment.

OCIE Considerations

As I discussed earlier, there is an ethical component to many of the federal securities laws. When NEP staff examines, for example, an investment adviser's adherence to its fiduciary obligations, or a broker-dealer's effective development, maintenance and testing of its compliance program, our examiners are looking at how well firms are meeting both the letter and spirit of these obligations. In addition, our examiners certainly examine specific requirements for ethical processes, such as business conduct standards.

There is another way in which the ethical environment within a firm matters to us. As you know, our examination program has greatly increased its emphasis on risk-based examinations. How we perceive a registrant's culture of compliance and ethics informs our view of the risks posed by particular entities. In this regard we have begun meeting boards of directors, CEOs and senior management to share perspectives on the key risks facing the firm, how those risks are being managed and the effectiveness of key risk management, compliance, ethics and control functions. It provides us an opportunity to emphasize the critical importance of compliance, ethics, risk management and other key control functions, and our expectation that these functions have sufficient resources, independence, standing and authority to be effective in their roles. These dialogues also provide us an opportunity to assess the tone at the top that is shaping the culture of compliance, ethics and risk management in the firm. If we believe that a firm tolerates a nonchalant attitude toward compliance, ethics and risk management, we will factor that into our analysis of which registrants to examine, what issues to focus on, and how deep to go in executing our examinations.

Finally, I would end by sharing with you that we are also embracing these leading practices. We recently created our own program around compliance and ethics. For the first time, we have a dedicated team focused on strengthening and monitoring how effectively we adhere to our own examination standards. We are in the process of finalizing our first Exam Manual, which we set forth all of our key policies and standards in one manual. We have also established a senior management committee with oversight responsibility for compliance, ethics and internal control. On the risk management front, we are also making good progress. We have recruited individuals with expertise and established a senior management oversight committee here as well. In short, we are also committing ourselves to a culture of ongoing improvement and leading practices.

Conclusion

Thank you for inviting me to speak here today. I hope that my remarks will be helpful to you and help you to perform your critical compliance functions more effectively. I invite your feedback, whether regarding the points that I made, or the points that you think I missed. I now invite your questions.

APPENDIX 2: SHINING A LIGHT ON EXPENDITURES OF SHAREHOLDER MONEY

Commissioner Luis A. Aguilar
U.S. Securities and Exchange Commission
Practising Law Institute's SEC Speaks in 2012 Program, Ronald Reagan Building and International Trade Center, Washington, D.C.
February 24, 2012

Good morning. It is my pleasure to be here today. This is my fourth SEC Speaks and my first after being sworn-in for a second term as an SEC Commissioner. I can report that the issues before the Commission and the magnitude of what is at stake remain of top concern, just as they have throughout my tenure. Before I begin, let me start by issuing the standard disclaimer that the views I express today are my own, and do not necessarily reflect the views of the Securities and Exchange Commission, my fellow Commissioners, or members of the staff.

In thinking through how to use my time with you today, many issues immediately came to mind. To name just a few, I thought of discussing:

- The SEC's work on Title VII to regulate the security-based derivatives industry – what has been proposed and the longer list of what has yet to be adopted;
- The SEC's new no admit/no deny policy involving parallel criminal proceedings,[1] and how it applies in so few situations that it needs to be revised to be more useful and effective; and
- The lengthy delay in re-establishing the Investor Advisory Committee, a committee required by Dodd-Frank to amplify the voices of investors and ensure that the Commission is carrying out its core mission.

However, I decided to focus my time today on one issue – an issue that highlights the Commission's fundamental responsibilities as a regulator.

The Commission's core mission is to protect investors. William O. Douglas, a former chairman of the Securities and Exchange Commission, who went on to serve as a Supreme Court Justice, described the SEC's role by contrasting it with a well-represented industry. Chairman Douglas said: 'We've got broker's advocates, we've got exchange advocates, we've got investment banker advocates, and we [the SEC] are the investor's advocate'.[2]

Not much has changed since Chairman Douglas spoke those words at his first press conference as SEC Chairman in 1937. The industry, with its lobbyists and spokespeople, remains the loudest voice – in fact, one could say that things have gotten much worse. As a result, investors need an advocate today more than ever.[3]

Given that this is so, a true investor's advocate would be focused on whether shareholders and investors receive adequate disclosure about the companies they own or may buy. In serving as an investor advocate, it is the responsibility of the Commission to promulgate rules to make sure that investors are armed with the appropriate information they need during each step of their investment decision – whether it is to buy, sell, or hold their securities, or to vote their securities. When it is clear that investors are in the dark and not receiving adequate disclosures, the Commission should act, and act swiftly, to ensure that investors have the information they require.

Background of Citizens United

I want to illustrate this point by looking at an issue that dominates the headlines on a daily basis. And that is the undisclosed corporate campaign spending arising from the Supreme Court's decision in *Citizens United v. Federal Election Commission*.[4] In January 2010, the Supreme Court struck down federal restrictions on the ability of corporations 'to use general treasury funds to make campaign expenditures defined as an "electioneering communication" or for speech expressly advocating the election or defeat of a candidate'.[5] The Court was quick to also say '[t]he Government may regulate corporate political speech through disclaimer and disclosure requirements, but it may not suppress speech altogether'.[6]

Fundamental Deprivation

The ramifications of this decision and its resulting impact on campaign finance laws and practices have been significant and swift.

For example, it has been reported that outside groups spent four times as much in 2010, after the Citizens United decision, as compared to in 2006.[7] A recently released poll found Americans across all parties oppose the ruling; and among all voters, sixty-two percent oppose the decision.[8] President Obama described the impact of the Supreme Court's decision as

> dealing a huge blow to [our] efforts to rein in this undue influence. In short, this decision gives corporations and other special interests the power to spend unlimited amounts of money – literally millions of dollars – to affect elections throughout our country. This, in turn, will multiply their influence over decision-making in our government.[9]

As to whether or not corporations should be making political contributions at all, that is a question I will leave to other agencies, corporations, institutions, and to the American public at large.

I want to focus on the shareholders of corporations and how they are often in the dark as to whether the companies they own, or contemplate owning, are making political expenditures. Withholding information from shareholders is a fundamental deprivation that undermines the securities regulatory framework which requires investors receive adequate and appropriate information, so that they can make informed decisions about whether to purchase, hold, or sell shares – and how to exercise their voting rights. Investors are not receiving adequate disclosure, and as the investor's advocate, the Commission should act swiftly to rectify the situation by requiring transparency.

Many interested parties have weighed in and enumerated significant reasons for requiring these disclosures.[10] These reasons include, but are not limited to, the following:

- Investors may not want to invest in companies that engage in any political expenditure.
- Individual investors may want to avoid investing in a company whose political spending advances causes or candidates with which that investor disagrees.
- To ensure that political spending decisions do not further the interests of corporate managers at the expense of shareholder interests. On this topic, John Bogle, founder of Vanguard, has stated, 'corporate managers are likely to try to shape government policy in a way that serves their own interests over the interests of their shareholders'.[11]
- The view that when corporations are able to obtain favorable conditions through political influence, rather than meritoriously adding value through a better product or service, it distorts the operation of the marketplace, which undercuts capital formation.
- A lack of transparency regarding political expenditures directly fosters destructive pay-to-play corruption. As just one example, nearly half the states have adopted pay-to-play bans, after corruption scandals revealed government officials demanding corporate payoffs in exchange for public contracts.[12]

Despite the abundance of reasons investors have for requiring this information and the transparency it would provide, the fact remains that no comprehensive disclosure framework exists.

There are tens of thousands that have urged the Commission to address this issue, ranging from investors, academics, non-profits, state treasurers, and businesses.[13] To highlight just a few of the requests, in August 2011, ten law professors from distinguished universities across the country filed a petition for rulemaking requesting that the Commission promulgate rules to require that public companies disclose political expenditures.[14] The Commission has also received letters from Members of Congress,[15] from elected government officials with fiduciary responsibility for nearly one trillion dollars in pension fund assets,[16] and from a coalition of United States Senators.[17] Each of these letters asked the Commission to take action to require public disclosure of corporate political spending.

In November 2011, a coalition of asset managers and investment professionals representing over $690 billion in assets wrote to the SEC to express their strong support for the SEC to promulgate rules requiring corporate political transparency. This coalition lamented that corporate political expenditures 'may be subject to a variety of state and federal rules, but there are no current rules that require that companies disclose this spending to their shareholders, and there are significant gaps in the type of spending that is required to be disclosed to anyone.'[18]

In a separate letter, the Council for Institutional Investors described the fundamental issue as

> Shareowners have a right to know whether and how their company uses its resources for political purposes. Yet the existing regulatory framework creates barriers to this information. Disclosure is either dispersed among several regulatory authorities or entirely absent in cases where political spending is channeled through independent organizations exempt from naming donors.[19]

Ted Wheeler, the State Treasurer of Oregon, and a vocal advocate for rules regarding corporate disclosure of political donations, stated '[c]ompanies have the ability to spend heavily on political causes and they have the right to do so. However, corporations also have the ability to obscure that spending from shareholders, such as Oregon beneficiaries of trust funds ... That's wrong.'[20] It is troubling that many companies are funding political campaigns without their shareholders' consent or even knowledge.

Evidence of Investors Trying to Obtain the Information

The importance of this topic to shareholders is evident. The Commission itself has received tens of thousands of letters requesting that it take action.[21] The record is replete with examples and evidence of investors trying to obtain information regarding corporate political expenditures.

For example, in 2011, out of the 465 shareholder proposals appearing on public company proxy statements, 50 proposals were related to political spending.[22] In fact, more proposals of this type were included in proxy statements than any other type of proposal.[23] During the 2011 proxy season, 25 of the companies in the S&P 100 included proposals on their proxy statements requesting disclosure of corporate spending on politics.[24]

The demand from investors has been so significant that large public companies have increasingly agreed to adopt policies requiring disclosure of companies' political expenditures. In the S&P 100, this number has risen from a trivial level in 2004 to close to 60% by 2011. However, it is important to keep in mind that while some companies are voluntarily providing disclosures, many others are not. In addition, the disclosure that is provided is not uniform and may not be adequate.

Unfortunately, there is no comprehensive system of disclosure related to corporate political expenditures – and that failure results in investors being deprived of uniform, reliable, and consistent disclosure regarding the political expenditures of the companies they own.

This is a Core Responsibility of the SEC

Arming investors with the information they need to facilitate informed decision-making is a core responsibility of the SEC. In fact, it is one of the factors that led to the creation of the SEC. It is one of the SEC's core functions to identify gaps in information that investors require, and then close that gap as quickly as possible.

Shareholders require uniform disclosures regarding corporate political expenditures for many reasons, including that it is impossible to have any corporate accountability or oversight without it. The Supreme Court recognized that need. For example, even as it struck down restrictions on corporate campaign contributions, the Supreme Court cited '[s]hareholder objections raised through the procedures of corporate democracy'[25] as a means through which investors could monitor the use of corporate resources on political activities. The Court envisioned that

> prompt disclosure of expenditures can provide shareholders and citizens with information needed to hold corporations and elected officials accountable for their positions and supporters. Shareholders can determine whether their corporation's political speech advances the corporation's interest in making profits, and citizens can see whether elected officials are 'in-the-pocket' of so-called moneyed interest.[26]

Unfortunately, the Court envisioned a mechanism that does not currently exist.

This is not the first time that the Commission has been faced with a lack of transparency regarding political expenditures. In 1999, the Commission proposed a pay-to-play rule in direct response to egregious pay-to-play conduct by investment advisers that had harmed investors with sweetheart deals and bribes.[27] The egregiousness of the conduct and the need for new rules was clear. It was obvious that depending solely on the SEC's ability to use its anti-fraud authority would be too little, too late. However, the pay-to-play rule was shelved – lost to the wasteland where un-adopted SEC rule proposals go. It took a decade of scathing scandals, egregious fraud, and significant harm, before the Commission made pay-to-play a priority, and acted on it in 2010.[28] If the Commission had adopted new rules in 1999, it is likely that much of the tremendous harm of the pay-to-play scandals from the last decade could have been averted. The cost of Commission inaction – particularly in the face of compelling evidence for the Commission to act – can be devastating, as we have seen over and over again.

Requiring transparency for corporate political expenditures cannot wait a decade. It is the Commission's responsibility to rectify this gap and ensure that investors are not left in the dark while their money is used without their knowledge or consent. The Commission should provide for disclosure of corporate political expenditures that results in uniform and consistent disclosure.

Conclusion

As Commissioners, it is crucially important that we listen, and respond, to the needs of investors. The Commission receives investor input in various forms, from comment letters on proposed rulemakings, to formal rulemaking petitions. Unfortunately, the voices of investors are often drowned out by the louder, better-funded, and often better-connected voices of issuers, financial institutions, and corporate lawyers. When that happens, it is incumbent upon us to not only remember, but also make evident by our actions, that the fundamental mission of the SEC is to protect investors.

In closing, I want to thank you for your kind attention.

I also want to thank the many SEC staffers who are participating at this year's SEC Speaks – as well as the many others who devote themselves to the protection of investors. I am proud to work at their side.

Thank you.

WORKS CITED

Acharya, V. V., T. F. Cooley, M. Richardson and I. Walter (eds), *Regulating Wall Street: The Dodd-Frank Act and the New Architecture of Global Finance* (Hoboken, NJ: John Wiley & Sons, Inc., 2011).

Akerlof, G. A. and R. Shiller, *Animal Spirits: How Human Psychology Drives the Economy, and Why It Matters for Global Capitalism* (Princeton, NJ: Princeton University Press, 2010).

Appiah, K. A., *The Ethics of Identity* (Princeton, NJ: Princeton University Press, 2005).

Aristotle, *Nicomachean Ethics*, at http://classics.mit.edu/Aristotle/nicomachaen.1.i.html [accessed 17 November 2014].

Boatright, J. R. (ed.), *Finance Ethics: Critical Issues in Theory and Practice* (Hoboken, NJ: John Wiley & Sons, 2010).

Bogle, J. C., *The Battle for the Soul of Capitalism: How the Financial System Undermined Social Ideals, Damaged Trust in the Markets, Robbed Investors of Trillions – and What to Do About It* (New Haven, CT: Yale University Press, 2005).

—, *The Clash of Cultures: Investment Vs. Speculation* (Hoboken, NJ: John C. Wiley, 2012).

Boylan, M. (ed.), *Business Ethics*, 2nd edn (Malden, MA: Wiley-Blackwell, 2013).

Chapman, G., 'Revenge for Honour', *The Comedies and Tragedies of George Chapman* (London: John Pearson, 1873).

Coleman, T. S., *A Practical Guide to Risk Management* (New York: Research Foundation of CFA Institute, 2011).

Daft, R. L. and D. Marcic, *Understanding Management*, 9th edn (Stamford, CT: Cengage Learning, 2013).

Drucker, P. F., *Landmarks of Tomorrow: A Report on the New 'Post-Modern' World* (New York: Harper & Brothers, 1959).

—, *The Daily Drucker* (New York: Harper Collins, 2004).

—, *Management*, revised edn (New York: Harper Collins, 2008).

Financial Crisis Inquiry Commission, *Financial Crisis Inquiry Report: Final Report of the National Commission on the Causes of the Financial and Economic Crisis in the United States* (Philadelphia, PA: Public Affairs Reports, 2011).

Friedman, B. (ed.), *Reforming U.S. Financial Markets: Reflections Before and Beyond Dodd-Frank* (Cambridge, MA: Massachusetts Institute of Technology Press, 2011).

Friedman, M., *Capitalism and Freedom* (Chicago, IL: University of Chicago Press, 1962).

Fukuyama, F., *Trust: The Social Virtues and the Making of Prosperity* (New York: Free Press, 1996).

Fullbrook, E. (ed.), *Real World Economics – A Post-Autistic Economics Reader* (London: Anthem Press, 2007).

Glover, J., *Humanity: A Moral History of the 20th Century* (New Haven, CT: Yale Nota Bene/ Yale University Press, 1999).

Goodpaster, K. E., *Conscience and Corporate Culture* (Malden, MA: Blackwell Publishers, 2007).

Halberstam, D., *The Reckoning* (New York: Open Road Integrated Media, 2012), p. 734.

Hoyk, R. and P. Hersey, *The Ethical Executive: Becoming Aware of the Root Causes of Unethical Behavior: 45 Psychological Traps that Every One of Us Falls Prey To* (Stanford, CA: Stanford University Press, 2008).

Kahneman, D., *Thinking Fast and Slow* (New York: Farrar, Strauss and Giroux, 2011).

—, and A. Tversky, *Choices, Values, and Frames* (Cambridge University Press, 2000).

Krutch, J. W. (ed.), *Walden and Other Writings by Henry David Thoreau* (New York: Bantam Books, 1981).

Liu, E. and N. Hanauer, *The Gardens of Democracy: A New American Story of Citizenship, Economy and the Role of Government* (Seattle, WA: Sasquatch Books, 2011).

Lowenstein, R., *Buffet: The Making of an American Capitalist* (New York: Random House, 2008).

MacDonald, S. B. and J. E. Hughes, *Separating Fools from their Money: A History of American Financial Scandals* (New Brunswick, NJ: Transaction Publishers, 2010).

McDermott, J. J. (ed.), *The Writings of William James* (Chicago, IL: University of Chicago Press, 1977).

McDonald, L. G. and P. Robinson, *A Colossal Failure of Common Sense: The Inside Story of the Collapse of Lehman Brothers* (New York: Crown Publishing, 2009).

Nussbaum, M. C., *Women and Human Development: The Capabilities Approach* (Cambridge: Cambridge University Press, 2000).

Partnoy, F., *Infectious Greed: How Deceit and Risk Corrupted The Financial Markets* (New York: Times Books, 2003).

Pine, J. T. (ed.), *Frederick Douglass on Slavery and the Civil War: Selections from His Writings* (New York: Dover Thrift Editions, 2003).

Plato, *The Republic*, at http://classics.mit.edu/Plato/republic.9.viii.html [accessed 17 November 2014].

Potter, W., *Deadly Spin: An Insurance Company Insider Speaks Out on How Corporate PR is Killing Health Care and Deceiving Americans* (New York: Bloomsbury Press, 2010).

Rorty, R., *Philosophy as Cultural Politics: Philosophical Papers, Volume 4* (New York: Cambridge University Press, 2007).

Roubini, N. and S. Mihm, *Crisis Economics: A Crash Course in the Future of Finance* (New York: Penguin Press, 2010).

Sackrey, C., J. Schneider and J. Knoedler, *Introduction to Political Economy*, 5th edn (Boston, MA: Dollars and Sense, 2008).

Sahlins, M., *Stone Age Economics* (New York: Routledge, 1974).

Seton, E. T. (ed.), *The Gospel of the Red Man: An Indian Bible* (San Diego, CA: Book Tree, 2006).

Shakespeare, W., *Macbeth,* at http://shakespeare.mit.edu/macbeth/full.html [accessed 19 November 2014].

Siegler, L. B. (ed.), *Insights into the Global Financial Crisis* (New York: Research Foundation of CFA Institute, 2009).

Singer, P. (ed.), *A Companion to Ethics* (Cambridge, MA: Basil Blackwell, 1993).

Smith, A., *An Inquiry into the Nature and Causes of the Wealth of Nations* (New York: P. F. Collier & Son, 1952), Part 2.

—, *The Theory of Moral Sentiments*, ed. K. Haakonssen (Cambridge: Cambridge University Press, 2002).

Sorkin, A. R., *Too Big to Fail: The Inside Story of How Wall Street and Washington Fought to Save the Financial System – and Themselves* (New York: Penguin Group, 2010).

Taleb, N., *The Black Swan: The Impact of the Highly Improbable* (New York: Random House, 2007).

Taylor, E. B., *Primitive Culture: Researches into the Development of Philosophy, Mythology, Religion, Art and Custom* (London: John Murray, 1871).

Wilkinson, R. and K. Pickett, *The Spirit Level: Why Greater Equality Makes Societies Stronger* (New York: Bloomsbury Press, 2009).

Will, G. F., *Statecraft as Soulcraft: What Government Does* (New York: Simon and Schuster, 1983).

NOTES

Glossary of Selected Terms

1. R. L. Daft and D. Marcic, *Understanding Management*, 9th ed. (Stamford, CT: Cengage Learning, 2013), pp. 511–12.

Introduction: A Citizen's Meditation on a Problem

1. G. A. Akerlof and R. J. Shiller, *Animal Spirits: How Human Psychology Drives the Economy, and Why It Matters for Global Capitalism* (Princeton, NJ: Princeton University Press, 2010), pp. xxiii–xxiv.
2. Aristotle, *Nicomachean Ethics*, trans. W. D. Ross, 10 vols (350 BC; Cambridge, MA: MIT Internet Classics Archive, 2000), vol. 1, at http://classics.mit.edu/Aristotle/nicomachaen.1.i.html [accessed 17 November 2014].
3. J. F. Kennedy, Commencement Address at American University, 10 June 1963, J. F. Kennedy Presidential Library and Museum, Film Reel, TNC-319-EX, at http://www.jfklibrary.org/Asset-Viewer/BWC7I4C9QUmLG9J6I8oy8w.aspx [accessed 17 November 2014].
4. Unless otherwise indicated, I use the words 'moral' and 'ethical' interchangeably and has having the same meaning, that is, as referring well-reasoned prescriptions for conduct that show due regard to the needs and dignity of both ourselves and of others.
5. M. Friedman, *Capitalism and Freedom* (Chicago, IL: University of Chicago Press, 1962), p. 202.
6. P. F. Drucker, *The Daily Drucker* (New York: Harper Collins, 2004), p. 319.
7. See E. Fullbrook (ed.), *Real World Economics – A Post-Autistic Economics Reader* (London: Anthem Press, 2007).
8. Fullbrook, *Real World Economics*, p. 485.
9. Sworn Again America, 'The Oath', at http://www.swornagainamerica.us/ [accessed 8 November 2014].
10. M. Gentile, 'Business Schools: A Failing Grade on Ethics', *Bloomberg Businessweek*, 5 February 2009, at http://www.businessweek.com/bschools/content/feb2009/bs2009025_129477.htm [accessed 1 March 2014].
11. G. Chapman, *Revenge for Honour*, III.ii, in *The Comedies and Tragedies of George Chapman* (London: John Pearson, 1873), p. 327.
12. N. Roubini and S. Mihm, *Crisis Economics: A Crash Course in the Future of Finance* (New York: Penguin Press, 2010), p. 219.

13. R. Hoyk and P. Hersey, *The Ethical Executive, Becoming Aware of the Root Causes of Unethical Behavior: 45 Psychological Traps that Every One of Us Falls Prey To* (Stanford, CA: Stanford University Press, 2008), p. 24.

14. R. Rorty, 'Justice as a Larger Loyalty', in *Philosophy as Cultural Politics: Philosophical Papers, Volume 4* (New York: Cambridge University Press, 2007), pp. 42–3.

15. For example, see D. Kahneman's *Thinking Fast and Slow* (New York: Farrar, Strauss and Giroux, 2011), and D. Kahneman's and A. Tversky's, *Choices, Values, and Frames* (Cambridge University Press, 2000).

16. Plato, *The Republic*, Book II, at http://classics.mit.edu/Plato/republic.3.ii.html [accessed 10 October 2014]; emphasis added.

17. G. A. Akerlof and R. J. Shiller, *Animal Spirits: How Human Psychology Drives the Economy, and Why It* Matters for Global Capitalism (Princeton, NJ: Princeton University Press, 2010), pp. 26–7.

18. L. G. McDonald and P. Robinson, *A Colossal Failure of Common Sense: The Inside Story of the Collapse of Lehman Brothers* (New York: Crown Publishing, 2009), p. 293.

19. W. Shakespeare, *Macbeth*, I.vii, at http://shakespeare.mit.edu/macbeth/full.html [accessed 19 November 2014].

20. K. E. Goodpaster, *Conscience and Corporate Culture* (Malden, MA: Blackwell Publishers, 2007).

21. P. F. Drucker, *Landmarks of Tomorrow – A Report on the New "Post-Modern" World* (New York: Harper & Brothers, 1959), p. 264.

22. E. Povoledo and D. Carvajal, 'Increasingly in Europe, Suicides "by Economic Crisis"', *New York Times,* 14 April 2012, at http://www.nytimes.com/2012/04/15/world/europe/increasingly-in-europe-suicides-by-economic-crisis.html?pagewanted=all&_r=0 [accessed 13 February 2014].

23. Y. Q. Mui, 'For black Americans, financial damage from sub-prime implosion is likely to last', *Washington Post*, 8 July 2012, at http://www.washingtonpost.com/business/economy/for-black-americans-financial-damage-from-subprime-implosion-is-likely-to-last/2012/07/08/gJQAwNmzWW_story.html [accessed 24 February 2014].

24. Organization for Economic Cooperation and Development ('OECD'), at http://www.oecd-ilibrary.org/economics/household-saving-rates-forecasts_2074384x-table7 [accessed 13 February 2014].

25. As of this writing in late 2014, however, there were signs of improvement in US household balance sheets, but the savings rate still remains anemic, and most Americans would be unable to withstand a sustained period of unemployment due to still-high household debt levels – not to mention student loan debt that has surpassed $1 trillion, with default rates at about 13.7 percent in the last quarter of 2014.

1 Human Beings and Markets

1. E. T. Seton (ed.), *The Gospel of the Red Man: An Indian Bible* (San Diego, CA: Book Tree, 2006), p. 73.

2. P. Hsieh, 'A Defense of High Frequency Trading', *Real Clear Markets*, 7 January 2011, at http://www.realclearmarkets.com/articles/2011/01/07/a_defense_of_high-frequency_trading_98822.html [accessed 7 November 2014].

3. M. C. Nussbaum, *Women and Human Development: The Capabilities Approach* (Cambridge: Cambridge University Press, 2000), pp. 78–81.

4. A. Smith, *An Inquiry into the Nature and Causes of the Wealth of Nations*, Part 2 (New

York: P. F. Collier & Son, 1952), p. 160, emphasis added. Originally published 1776.

5.   J. W. Krutch (ed.), *Walden and Other Writings by Henry David Thoreau* (New York: Bantam Books, 1981), p. 160.

6.   A. Smith, *The Theory of Moral Sentiments*, ed. K. Haakonssen (Cambridge: Cambridge University Press, 2002), p 105.

7.   E. Liu and N. Hanauer, *The Gardens of Democracy: A New American Story of Citizenship, Economy and the Role of Government* (Seattle, WA: Sasquatch Books, 2011), pp. 7–8.

8.   D. E. McClean, 'McClean: Goldman Charges No Surprise', *Newsday*, 19 March 2012, at http://www.newsday.com/opinion/oped/mcclean-goldman-charges-are-no-surprise-1.3612309 [accessed 13 October 2014].

9.   J. F. Kennedy, Commencement Address at American University, 10 June 1963, J. F. Kennedy Presidential Library and Museum, Film Reel, TNC-319-EX, at http://www.jfklibrary.org/Asset-Viewer/BWC7I4C9QUmLG9J6I8oy8w.aspx [accessed 17 November 2014].

10. 'Report Pursuant to Section 21(a) of the Securities Exchange Act of 1934 Regarding the NASD and the NASDAQ Market', 8 August 1996, at https://www.sec.gov/litigation/investreport/nd21a-report.txt [accessed 2 February 2014].

11. Securities and Exchange Commission Press Release, 'SEC Charges New York-Based High Frequency Trading Firm With Fraudulent Trading to Manipulate Closing Prices: First High Frequency Trading Manipulation Case', 16 October 2014, at http://www.sec.gov/News/PressRelease/Detail/PressRelease/1370543184457#.VEGsQTh0zIU [accessed 18 October 2014].

12. T. Gilroy, *Michael Clayton: Final Shooting Script* , 11 February 2006, at http://www.screenplaydb.com/film/scripts/michaelclayton/ [accessed 5 July 2014].

13. W. Potter, *Deadly Spin: An Insurance Company Insider Speaks Out on How Corporate PR is Killing Health Care and Deceiving Americans* (New York: Bloomsbury Press, 2010), pp. 11–12.

14. The Financial Crisis Inquiry Commission, which authored the report, was established as part of the Fraud Enforcement and Recovery Act (Public Law 111–21) passed by Congress and signed by the President of the United States in May 2009.

15. Financial Crisis Inquiry Commission, *Financial Crisis Inquiry Report: Final Report of the National Commission on the Causes of the Financial and Economic Crisis in the United States* (Philadelphia, PA: Public Affairs Reports, 2011), pp. 390–1.

16. E. B. Taylor, *Primitive Culture: Researches into the Development of Philosophy, Mythology, Religion, Art and Custom* (London: John Murray, 1871), p. 1.

17. B. Dylan, 'Gotta Serve Somebody' lyrics, at http://www.bobdylan.com/us/songs/gotta-serve-somebody [accessed 19 November 2014].

18. W. W. George, 'Why Leaders Lose Their Way', *Harvard Business School Working Knowledge: Research and Ideas*, 6 June 2011, at http://hbswk.hbs.edu/item/6741.html [accessed 29 December 2013].

19. 'Market', BusinessDictionary.com, at http://www.businessdictionary.com/definition/market.html#ixzz2tJmwMYRW [accessed 17 November 2014].

20. P. F. Drucker, *Management*, revised edn (New York: Harper Collins, 2008), p. 97, emphasis added.

21. J. Glover, *Humanity: A Moral History of the 20th Century* (New Haven, CT: Yale University Press, 1999), p. 265.

22. R. Wilkinson and K. Pickett, *The Spirit Level: Why Greater Equality Makes Societies*

Stronger (New York: Bloomsbury Press, 2009).

23. T. Winter, *The Wolf of Wall Street*, screenplay, p. 68, at http://www.paramountguilds. com/pdf/the_wolf_of_wall_street_screenplay.pdf [accessed 16 February 2014].

24. M. Sahlins, *Stone Age Economics* (New York: Routledge, 1974), p. 37.

2 Recent Scandals and the Cultures that Created Them

1. M. Smith and N. Verbitsky, 'To Catch a Trader', *Frontline*, television programme transcript, 7 January 2014, at http://www.pbs.org/wgbh/pages/frontline/business-economy-financial-crisis/to-catch-a-trader/transcript-54/ [accessed 19 November 2014].

2. J. Lanchester, 'Money Talks: Learning the Language of Finance', *New Yorker* (4 August 2014), at http://www.newyorker.com/magazine/2014/08/04/money-talks-6 [accessed 19 November 2014].

3. Financial Crisis Inquiry Commission, *Financial Crisis Inquiry Report: Final Report of the National Commission on the Causes of the Financial and Economic Crisis in the United States* (Philadelphia, PA: Public Affairs Reports, 2011), p. 361.

4. D. Gleason, 'Insider Trading is a Victimless Crime', *BD Live*, 12 September 2013, at http://www.bdlive.co.za/opinion/columnists/2013/09/12/insider-trading-is-a-victimless-crime [accessed 19 November 2014].

5. P.-J. Engelen and L. Van Liedekerke, 'Insider Trading', in J. Boatright (ed.), *Finance Ethics: Critical Issues in Theory and Practice* (Hoboken, NJ: John Wiley & Sons, 2010), pp. 199–221.

6. Securities and Exchange Commission, 'Insider Trading', at http://www.sec.gov/answers/insider.htm [accessed 19 November 2014].

7. Engelen and Van Liedekerke, 'Insider Trading', p. 214.

8. P. Lattman and B. Protess, 'SAC Capital Is Indicted, and Called a Magnet for Cheating', *New York Times: DealB%k*, 25 July 2013, at http://dealbook.nytimes. com/2013/07/25/sac-capital-is-indicted/?_php=true&_type=blogs&_r=0 [accessed 1 November 2014].

9. United States Department of Justice, Indictment of SAC, p. 3, at http://www.justice. gov/usao/nys/pressreleases/July13/SACChargingAndSupportingDocuments.php [accessed 5 July 2014].

10. United States Department of Justice, Indictment of SAC, p. 4, at http://www.justice. gov/usao/nys/pressreleases/July13/SACChargingAndSupportingDocuments.php [accessed 5 July 2014].

11. L. Thomas Jr, 'Who Wins from an Analysts Rich Deal', New York Times, 8 April 2003, at http://www.nytimes.com/2003/04/08/business/who-wins-from-an-analyst-s-rich-deal.html [accessed 7 October 2013].

12. United States Securities and Exchange Commission, 'SEC Fact Sheet on Global Analyst Research Settlements', at http://www.sec.gov/news/speech/factsheet.htm [accessed 19 November 2014].

13. R. Hoyk and P. Hersey, *The Ethical Executive – Becoming Aware of the Root Causes of Unethical Behavior: 45 Psychological Traps that Every One of Us Falls Prey To* (Stanford, CA: Stanford University Press, 2008), p. 32.

14. B. McLean and J. Nocera, 'How the Roof Fell in on Countrywide', at http://fortune. com/2010/12/23/how-the-roof-fell-in-on-countrywide/ [accessed 8 August 2014].

15. M. Farrell, 'JPMorgan Posts Loss on Big Legal Costs, But ...', *CNN Money*, 11 October 2013, at http://money.cnn.com/2013/10/11/investing/jpmorgan-earnings/ [accessed

10 November 2014].
16. R. Lowenstein, *Buffet: The Making of an American Capitalist* (New York: Random House, 2008), p. 111.
17. J. Bogle, *The Battle for the Soul of Capitalism: How the Financial System Undermined Social Ideals, Damaged Trust in the Markets, Robbed Investors of Trillions – and What to Do About It* (New Haven, CT: Yale University Press, 2005), pp. 42–3.
18. Financial Crisis Inquiry Commission, *Financial Crisis Inquiry Report: Final Report of the National Commission on the Causes of the Financial and Economic Crisis in the United States* (Philadelphia, PA: Public Affairs Reports, 2011), pp. xxii–xxiii.

3 Corporate Soulcraft

1. G. F. Will, *Statecraft as Soulcraft: What Government Does* (New York: Simon and Schuster, 1983), p. 98.
2. E. Liu and N. Hanauer, *The Gardens of Democracy: A New American Story of Citizenship, Economy and the Role of Government* (Seattle, WA: Sasquatch Books, 2011), pp. 10–11.
3. Will, *Statecraft as Soulcraft*, p. 22.
4. J. Burns, 'Is Sarbanes-Oxley Working?', *Wall Street Journal*, 21 June 2004, at http://online.wsj.com/articles/SB108750495035740487 [accessed 13 February 2014].
5. CNBC, 'Cramer Rages on Banks: "Where's the SEC?!"', 17 January 2008, at http://www.cnbc.com/id/22706231 [accessed 13 October 2013].
6. Senator C. Dodd, remarks on the floor of the Senate, *mefeedia.com*, 15 July 2010, at http://www.mefeedia.com/news/31992913 [accessed 21 November 2014].
7. P. F. Drucker, *Management*, revised edn (New York: Harper Collins, 2008), p. 466.
8. P. F. Drucker, *Management*, p. 511.
9. J. E. Stiglitz, *Freefall: America, Free Markets, and the Sinking of the World Economy* (New York: W. W. Norton, 2010), p. 275.
10. R. Barker, 'No, Management is Not a Profession', *Harvard Business Review*, 88 (July–August 2010), pp. 52–60, on p. 53.
11. G. Pence, 'Virtue Theory', in P. Singer (ed.), *A Companion to Ethics* (Cambridge, MA: Basil Blackwell, 1993), pp. 249–58, on p. 251.
12. C. Sackrey, J. Schneider and J. Knoedler, *Introduction to Political Economy*, 5th edn (Boston, MA: Dollars and Sense, 2008), pp. 17–18.

4 The Other Wall Street: A Look at Our Animal Spirits

1. J. Gates, *Democracy at Risk, Rescuing Main Street from Wall Street: A Populist Vision for the Twentieth Century* (Cambridge, MA: Perseus Pub., 2000), p. 250.
2. J. Charkham, *Keeping Good Company: A Study of Corporate Governance in Five Countries* (Oxford: Oxford University Press, 1994), pp. 1–2.
3. J. Royce, *The Philosophy of Loyalty* (New York: Macmillan, 1916), p. 282.
4. K. Anthony Appiah, *The Ethics of Identity* (Princeton, NJ: Princeton University Press, 2005), pp. 203, 211; emphasis added.
5. C. Handy, 'What's a Business For?', *Harvard Business Review on Corporate Responsibility* (Cambridge, MA: Harvard Business Review Publishing Corporation, 2003), pp. 65–82, on p. 65.
6. P. Sen, 'Volcker Rule Still Under Attack from Republicans', at www.upi.com/2662586

[accessed 21 November 2014].

7. S. B. MacDonald and J. E. Hughes, *Separating Fools from their Money: A History of American Financial Scandals* (New Brunswick, NJ: Transaction Publishers, 2010).

8. 'Enron's "Code of Ethics": 64-Page Guide is "Exhibit 1" as Trial Gets Underway', *Smoking Gun*, at http://www.thesmokinggun.com/documents/crime/enrons-code-ethics [accessed 21 November 2014].

9. S. B. MacDonald and J. E. Hughes, *Separating Fools from their Money: A History of American Financial Scandals* (New Brunswick, NJ: Transaction Publishers, 2010), p. 10, emphasis added.

10. MacDonald and Hughes, *Separating Fools from their Money*, p. 248.

11. G. F. Will, *Statecraft as Soulcraft: What Government Does* (New York: Simon and Schuster, 1983), p. 98.

12. 'Greenspan Concedes Error in Regulation', *New York Times*, 23 October 2008, at http://www.nytimes.com/2008/10/24/business/economy/24panel. html?mabReward=relbias:r,{%222%22:%22RI:14%22}&adxnnl=1&module=Search &adxnnlx=1418658060-qNOg22ArfxDYYgQfwdfkzg [accessed 1 January 2013].

13. 'FSA Tells City Banks to Claw Back Bonuses', *Daily Telegraph*, 15 November 2012, at http://www.telegraph.co.uk/finance/newsbysector/banksandfinance/9679411/FSA-tells-City-banks-to-claw-back-bonuses.html [accessed 21 February 2014].

14. M. Friedman, 'The Social Responsibility of Business is to Increase its Profits', *New York Times*, 13 September 1970, at http://query.nytimes.com/mem/archive-free/pdf?res= 9E05E0DA153CE531A15750C1A96F9C946190D6CF&module=Search&mabRe ward=relbias%3As%2C%7B%222%22%3A%22RI%3A14%22%7D [accessed 7 July 2014].

15. See 'Dodd-Frank Wall Street Reform and Consumer Protection Act' (2010), section 165(d).

16. M. Anderson and P. Escher, *The MBA Oath* (New York: Portfolio/Penguin Books, 2010), pp. xv–xvi.

17. S. B. MacDonald and J. E. Hughes, *Separating Fools from their Money: A History of American Financial Scandals* (New Brunswick, NJ: Transaction Publishers, 2010), p. 10.

18. R. Rorty, 'Is Philosophy Relevant to Applied Ethics?', *Business Ethics Quarterly*, 16:3 (2006), pp. 369–80.

19. F. Fukuyama, *Trust: The Social Virtues and the Making of Prosperity* (New York: Free Press, 1996).

20. D. Halberstam, *The Reckoning* (New York: Open Road Integrated Media, 2012), p. 734.

21. L. A. Bebchuk and J. M. Fried, 'Pay Without Performance: Overview of the Issues', *Journal of Applied Corporate Finance*, 17:4 (2005), pp. 8–23.

22. C. M. Elison and C. K. Ferrere, 'Executive Superstars, Peer Groups and Over-Compensation – Cause, Effect and Solution', at http://sites.udel.edu/wccg/files/2012/10/ Executive-Superstars-Peer-Groups-and-Over-Compensation10–10.pdf [accessed 27 October 2014].

23. Sir R. Cohen and M. Bannick, 'Is Social Impact Investing the Next Venture Capital?', at http://www.forbes.com/sites/realspin/2014/09/20/is-social-impact-investing-the-next-venture-capital/ [accessed 21 November 2014].

24. One such investment vehicle is the Trilinc Global Impact Fund, which has hopes for a maximum capital raise of $1.5 billion. Information about its public offering is avail-

able at http://www.sec.gov/Archives/edgar/data/1550453/000119312513079541/
d458085d424b3.htm [accessed 27 October 2014]. Disclosure Note: The author was, at
the time of publication, affiliated with a sub-adviser to this fund.

25. P. Vigna, 'The Best Indicator of US Health is Wage Growth (or Lack Thereof)', *Wall
Street Journal's* blog *Moneybeat*, 16 April 2014, at http://blogs.wsj.com/moneyb-
eat/2013/04/16/the-best-indicator-of-u-s-health-is-wage-growth-or-lack-thereof/
[accessed 13 November 2014].

5 Reform or *Metanoia*? – Beyond Dodd-Frank

1. J. J. McDermott (ed.), *The Writings of William James* (Chicago, IL: University of Chicago Press, 1977), p. 661.
2. Ill Bill, 'Gangsta Rap', *LyricsFreak.com*, at http://www.lyricsfreak.com/i/ill+bill/
gangsta+rap_20206697.html [accessed 23 November 2014].
3. T. Winter, *The Wolf of Wall Street*, screenplay, p. 68, at http://www.paramountguilds.
com/pdf/the_wolf_of_wall_street_screenplay.pdf [accessed 16 February 2014] p. 68.
4. S. Weiser and O. Stone, 'Wall Street: Original Screenplay', at http://www.imsdb.com/
scripts/Wall-Street.html [accessed 13 February 2014].

6 Wall Streets, 2025

1. Interview of Arthur Levitt, former Chairman of the Securities and Exchange Commission: PBS, 'The Wall Street Fix', *Frontline*, 13 January 2003, at http://www.pbs.org/
wgbh/pages/frontline/shows/wallstreet/interviews/levitt.html, [accessed 2 January
2014].
2. *Citizens United v. Federal Election Commission*, at http://www.supremecourt.gov/
opinions/09pdf/08–205.pdf [accessed 10 September 2014].
3. 'The Court's Blow to Democracy', *New York Times*, 21 January 2010 [accessed 21
November 2014].
4. *Citizens United v. Federal Election Commission*, at http://www.supremecourt.gov/
opinions/09pdf/08–205.pdf [accessed 10 September 2014].
5. *Lochner v. New York*, 198 U.S. 45, 25 S. Ct. 539, 49 L. Ed. 937 (1905).
6. 'Dissenting Opinion of John Paul Stevens, Supreme Court of the United States, in
Citizens United, Appellant v. Federal Election Commission', 21 January 2010, at http://
www.law.cornell.edu/supct/html/08–205.ZX.html [accessed 23 November 2014].
7. Financial Crisis Inquiry Commission, *Financial Crisis Inquiry Report: Final Report
of the National Commission on the Causes of the Financial and Economic Crisis in the
United States* (Philadelphia, PA: Public Affairs Reports, 2011), p. xviii.
8. J. Lardner, 'How Will the Volcker Rule Stand Up Against the Armies of Wall Street?:
Implementation of the Volcker Rule Must be Overseen by Regulators and the Public',
U.S. News and World Report, 19 December 2013, at http://www.usnews.com/opinion/
blogs/economic-intelligence/2013/12/19/how-will-the-volcker-rule-stand-up-against-
the-armies-of-wall-street [accessed 13 February 2014].
9. Justice Scalia, 'Concluding Remarks', *Citizens United v. Federal Election Commission*, at
http://www.supremecourt.gov/opinions/09pdf/08–205.pdf [accessed September 10,
2014].
10. Dissenting Opinion of John Paul Stevens, Supreme Court of the United States, in
Citizens United, Appellant v. Federal Election Commission (21 January 2010), at http://

www.law.cornell.edu/supct/html/08–205.ZX.html [accessed 23 November 2014].

11. J. C. Bogle, *The Clash of Cultures: Investment vs. Speculation* (Hoboken, NJ: John C. Wiley, 2012), p. 34.

12. 'Community Giving: ADM Cares', at http://www.adm.com/en-US/company/CommunityGiving/Pages/default.aspx [accessed 13 February 2014].

13. M. Giddings, 'The End of Sole Corporate Directors', 22 September 2010, at http://www.growthbusiness.co.uk/growing-a-business/business-regulations/1285728/the-end-of-sole-corporate-directors.thtml [accessed 12 February 2014].

14. L. A. Aguilar, 'The Power of the Shareholder & the Rise of Corporate Democracy', 2009 New America Alliance Latino Economic Forum, Waldorf Astoria Hotel, New York City, 29 October 2009, at http://www.sec.gov/news/speech/2009/spch-102909laa.htm [accessed 1 November 2014].

15. For a fuller discussion of the problem of regulatory capture, see C. Coglianese (ed.), *Regulatory Breakdown: The Crisis of Confidence in U.S. Regulation* (Philadelphia, PA: University of Pennsylvania Press, 2012).

16. My letter, now a public record, may be found at http://www.sec.gov/comments/s714–10/s71410–86.pdf.

17. 'Remarks of Brooksley Born on Accepting the 2009 Profile in Courage Award', 18 May 2009, at http://www.jfklibrary.org/Events-and-Awards/Profile-in-Courage-Award/Award-Recipients/Brooksley-Born-2009.aspx?t=3 [accessed 5 January 2014].

18. D. E. McClean, 'Derivatives and the Financial Crisis: Ethics, Stewardship, and Cultural Politics', in M. Boylan (ed.), *Business Ethics*, 2nd edn (Malden, MA: Wiley-Blackwell, 2013), pp. 339–56.

19. European Commission, 'Adoption of Regulatory Technical Standards for the Regulation on OTC Derivatives, Central Counterparties and Trade Repositories – 13.02.2014', at http://ec.europa.eu/internal_market/financial-markets/derivatives/index_en.htm [accessed 5 July 2014].

20. N. McCulloch and G. Pacillo, 'Is a Financial Transaction Tax a Good Idea?', *IDS in Focus Policy Briefing – Institute of Development Studies*, 14:2 (2010), at http://www.ids.ac.uk/publication/is-a-financial-transaction-tax-a-good-idea-a-review-of-the-evidence [accessed 12 February 2014].

21. 'Robin Hood Tax that Could Raise $26bn a Year Worldwide is Viable, Says Report', *Guardian*, 9 November 2010, at http://www.theguardian.com/business/2010/nov/09/robin-hood-tax-viable [accessed 13 February 2014].

22. 10 European Union (EU) member states – Bulgaria, Czech Republic, Estonia, Hungary, Latvia, Lithuania, Poland, Romania, the Slovak Republic, and Slovenia – and one forthcoming member, Croatia, although the report does not consider the inclusion of Croatia, in July 2013.

23. PriceWaterhouseCoopers, *Financial Transaction Tax: The Impacts and Arguments – A Literature Review*, 21 November 2013, at https://www.abi.org.uk//media/Files/Documents/Publications/Public/2013/Taxation/Financial%20Transaction%20Tax%20Literature%20Review.pdf [accessed January 2015].

24. E. Liu and N. Hanauer, *The True Patriot: A Pamphlet* (Seattle, WA: Sasquatch Books, 2007), p. 8.

25. J. McCain and M. Salter, *Worth the Fighting For* (New York: Random House, 2002), p. 337.

26. 'Testimony of Arthur Levitt, Chairman US Securities and Exchange Commission, Concerning The Large Firm Project, Before The Subcommittee on Telecommuni-

cations and Finance of The Committee on Energy and Commerce, US House Of Representatives', 14 September 1994, at http://edgar.sec.gov/news/studies/rogue2.txt [accessed 10 February 2014].

27. Securities and Exchange Commission, 'Report of the Committee on Compensation Practices', 10 April 1995, p. 3, at https://www.sec.gov/news/studies/bkrcomp.txt [accessed 12 February 2014].
28. Securities and Exchange Commission, 'Report of the Committee on Compensation Practices', p. 4.
29. A. Levitt, *Take on the Street: What Wall Street and Corporate America Don't Want You to Know – What You Can Do to Fight Back* (New York: Pantheon Books, 2002), p. 17.
30. CFA Institute, 'Restricting Sales Inducements: Perspectives on the Availability and Quality of Financial Advice for Investors', February 2014, p. 2, at http://blogs.cfainstitute.org/marketintegrity/2014/02/18/restricting-investment-sales-inducements-impact-of-reform-other-mis-selling-solutions/ [accessed 23 November 2014].
31. J. Henizl, 'The Tyranny of Fees: How Costs Kill Investment Returns', *Globe and Mail*, 26 April 2013, at http://www.theglobeandmail.com/globe-investor/the-tyranny-of-fees-how-costs-kill-investment-returns/article11578254/ [accessed 24 November 2014].
32. B. Mattlin, 'In Europe, Unbundling Proposals Spark Anxiety, Opposition', *Institutional Investor*, 13 October 2014, at http://www.institutionalinvestor.com/article/3386604/research-and-rankings/in-europe-unbundling-proposals-spark-anxiety-opposition.html#.VDWFDjh0zIW [accessed 23 November 2014].
33. J. Keefe, 'Retirement Programs: Soft Dollar: Fixing the Leaks', *Plan Sponsor*, 18 April 2005, at http://www.plansponsor.com/MagazineArticle.aspx?id=4294991728 [accessed 23 November 2014].
34. M. Samelson, 'Soft Dollars: Are the US Equity Markets in Denial?', *Plan Sponsor*, 11 December 2012, at http://www.plansponsor.com/MagazineArticle.aspx?id=4294991728 [accessed 23 November 2014].
35. FINRA, 'FINRA Provides Guidance on Prohibition Against Offering Favorable Research to Induce Investment Banking Business', *Regulatory Notice 11–41*, September 2011, at http://www.finra.org/Industry/Regulation/Notices/2011/P124424 [accessed 20 November 2014].
36. T. S. Coleman, *A Practical Guide to Risk Management* (New York: Research Foundation of CFA Institute, 2011), p. 57.

Conclusion

1. R. Rorty, 'Is Philosophy Relevant to Applied Ethics?', *Business Ethics Quarterly*, 16:3 (2006), pp. 369–80, on p. 379.
2. F. Douglass, 'No Progress Without Struggle!', in J. T. Pine (ed.), *Frederick Douglass on Slavery and the Civil War: Selections from His Writings* (New York: Dover Thrift Editions, 2003), p. 42.
3. S. B. MacDonald and J. E. Hughes, *Separating Fools from their Money: A History of American Financial Scandals* (New Brunswick, NJ: Transaction Publishers, 2010), pp. 248–9.
4. G. F. Will, *Statecraft as Soulcraft: What Government Does* (New York: Simon and Schuster, 1983), pp. 136–7.

Appendix 1: The Role of Compliance and Ethics in Risk Management

1. The Securities and Exchange Commission, as a matter of policy, disclaims responsibility for any private statements by its employees.
2. For a deeper plunge into the relationship between law and ethics, a classic exchange on this subject can be found in *Positivism and the Separation of Law and Morals*, H.L.A. Hart, 71 Harvard L. Rev. 529 (1958) and *Positivism and Fidelity to Law: A Reply to Professor Hart*, L.L. Fuller, 71 Harvard L. Rev. 630 (1958).
3. *SEC v. Investment Research Bureau, Inc.*, 375 U.S. 180, 186–7 (1963), quoting *Silver v. New York Stock Exchange*, 373 U.S. 341, 366 (1963).
4. 'Study on Investment Advisers and Broker-Dealers: As Required by Section 913 of the Dodd-Frank Wall Street Reform and Consumer Protection Act', January 2011, p. 62, at http://www.sec.gov/news/studies/2011/913studyfinal.pdf.
5. Advisers Act Section 204A, and Advisers Act Rule 204A–1.
6. 'Study on Investment Advisers and Broker-Dealers', p. 51.
7. 'Study on Investment Advisers and Broker-Dealers', p. 51.
8. 'Study on Investment Advisers and Broker-Dealers', p. 66.
9. 'Study on Investment Advisers and Broker-Dealers', p. 52.
10. 'Study on Investment Advisers and Broker-Dealers', pp. 52–3 and cases cited therein.
11. 'Study on Investment Advisers and Broker-Dealers', p. 51; and 'Guide to Broker-Dealer Registration', April 2008, at http://www.sec.gov/divisions/marketreg/bdguide.htm.
12. *SEC v. Capital Gains Research Bureau, Inc.*, 375 U.S. 180, 194 (1963); and 'Study on Investment Advisers and Broker-Dealers', p. 21.
13. 'Study on Investment Advisers and Broker-Dealers', p. 22 (quoting Concept Release on the U.S. Proxy System, Investment Advisers Act Release No. 3052 (14 July 2010) at p. 119.
14. 'Study on Investment Advisers and Broker-Dealers', p. 54 and cases cited therein.
15. Committee of Sponsoring Organizations of the Treadway Commission,'Enterprise Risk Management: Integrated Framework', September 2004, p. 29, at http://www.coso.org/documents/coso_erm_executivesummary.pdf [accessed 16 December 2014].
16. 'Study on Investment Advisers and Broker-Dealers: As Required by Section 913 of the Dodd-Frank Wall Street Reform and Consumer Protection Act', January 2011, pp. 29–30, at http://www.sec.gov/news/studies/2011/913studyfinal.pdf.
17. Basel Committee on Banking Supervision, 'Principles for Enhancing Corporate Governance', October 2010, p. 8, at http://www.bis.org/publ/bcbs176.pdf [accessed 16 December 2014].

Appendix 2: Shining a Light on Expenditures of Shareholder Money

1. See D. S. Hilzenrath, 'SEC Changes Settlement Rules for Companies Found Guilty of Crimes', *Washington Post*, 6 January 2012, at http://www.washingtonpost.com/business/economy/sec-settlements-with-companies-found-guilty-of-crimes-will-acknowledge-wrongdoing/2012/01/06/gIQAf9yRfP_story.html.
2. See Transcript of Douglas's press conference, 22 September 1937, Douglas Papers, container No. 21, Library of Congress, container no. 21, cited in J. Seligman, *The Transformation of Wall Street*, 2nd edn (Boston, MA: Northeastern University Press, 1995), p. 157. See also, 'Douglas Wants a Free Market, He Tells Press', *Washington Post*,

23 September 1937, p. 3.

3. Congress has recognized the need to ensure that investor voices are heard at the SEC. The Dodd-Frank Wall Street Reform and Consumer Protection Act ('Dodd-Frank') amended the Securities Exchange Act to establish within the Commission an Investor Advisory Committee, an Office of the Investor Advocate, and an Ombudsman to act as liaison between the Commission and retail investors. See 'Dodd-Frank Wall Street Reform and Consumer Protection Act' (2010), sections 911, 915 and 919D.

4. *Citizens United v. Federal Election Commission*, 130 S. Ct. 876, 175 L. Ed. 2d 753 (2010).

5. *Citizens United v. Federal Election Commission*, p. 886.

6. *Citizens United v. Federal Election Commission*, p. 886.

7. J. Crewdson, A. Fitzgerald, J. Salant and C. Babcock, 'Secret Donors Multiply in U.S. Election Spending', *Bloomberg*, 19 May 2011, at http://www.bloomberg.com/news/2011-05-19/secret-donors-multiply-in-u-s-with-finances-dwarfing-watergate.html.

8. 'Two Years After Citizens United, Voters Fed Up with Money in Politics', 19 January 2012, at http://www.democracycorps.com/National-Surveys/two-years-after-citizens-united-voters-fed-up-with-money-in-politics/. This article cites a national survey of 1000 likely 2012 voters conducted 8–11 January 2012 by Greenberg Quinlan Rosner Research for Democracy Corps and Public Campaign Action Fund.

9. 'Weekly Address: President Obama Calls on Congress to Enact Reforms to Stop a "Potential Corporate Takeover of Our Elections", 1 May 2010, at http://www.whitehouse.gov/the-press-office/weekly-address-president-obama-calls-congress-enact-reforms-stop-a-potential-corpor.

10. Brennan Center for Justice, Letter to Ms Elizabeth M. Murphy, Secretary of Securities and Exchange Commission, 21 December 2011, SEC file no. 4–637, at http://www.sec.gov/comments/4-637/4637-20.pdf [accessed 16 December 2014].

11. Bogle Financial Markets Research Center, Letter to Ms Elizabeth M. Murphy, Secretary of Securities and Exchange Commission, 17 January 2012, SEC file no. 4–637, at https://www.sec.gov/comments/4-637/4637-22.pdf [accessed 16 December 2014].

12. See, for example, Karl J. Sandstrom and Michael T. Liburdi, 'Overview of State Pay-to-Play Statutes', 5 May 2010, at http://www.perkinscoie.com/images/content/2/1/v2/21769/wp-10-05-pay-to-play.pdf.

13. See 'Comments on Rulemaking Petition: Petition to Require Public Companies to Disclose to Shareholders the Use of Corporate Resources for Political Activities', SEC file no. 4–637, at http://www.sec.gov/comments/4-637/4-637.shtml.

14. For more on this petition to require public companies to disclose to shareholders the use of corporate resources for political activities, submitted by Lucian A. Bebchuk, Co-Chair, Bernard S. Black, John C. Coffee Jr., James D. Cox, Jeffrey N. Gordon, Ronald J. Gilson, Henry Hansmann, Robert J. Jackson Jr., Co-Chair, Donald C. Langevoort, and Hillary A. Sale, see 'Petition for Rulemaking', 3 August 2011, The Committee on Disclosure of Corporate Political Spending, SEC file no. 4–637, at http://www.sec.gov/rules/petitions/2011/petn4-637.pdf.

15. See Letter from Rep. Michael E. Capuano, US House of Representatives, 18 January 2012, SEC file no. 4–637, at http://capuano.house.gov/news/2012/pr011812.pdf [accessed 16 December 2014]. Representative Capuano's letter states, 'I joined with 42 of my colleagues in writing to you in October 2011, urging the Securities and Exchange Commission ... to promulgate rules requiring public disclosure of corporate spending

in elections'.

16. Letter from Governor Pat Quinn, Illinois; State Treasurer Janet Cowell, North Carolina; State Comptroller Tom DiNapoli, New York; State Treasurer Bill Lockyer, California; State Treasurer Rob McCord, Pennsylvania; Public Advocate Bill De Blasio, New York City; City Controller Wendy Greuel, Los Angeles; Rep. William A. Current, Sr., North Carolina House of Representatives; Rep. James Pilliod, New Hampshire House of Representatives; and Commissioner Toni Pappas, Hillsborough County, New Hampshire, 19 January 2012, SEC file no. 4–637.

17. Letter from US Senators Robert Menendez, Jeff Bingaman, Sherrod Brown, Tom Udall, Patrick Leahy, Sheldon Whitehouse, Dick Durbin, Jeanne Shaheen, Tom Harkin, Mark Begich, Richard Blumenthal, Jeffrey Merkley, Frank R. Lautenberg, Bernie Sanders, and Al Franken, to SEC Chairman Mary Schapiro, 19 January 2012, at http://www.votesmart.org/public-statement/663201/letter-to-chairwoman-schapiro-us-securities-and-exchange-commission.

18. Letter from coalition of investment professionals, 1 November 2011, SEC File No 4–637.

19. Letter from Council for Institutional Investors, 19 October 2011, SEC File No. 4–637.

20. R.Chebium, 'Wheeler Presses for Additional Corporate Disclosures of Political Activity', *Statesman Journal*, 19 January 2011, at http://www.statesmanjournal.com/article/20120119/UPDATE/120119068/Wheeler-presses-additional-corporate-disclosures-political-activity.

21. See 'Comments on Rulemaking Petition: Petition to Require Public Companies to Disclose to Shareholders the Use of Corporate Resources for Political Activities', SEC file no. 4–637, at http://www.sec.gov/comments/4-637/4-637.shtml.

22. Lucian A. Bebchuk, Co-Chair, Bernard S. Black, John C. Coffee Jr., James D. Cox, Jeffrey N. Gordon, Ronald J. Gilson, Henry Hansmann, Robert J. Jackson Jr., Co-Chair, Donald C. Langevoort, and Hillary A. Sale, 'Petition for Rulemaking', 3 August 2011, The Committee on Disclosure of Corporate Political Spending, SEC file no. 4–637, at http://www.sec.gov/rules/petitions/2011/petn4-637.pdf, p. 4 cites a 25 July 2011 search of the Sharkrepellent Dataset of Factset Research Systems, for Proxy Proposals.

23. 'Petition for Rulemaking', p. 4.

24. 'Petition for Rulemaking', p. 5.

25. *Citizens United v. Federal Election Commission*, 130 S. Ct. 876, 916, citing *First National Bank v. Bellotti*, 435 U.S. 765, 794, 98 S. Ct. 1407, 55 L. Ed. 2d 707 (1978).

26. *Citizens United v. Federal Election Commission* citing McConnell v. Federal Election Commission, 540 U.S. 93, 259, 124 S. Ct. 619, 157 L. Ed. 2d 491 (2003).

27. *Political Contributions by Certain Investment Advisers*, release no. IA–1812, file no. S7–19–99, at http://www.sec.gov/rules/proposed/ia-1812.htm.

28. *Political Contributions by Certain Investment Advisers*, release no. IA–3043, file no. S7–18–09, at http://www.sec.gov/rules/final/2010/ia-3043.pdf.

INDEX